D0439489

Daughter

of the Regiment

Daughter
of the Regiment

Memoirs of a Childhood in the Frontier Army, 1878–1898

Mary Leefe Laurence

Edited by Thomas T. Smith

University of Nebraska Press

Lincoln & London

The paper in this book meets the minimum
requirements of American National Standard for
Information Sciences—Permanence of Paper
for Printed Library Materials, ANSI Z39.48-1984.

Library of Congress Cataloging-in-Publication Data
Laurence, Mary Leefe, 1872–1945.
    Daughter of the regiment : memoirs of a
childhood in the Frontier Army, 1878–1898 /
Mary Leefe Laurence : edited by Thomas T. Smith.
        p.   cm.
    Includes bibliographical references and index.
    1. Laurence, Mary Leefe, 1872–1945. 2. West
(U.S.)—History—1860–1890. 3. West (U.S.)—
History—1890–1945.   4. United States. Army—
Military life.   5. Army spouses—West (U.S.)—Bi-
ography.   I. Smith, Thomas T., 1950-   . II. Title.
F594.L38 1996
978'.02–dc20   95—24896
                                              CIP

CONTENTS

ILLUSTRATIONS

Photographs following page 94

vii

EDITOR'S ACKNOWLEDGMENTS

THANKS TO John F. Laurence of Glen Head, New York, son of Mary Leefe Laurence, who gave of his memory and trust for this work. Many thanks are due to my friend Alan C. Aimone, chief of Special Collections Division, United States Military Academy Library, West Point, New York, for sharing both his encyclopedic knowledge of sources and his enthusiasm for the project. Additional thanks to Don Rickey Jr., Shirley L. Leckie, Patricia Y. Stallard, Edward M. Coffman, Sherry L. Smith, and Joseph G. Dawson III, all scholars of the nineteenth century who generously offered their time, advice, and sources at various stages of the project. Finally, eternal gratitude to my own army brats, my son, Miles and daughter, Dustin, camp followers who have been good soldiers, faithfully following the regiment across continents and oceans.

The views expressed herein are those of the author and editor and do not purport to reflect the positions of the Department of the Army or the Department of Defense.

INTRODUCTION

MARY LEEFE LAURENCE, called "Mamie" by her family, offers the reader a rare view into the domestic and family aspects of the post–Civil War frontier army. Her memoirs are the most extensive and detailed recollections of an army child of the nineteenth century, focusing on the period of her sixth to twenty-sixth year, roughly 1878 to 1898.[1]

In 1944 she began the original manuscript, entitled "A Rainbow Passes," at Port Washington on Long Island, New York, completing it just prior to her death in the summer of 1945. Her friend, Major General Guy V. Henry Jr., wrote the preface to the manuscript. Like her, Henry spent his childhood in the frontier army, the son of a famous cavalry officer of the Indian Wars. Like her, he left his own vivid memoirs, although in much briefer form.[2]

The odyssey of the manuscript written by Mary Leefe Laurence offers an insight to the sometimes oddly circuitous path of the historical process. Shortly after her death, Stanley Vestal began to edit the typescript for publication. Vestal, professor of writing at the University of Oklahoma, had published many books on the American West, usually under his adopted name, Walter S. Campbell. The project was not typical of Vestal, who, as Sherry L. Smith noted in a recent biographical essay, usually concentrated on the masculine heroes of the West, and thus his writing left "no room for the qualities which Vestal would label more feminine."[3] The very fact that he undertook the project, albeit unsuccessfully, might come as a bit of a surprise to Vestal scholars. Mary Leefe Laurence's original typescript was very polished, but Vestal did make a few paragraph marks and the occasional word correction, as well as adding an appendix on the histories of the forts at which she was stationed. Vestal did not see the manuscript through to publication, probably because at that time there was not a strong market for women's history or for studies of the more domestic aspects of the Indian-fighting army.

In 1964 Mary's son, John F. Laurence, gave a copy of the typescript to Special Collections, United States Military Academy Library, West Point, where it gathered dust in obscurity for thirty years until it was rediscovered by Alan C. Aimone, the chief of Special Collections. In the process of entirely rearranging the storage of the books and manuscripts, he and his staff found a few items from previous decades that needed to be cataloged and added to the manuscript guide. These were put in a small stack near his desk, the Mary Leefe Laurence typescript among them.

At that time, November 1993, I was teaching military history at West Point and researching and writing a broad survey history of the activities of the U.S. Army in nineteenth-century Texas. I had been working on this pet project off and on for five years. In the process of researching primary material at Texas A&M University on army exploration in Texas I had examined what initially appeared to be an army surveyor's journal. The journal turned out to contain the detailed memoirs of a German immigrant who served as a foot soldier in the frontier army, a relatively rare find. Work on the "Texas" book ceased for over two years while I edited and published with the University of Nebraska Press that memoir titled *A Dose of Frontier Soldiering: The Memoirs of Corporal E. A. Bode, Frontier Regular Infantry, 1877–1882.*

With the Bode book finally completed I was anxious to return to research on the original project on the army in Texas. I decided to spend the Thanksgiving holidays mining the excellent manuscript collection at West Point for sources on the family and garrison aspects of the military experience in Texas. While visiting with Alan Aimone and sharing an enthusiastic mutual interest in the "old army," I noticed a small stack of books and manuscripts he had put aside for cataloging. Anyone with the slightest interest in history cannot resist picking up and thumbing through a dusty book pile, and I am no exception.

I randomly opened a black-covered typescript to a section on Fort Clark and was delighted to encounter exactly what I had come to find, primary material from the Texas frontier. The name on the title page was unfamiliar, and I was reasonably sure that material from this Mary Leefe Laurence had not been used by any of the relatively small cadre of historians exploring the garrison life of the nineteenth-century army. I had hardly finished scanning Guy V. Henry's preface and Mary's foreword when I realized with certainty my beloved army-in-Texas project was once again going to have to wait.

The address for Mary's son, who had donated the manuscript, was thirty years old, and there was no longer a village of Glen Head on any of my New York maps. I geared up for a monumental task of a month or two search to find him while reminding myself that good historians are nothing if not half-bloodhound. I decided to start by calling information in every area code in New York and expanding from there. There were many town names beginning with "Glen" on Long Island, so I started with that area code. I had John Laurence's number on the first try, and he answered the phone on the second ring. The whole process took less than five minutes. Sometimes the historian just gets lucky.

For this publication the manuscript is presented with its original grammar and punctuation, and the few spelling errors silently corrected. The few words I added for clarification are identified with enclosing brackets.

Mary Comfort Pinckney, the mother of Mary Leefe Laurence, was born in Vernon, New York. Her father, the grandfather of Mary Leefe Laurence, was an Englishman, Charles Clarence Pinckney, who married Emily Keene of New Hampshire. The Pinckneys were Tennessee planters until the American Civil War. At the outbreak of war they gave freedom to their slaves and moved north. During the war Charles Clarence Pinckney served as a captain in the First Michigan Infantry, and after the war the Pinckneys settled on a plantation estate on Frog Bayou of the Arkansas River near Van Buren and Fort Smith, Arkansas. It was here in 1866 that the Pinckney daughter, Mary Comfort Pinckney, met a lieutenant of the postwar Union occupation forces, John George Leefe, pronounced "leaf." Mary and John were married, had a daughter Katherine, called Kate, and a son Fred, called Dick, and transferred to Louisiana in 1870. On 2 October 1872, while in Louisiana, they had their third of four children, Mary Leefe.[4]

John George Leefe, the father of Mary Leefe Laurence, was also an Englishman, like Mary's maternal grandfather Pinckney. Born in London in 1837, Leefe immigrated to New York City at four years of age. His father was a lithographic artist with a studio in Manhattan. John G. Leefe began his path to a career in the army during the Civil War. Commissioned as a lieutenant in the 162nd New York Infantry in 1862, Leefe earned promotions and brevets to the rank of lieutenant colonel by 1865, serving as an infantry officer, adjutant, and ordnance officer. His brevet promotions for gallant service came at the Battle of Opequan and the Battle of Fisher's Hill, Virginia. Leefe served in both the Eastern and Western Theaters, including the siege of Port Hudson, Louisiana and the Sabine, Texas, Expedition, and he was wounded at Fort De Russey, Louisiana. Leefe was also in the Battles of Winchester and Cedar Creek during Phil Sheridan's Shenandoah Valley Campaign. During the postwar reduction in force Leefe earned a regular army

The Army Life of
Mary Leefe
1874-1898

Fort Brady MI
1890-96

Fort Wayne MI 1896-98

Davids Island NY
1881-82

Fort Lyon CO
1874-76

Fort Dodge KS
1876-80

Fort Leavenworth KS
1880-81

Fort Gibson OK 1881

Fort Clark TX 1886-89

Mount Vernon Bks. AL
1889-90

Fort Duncan TX 1886

Fort Ringgold TX
1883-86

T. Smith

second lieutenant commission in the Nineteenth Infantry, a regiment in which he would serve for the following thirty-three years.

In the regular army, with family in tow, Leefe served throughout the Great Plains and Texas, with an occasional assignment in the East or South until the 1890 assignment to Michigan. From there, in 1898 he led a battalion to Puerto Rico during the Spanish-American War, where, in 1899, as a major, he had field command of the regiment. From the Caribbean his unit was moved in 1899 to the Philippine Islands during the Philippine Occupation and Insurrection. In the Philippines Major Leefe commanded several posts and eventually the regiment, which he led against insurgent positions at Sudlon on the island of Cebu in January 1900. Returning to the United States in 1901, Leefe gained the lieutenant colonelcy of the Thirtieth Infantry Regiment. Finally, in September 1901 Lieutenant Colonel Leefe was ordered to retire by reason of age. He was then sixty-four years old and had been in military service as a volunteer or regular soldier for thirty-eight years.

Even upon retirement Leefe did not quite leave the service.

For two years afterward he served as the professor of military science and tactics at the De La Salle Institute in New York City. While on that duty he died of pneumonia on 9 June 1903 and was buried at Cypress Hill Cemetery. In 1905 Leefe's body was moved and interred with military honors in Arlington National Cemetery.[5]

John G. Leefe was a good soldier according to the efficiency reports of his commanders and superior officers. It is evident from this memoir by his daughter that he was also a devoted father and family man. While not a musician (among a very musical family), Leefe was a writer. Mary Leefe Laurence recounts the short stories he published, all on some aspect of army life. It was during this period in the 1880s and 1890s that Captain Charles King popularized the genre of American frontier army fiction. King became a best-selling author and his stories the genesis of the same type of romantic soldier tale brought to the movie screen by John Ford and others. It is worth noting that Leefe published one of his short stories in a volume of King's collections of fiction in 1895. It is a tale called "Buttons," a light romance about a young West Point officer who does the right thing by marrying the wrong girl after he inadvertently put her reputation at risk, and then goes off to die in battle in the Indian Wars.[6]

After a childhood spent primarily on remote military posts Mary Leefe became, in her young adult years, a voice and diction teacher with a studio on F Street in Washington D.C. She was an accomplished professional concert soprano, often accompanying the Marine Corps Band. Between 1905 and 1910 she gave recitals in the Willard Hotel, the Washington Club, the Library of Congress, and Constitution Hall, where she opened the 1908 session of the Congress of the Daughters of the American Revolution. For a woman of her era she married late in life, at age thirty-nine. In New York City on 24 June 1911 she wed her cousin, Frederick Sturgis Laurence. Although he served as an army major during World War I, he was not a career soldier. Laurence trained as an artist under Frank Duvenck and spent a career using his artistic talent in construction projects involving terra cotta and decorative tile. Their only child, John F., was born in New York City on 28

October 1912. Mary spent her later life in New York, where she died on 19 July 1945. She is buried beside her mother, father, brother, and husband in Arlington National Cemetery.[7]

The biographical details available on the professional careers of Mary Leefe Laurence and her father provide insight into the relative challenges of various schools of history, specifically between American military history and women's history. The discipline of history is anchored upon the written record, the primary source document. The U.S. Army, perhaps more than any other nineteenth-century American institution, kept fairly meticulous records of its organizational activities and its members such as John G. Leefe. Through that wealth of documentation it was possible to accurately outline a portrait of Leefe's professional military life, the challenge being which of the voluminous details to omit.

In contrast, the personal and professional life of Mary Leefe Laurence remains incomplete because of the very lack of historical record. As a result of her unofficial status as camp follower her name was completely absent from the sheaf of military documents concerning her father. The sketch of her professional career as a concert soprano was cobbled from the few comments she offers in this memoir or from bits and pieces gleaned from family scrapbooks and brief newspaper clippings. By turning to the oral tradition, the antecedent of the written record, I fleshed out these thin details with interviews of aging family members who had direct contact with her. Thus, in the end, her father's professional biography required following a relatively straight line through the record, while hers demanded loops and circles and many more of the wily tricks and techniques of the historian.

While Mary Leefe Laurence provides the most lengthy and detailed recording of the army childhood experience, others have offered important glimpses, usually as smaller portions of autobiographical narratives. Guy V. Henry Jr., the son and grandson of army officers, wrote an unpublished memoir that provides seventeen pages on his life as a youth in the 1870s and 1880s on frontier cavalry posts in Nebraska, Kansas, Oklahoma, and Wyoming. General Douglas MacArthur, the son of a Thirteenth Infantry officer, included in his *Reminiscences* a few pages on his life at forts in the 1880s in New Mexico, Kansas, and Texas. Jack W. Heard, the son of a Third Cavalry officer, briefly records in *Pictorial Military Life History* his young experiences in Texas and Vermont in the 1880s and, more unusually, the Philippines during the insurrection of 1900. While most of the existing childhood memoirs are by white males, "*Three Score Years and Ten*" by Charlotte Ouisconsin Van Cleve, daughter of a Fifth Infantry officer, offers one hundred pages on her antebellum childhood, much of it at Fort Snelling, Minnesota, in the 1820s. Most unusual are childhood accounts by the children of enlisted men, such as the Eleventh Infantry bandmaster son in Arizona in the 1880s, Fiorello La Guardia, in his *The Making of an Insurgent*. Rarest of all are the recorded experiences of the offspring of black soldiers in the nineteenth century.[8]

These autobiographies share certain facets of their recollections. Particularly interesting are powerful first memories in military settings, all at about the age of four or five years. For MacArthur it was the three-hundred-mile overland march from Fort Wingate to Fort Selden, New Mexico, at the height of the Apache Wars. MacArthur marched at the head of the column beside the company first sergeant. Henry, born in a tent at Fort Robinson, Nebraska, recounts, "One of my earliest recollections is travelling on some Union Pacific train and having Colonel William Cody (Buffalo Bill) give me a box of candy." For Charlotte Van Cleve it was the first steamboat to deliver mail to her garrison in 1823. Jack Heard remembered the bats in the ceiling of their adobe quarters at Fort Ringgold, Texas.[9]

The first permanent memory for Mary Leefe Laurence was a bloody blanket in the yard and a solemn crowd of soldiers on the porch of the commanding officer's quarters of Fort Dodge, Kansas. Inside the house lay the lifeless body of the colonel of the regiment, killed by the Cheyennes in 1878. "The first scene I can remember on the stage set for my childhood eyes was one of tragedy. . . . The meaning of it did not come to me till the following day when the silence of the fort was broken by a clear bugle call and a column of troops with arms reversed marching out with a caisson bearing a long box covered with an American flag. Muffled drums beat out a slow measured cadence as the procession moved out toward the river. . . . Then I knew, the first occasion when the fact of death registered itself in my baby brain as an incident of life to be expected."[10]

Mary Leefe Laurence, though a woman, shared with Henry and MacArthur a common class, the officer caste, as well as many similar views. She believed she was a part of her father's unit, always referring to "our" regiment and speaking of the infantry company or its parent organization, the Nineteenth Infantry, in tones of a permanent extended family. Henry writes, "I first put on the uniform . . . at the age of four and considered myself a full-fledged member of Troop D, 3rd Cavalry." Mary Leefe Laurence records the sense of adventure that permeated her life as army child, the thrill of the evening retreat ceremony, and the fun of rides on army wagons, all sentiments echoed by Henry, Heard, and MacArthur. Heard stated, "I can't help but feel sorry for any child not brought up on a post."[11]

There were of course noticeable gender differences. Mary Leefe Laurence, being female, faced more protective and restrictive rules on her movements. She was always confined to the boundaries of the post unless escorted. Henry had nearly complete freedom and began to accompany his father as his orderly in the field on military expeditions at the age of six. MacArthur and Heard write of firing ranges and cavalry drill, events observed but seldom experienced by Mary Leefe Laurence. However, when in her teens at Fort Clark, she does challenge one aspect of conventional gender restriction by insisting on riding her horse astride rather than side-saddle as was done by proper young ladies of the period.[12]

Army children of the officer caste, regardless of gender, are nearly universal in their memory of affectionate relations with enlisted men, many of whom treated the children as favored pets. "A great bond between us and the enlisted men grew up and has never passed," recalled Mary Leefe Laurence, offering in her memoir many examples of this relationship. Heard recalled, "One of my favorites was a waggoner named George. He drove the wagon that took coffins to the graveyard. I always rode beside him." Henry wrote fondly of his constant companion Gibson, a black soldier who came to cook for his family and remained for fifteen years, and of Dougherty and McShane, "probably the two worst men in the troop, but they were, however, our best friends."[13]

These relationships did have complications. Henry believed that at times the enlisted men cultivated his friendship because he was the son of the commander and could get them out of trouble should the need arise. It did, and he did. Mary Leefe Laurence, however, reflects more of a class aspect and a sense of, as she states, "the heritage of noblesse oblige." This ruling-class attitude is unconsciously expressed when she speaks of her father's relationship to his soldiers: "He loved his men and they, like children, intuitively knew it." Her father, after all, was of English middle-class birth within the British class system. Of all American institutions the military, by necessity, retained a clear and compelling hierarchy and a class structure.[14]

In time gender and class differences would naturally come to affect relationships with enlisted men. "My father and mother both had a very strong sense of class," she wrote, recalling being sixteen years old at Fort Clark, Texas, and "reaching the age when that bar between enlisted men and officers had to come down for us children." Nowhere in the memoirs of Mary Leefe Laurence is the military class system more evident than at Fort Clark when she is smitten, for the first time, with a handsome cavalry trooper from the ranks. Even though it was acknowledged that he was a gentleman from a fine family, and though her parents were kind about it and the garrison was mostly unaware, she felt a sense of guilt. This sort of relationship "was not to be spoken of, at least publicly." On the advice of her mother she was extremely circumspect with him. This unrequited relationship ended shortly when her family and infantry unit transferred to Alabama.[15]

The class distinction between the epaulets and the ranks often extended to the backyards and playgrounds, as enlisted man's son La Guardia was acutely aware. "That distinction went all the way down to the kids on post," he recorded of Whipple Barracks, Arizona. When Jack Heard recalled, "I made friendships with army children [with] whom I would be associated all my life," he includes mention of only officers' children in his memoirs, except at an outpost in the Philippines, where "there were no other American children in Vigan so perforce, our random playmates were natives."[16]

Whether male or female, army children were often inculcated with patriotic values and a strong sense of social responsibility. "Our teaching," recalled MacArthur, "included not only the simple rudiments, but above all else, a sense of obligation. We were to do what was right no matter what the personal sacrifice might be. Our country was always to come first." Mary Leefe Laurence mirrors the same in the passage, "There were also the restraints of rigid army discipline. . . . These brought devotion to something higher than self as the object of life. Without them we children might never have grown up to always put our country first when the choice had to be made, and from this to respect the rights of others."[17]

There are no monograph-length studies of army children on the frontier, but there are a few examinations of the experiences of civilian youngsters, most of which virtually ignore army families. Lillian Schissel, Byrd Gibbens, and Elizabeth Hampsten's *Far from Home: Families of the Westward Journey* (1989) by and large presents a negative image of the frontier experience; as noted in the introduction, the book "offers three tales of immense suffering." Through three case studies involving families in Oregon Territory, Colorado–New Mexico, and North Dakota the authors find that the reality of the westering experience does not hold up to the mythical image. *Far from Home* presents childhoods tormented by starvation, abuse, neglect, disease, and backbreaking toil, all products of "disassembled" families. Schissel observes, "These histories are not heroic."[18]

Elizabeth Hampsten's later work, *Settlers' Children: Growing Up on the Great Plains* (1991), is also rather narrowly focused in late-nineteenth- and early-twentieth-century North Dakota. She reinforces the unheroic image, but she does include a brief glimpse of the experience of an army doctor's daughter on the frontier of the late 1860s. Hampsten finds that the quality of the children's lives was directly related to their parents' economic status, and that children's forced labor was found mainly among the poor families. For the middle class, norms, values, and, above all, income protected children from much of the brutal harshness of life on the frontier. Pioneering, she concludes, was a diversity of experiences, for some good, for others harsh, depending on age, income, and region. It was most difficult, however, for families with small children, the group most vulnerable to disease. In many respects the memory of Mary Leefe Laurence confirms Hampsten's findings of the influence of class and social position. For this officer's daughter, within Hampsten's middle-class bracket, frontier life was clearly a positive experience.[19]

The childhood of Mary Leefe Laurence, as presented in her memoirs, has little in common with the general historiographic image offered in either *Far from Home* or *Settlers' Children*. A much broader study, and more complete scholarship, is found in Elliott West's *Growing Up with the Country: Childhood on the Far Western Frontier* (1989). "Until its children are heard," writes West, "the frontier's history cannot truly be written." Although West does not deal with army offspring, his more positive findings, or "happier heritage" as he puts it, resemble in many respects the portrait presented by Mary Leefe Laurence. West's study of the young, primarily Anglo inhabitants of the Great Plains in the period from 1850 to 1900 finds that children grew up with a sense of place and an affinity for the land. Children were a conservative force, encouraging parents to preserve aspects of their prefrontier immigration culture. The concern of parents for children's values was a mainspring for the creation of churches and schools.[20]

The voices that speak in West's *Growing Up with the Country* at times bear an uncanny resemblance to the recollections of Mary Leefe Laurence. West discovers pioneer children experiencing disturbing fears at the vast sameness of the plains, sometimes creating a deep sense of foreboding, the great open space leaving them afraid and vulnerable. Mary Leefe Laurence recalled this psychological effect of the environment on her young mind. "I had the feeling in looking at the plains that they stretched away to the end of the world—that they encircled us in a close and, at times, suffocating embrace. . . . Always there was the feeling of some nameless dread lurking unseen in their vast solitude." [21]

West's study reveals that a dreadful fear of Indians was almost born into pioneer children. Mothers, he writes, would shear closely the hair of their girls to make them less attractive to Indians. Mary Leefe Laurence shares a similar memory. "It has taken many years for those of us who were children of the old army to overcome the dread and hatred we had for the Indians of those days. With the threat of terrible outbreaks and the death and torture of our loved ones hovering at the back of our minds, it is not so surprising that we did feel so, and failed perhaps to appreciate the flagrant injustices perpetrated on the Indians by our own government." Before visiting a nearby Ute camp she records, "We children must all have our hair cut close lest some of the captive warriors be tempted to fall upon us and scalp us. . . . I myself wore a boy's haircut up to my sixteenth birthday." [22]

For the nomadic pioneer children of *Growing Up with the Country* the crucial element of stability was the extended family. The transient nature of frontier society tended to dilute the influence of hometown public opinion on these young minds. Army children likewise lived a nomadic existence, from post to post, assignment to assignment, but with a stability provided by their nuclear family and, perhaps as important, an ever-watchful public eye provided by the regimental family. Most post moves usually involved the reassignment of the unit rather than individuals; thus friends and neighbors often packed and traveled together, as well as shared the problems of adjusting to the environment of a new fort. [23]

The horse gave a sense of freedom and independence to the pioneer children, as it did to youngsters of the army such as Mary Leefe Laurence. West finds that in general the experience of the frontier gave pioneer children a remarkable sense of adventure and independence and an early maturity. However, in the view of Mary

Leefe, offspring of the military were more sheltered, and the taut social restrictions within the military subculture of the garrison tended to discourage, rather than encourage, early independence. "Army children," she writes, "were taught early to observe the rules of the garrison."[24]

There were other important differences between civilian pioneer and army children. Army quarters, especially by the 1870s, generally offered a more comfortable domestic situation than the farmer's sod house or the rancher's jacal. Unlike that of the frontier civilian child, the army offspring's labor was not an important economic factor in the survival of the family. Education in the sparse regions of the plains was a challenge for everyone. Settlers often solved the problem by free market education, creating local private schools by subscription. Army families sometimes were required to resort to this, but normally after the Civil War the federal government subsidized schools on post for the illiterate troops and the army children. In remote locations medical care was better for the army child, who had access to the post surgeon. Nevertheless both sets of children were equally vulnerable to the frontier's greatest child killer, laryngeal diphtheria.[25]

Although there is little detailed survey scholarship on the lives of nineteenth-century army children, the subject has been very well treated within a number of excellent broad studies of the army of the period. Patricia E. Stallard's *Glittering Misery* (1978) became the benchmark study that launched a new interest in research on military dependents, or "camp followers," on the frontier. Stallard includes a chapter on the lives of children of the army. Two chapters of Edward M. Coffman's excellent *The Old Army* (1986) explore the roles of women and children, contrasting the antebellum and post-Civil War periods. In *Life and Manners in the Frontier Army* (1978) Oliver Knight uses the novels of Captain Charles King to detail the social aspects of army garrison life.[26]

As Mary Leefe Laurence opens her story in 1878 the army of which she was a part had a composition of 23,254 enlisted men and 2,153 officers scattered in 110 posts across the United States. About two-thirds of the soldiers were stationed at the more remote frontier garrisons of the West. Of forty regiments in the army, twenty-five were infantry, ten were cavalry, and five were artillery. The army was fundamentally a small constabulary force concerned with nation building and peace keeping on the frontier. Most of the officers had combat experience in the great crusade of the previous decade but after the Civil War faced professional stagnation in the form of slow promotion and low pay. Mary's father, for example, had been a volunteer brevet lieutenant colonel, reduced in regular rank after the war, like the majority of his peers. Leefe served the next three decades in the company grade ranks as a lieutenant or captain. Although his family accompanied him to various posts, it was not until 1891 that the U.S. Army as an institution began to acknowledge its official responsibility toward the twelve thousand women and children constituting the families of officers and soldiers in that year.[27]

The daily lives of the "camp followers," as the family members were called, revolved around the military schedule of the fort. All posts shared common customs and routine, but each might have a unique atmosphere based on the personality of the commander, the size of the garrison, or the deployment of the unit to campaign duties. Distinct bugle or drum signals governed the daily routine. Reveille began the day at dawn, followed by breakfast call or stable call for cavalry posts, and then guard mount. After breakfast adjutant's call brought the officers to headquarters for orders and assignments. Sick call, fatigue call, drill, and a light supper filled out the day. The evening began with a dress parade and retreat to lower the flag at sundown. The soldiers had a tattoo or role call about 8:00 PM followed half an hour later by taps and slumber, except for the officer of the day and those soldiers on the nightly guard duty. The routine varied on Sundays to include a full dress inspection.[28]

Garrison life was somewhat of a closed society, described by one historian as an anachronistic "Arthurian court," with a social hierarchy based on rank, enforcing comparatively strict values and an idealized ethical code more demanding than the cultural norm in America. The ladies, rather than the men, tended to enforce the social stratification, with the post commander's wife being the queen bee in most situations. Mary observed this of the post commander's wife at Mount Vernon Barracks: "we felt some tact necessary in dealing with her."[29]

These army ladies had a salutary effect and were a restraining and refining influence in a male-dominated culture. Most officers' wives originated from middle- or upper-middle-class eastern homes and carried their values to the frontier, but they faced a constant battle with the forces of nature and the indifference of army bureaucracy. Army quarters and children's education presented them with their most difficult challenges. Quarters were varied, ranging from damp dugouts to elegant wood-framed multi-story houses, and depended on the seniority of the officer, the age of the post, and its proximity to the railroad. The Leefes generally had fair quarters and, except for the fear of rattlesnakes in the houses in posts along the Mexican border, found them satisfactory.[30]

Like quarters, the quality of children's education varied from post to post. Some officers sought assignments near good schools or solved the education problem by sending wives and children back East, but most stuck out the makeshift nature of frontier schooling. There were a wide variety of expedient methods, and a child might have an education over the years that was a hodgepodge of boarding schools, public schools, church schools, private tutors, home school, and post schools taught by a semiqualified soldier or army chaplain. While it may be generally true that army children suffered from educational deficiencies, Mary Leefe Laurence seems to have lost little in the long run. She had practically every type of schooling except boarding school. At Fort Leavenworth she attended a Catholic private school, even though she was Episcopalian. At Davids Island, New York, she went to a good public school, and at Fort Ringgold, Texas, the local school was considered dismally run by a "paddle-wielding testy old civilian school master." There her mother taught the Leefe children most subjects at home and hired a private tutor, an English enlisted man, to instruct them in grammar and mathematics. When circumstances closed the good little public school at Brackettville, Texas, near Fort Clark, the officers pooled their resources to hire a young female teacher from New Jersey to teach the children in one of the senior officers' quarters.[31]

The post social life consisted of an astonishing variety of diversions. In common with accounts from officers' wives of the period, these memoirs are filled with lively incidents of parties, picnics, buggy rides, card playing, group dinners, dances, amateur theater, and impromptu concerts around the Leefe piano. Music was a major part of the Leefe family life and, surprisingly but not unusually, the family piano was hauled across the Texas frontier to Fort Ringgold. Sports were popular, especially baseball and, as Mary records, tennis among the officer set at Fort Clark. The children and families of Fort Ringgold, as was typical of border posts, attended fiestas in Mexico, and after a visit by a traveling circus the children made their own circus, complete with trapeze act and bareback horse riding.[32]

Although the children tended to have free rein of the post, there were norms that circumscribed their behavior. Their parents could earn a rebuke from the post commander if the children misbehaved, for the soldiers were responsible for the actions of their families. Mary's tennis playing during guard mount at Fort Clark was a pleasant distraction for the guard but earned the displeasure of the post commander, who subsequently created a regulation prohibiting tennis during parade and guard mounting. On another occasion the Leefes' pet goat did enough damage to the ornamental trees that the post commander banned goats from the fort. "My escapades," she admits, "certainly kept the headquarters' press working."[33]

Maintenance of a proper middle-class lifestyle on low army pay was obviously another major family concern. Officers such as Leefe, although poorly paid, did have enough extra allowances and access to cheap labor to maintain the position expected of their station. "In the army we always had a retinue of servants," recorded Mary, "some from the enlisted ranks and some from the outside." The Leefes usually had a cook, housemaid, or nurse and a handyman or soldier striker. Male servants were more dependable in the long run than females. Young female servants of a marriageable age didn't last long before they found a husband among the ranks. With the constant expense of travel and the frequency of moves the life-style of the average army officer's family might best be described as a state of genteel poverty.[34]

In general the memory of Mary Leefe Laurence confirms the scholarship of historians of the old army. However, if there is one area of the historiography that these memoirs would challenge it is the issue of the isolated officer corps. In his classic *The Soldier and the State* (1957) Samuel P. Huntington practically carved in stone the historical generality that the army as a nineteenth-century in-stitution was physically, intellectually, and socially isolated from the very society it was supposed to protect. A few historians have since challenged this notion of an isolated military subculture, pointing out that in 1881, for example, almost a third of the officer corps was stationed in the East or in the urban West and that social contact with civilians was considered a part of military life. These memoirs by Mary Leefe Laurence provide excellent primary evi-dence for the latter view. Even in isolated posts, her family mixed freely with the local elites, and she offers numerous recollections of such social interaction.[35]

At Fort Gibson she records that her parents made many friends in Muskogee and often received invitations from them. At Davids Island, New York, a visiting houseguest, the rather eccentric poet and composer Stephen Massett, caused no end of embarrassment by being arrested by the guard for swimming nude at the enlisted beach in daylight. At Fort Ringgold, Texas, she recalls spending many afternoons at the home of one of the leading families of the town, whom she refers to as "cultured people." After a storm and facing a miserably soggy and undignified entrance to their new post of Fort Duncan, Texas, the Leefes were rescued in the street by a leading townsman who insisted they share his home and clean up before reporting for duty. Afterward, "our hosts sent us on to the fort in their own carriage." At Fort Wayne "life there with the big city of Detroit to draw on for social pleasures was a continual round of dinners, dances, and other diversions inside and outside the post." She found herself "much sought after in the younger set of Detroit society."[36]

Although she demonstrates that her army family interacted socially with civilian elites and was not entirely isolated from society, she also, at times, forcefully expresses the view that the hardships and sacrifices of the regular soldier were lost on an unappreciative and ungrateful public. Don Rickey Jr. labeled the frontier army the "stepchild of the Republic," a pathos shared by Mary Leefe Laurence. Likewise, she often reflects the regulars' general disdain and mistrust of the competence of the volunteer citizen as a soldier, particularly the state volunteers on frontier campaigns or state militia on urban riot duty. However, this judgment seems to have been tempered somewhat when, at age eighteen, she accompanied her father on an inspection of a state militia regiment in camp outside Mobile. She was clearly charmed by the attention and manners of the young officers of the "crack militia outfit," whom she called, reflecting her sense of class, the "best blood of Alabama."[37]

In her views toward Indians of the Great Plains Mary Leefe Laurence generally supports the scholarship of Sherry L. Smith in *The View from Officers' Row: Army Perceptions of Western Indians* (1990). Although Smith found a diversity of views among the officer caste, she noted that most officers' wives believed that Indian wives were swapped and traded like horses and that Indian men enslaved their women. Mary Leefe Laurence conforms to this perception by noting the story of the Indian who attempted to buy the attractive wife of a lieutenant. When the officer refused, the angry Indian was supposed to have declared that no wife was worth more than five dogs. "So, in that day did the Indians of the plains hold their womankind." She records, "They swapped and traded them freely."[38]

Smith also describes officers who were sympathetic to the general plight of the Indians and even identified with their fight to protect their homes and property. Mary Leefe Laurence, probably reflecting the views of her parents, writes, "In the army, there was a certain friendly feeling intermixed, as we understood the Indian better than those on the outside. The Indians themselves had more respect for the army than for the civilian population . . . A soldier was a warrior, like themselves, and usually a fair one."[39]

Within these memoirs there is little evidence of the serious social problems of the army. There is no mention of alcoholism, family abuse, marital infidelity, sexual indiscretions and affairs, or the scandals that occurred in some garrisons and were widely known by the rest of the army. For example, while the Leefes were at Fort Dodge a major of the regiment shot the regimental assistant surgeon, whom he apparently caught with his wife. The children were naturally sheltered from such knowledge, but, more realistically, Mary's discretion is the product of a military subculture that carefully guarded its image, closed ranks around scandal, and avoided the airing of dirty linen in public. In this respect her silence on these unpleasant subjects speaks volumes and proves her the quintessential army offspring.[40]

Mary Leefe Laurence is somewhat unusual because she did not marry into the army and because she pursued her own successful professional career until fairly late in life. Additionally, issues of gender and class within the military caste concerned her and are subtly addressed in these memoirs. However, Mary Leefe Laurence does represent an excellent case study of an officer's child reared in the post–Civil War frontier army. By and large, like other army children she thrived in the West and, in later years, was nostalgic for the experience, as were many of the wives and children who learned to adapt to the challenge of army life in the late nineteenth century. The title of this memoir, borrowed from the Donizetti opera, is apropos of her professional concert career and the classical vocal interest of Mary Leefe Laurence, but it is as well aptly descriptive of her personal worldview toward the army and her father's unit. She was in every sense a daughter of the regiment.[41]

DAUGHTER
OF THE REGIMENT

Good-bye Old Regulars. Your voluntary recruitment in the army of an earlier day upheld in its performance the ideas of our American heritage, perpetuated in its present-day system and aims. It is hoped these pages may reveal in part what manner of men they were who preserved for us these hopes and ideas, imparting to those born and brought up in the raw conditions faced on the Western frontier in its pioneer era.

MARY LEEFE LAURENCE

1945

Preface

MARY LEEFE LAURENCE was the daughter of an officer in the regular army of the United States. She has very truly recorded the recollections of her life from childhood to young womanhood. I can say truly recorded, for my childhood and youth were under like conditions.

Her recollections cover the period from 1876 to 1900, during which the greater portion of the regular army was stationed in small, isolated frontier garrisons, engaged in holding the Indians under control and in the development of our great West. Life was not all the beautiful rainbow of youthful recollections. For the parents much was stern reality, Indian conflicts, homes with scant comforts, and constant changes of station, frequently by mule wagon over hundreds of miles of the arid Southwest or by slow, dirty, uncomfortable troop trains of that period.

In spite of all of this, these parents were proud of their soldier's life and, with the passage of time, remembered it all as a rainbow passes.

Guy V. Henry Jr.
Major General, U.S. Army (Ret.)
1945

Author's Foreword

IN THE CHRONICLES of vanished years which have marked stages in our national growth, little or nothing factual has been written of the particular time and aspect of life I hope to picture in these memoirs. Since Mrs. Custer laid down her pen most of it has been fictional and far from accurate, none covering the scenes of my own experience. These I have tried to give with strict adherence to the truth so far as recollection preserves it through the mists of passing years. Scenes observed through a child's eyes are received as rapidly changing pictures, the clearness of which remains until the interest of later life causes these to fade and become obscure. It may well be asked then how could I remember so clearly in late life all the things I picture in this narrative.

Were it not that so many of these occurrences became traditions and have been so perpetuated in our family life, I might not have been able to do so. My mother's memory has helped in many events of my earliest childhood life and it is thus that I have been able to fill in where my own memory has been a bit hazy. So also, the testimony of my father about the events in which he was either a participant or observer. Our dinner table brought out much that has been remembered as dinner in our family was always somewhat formal and an event in itself.

If I cannot aspire to favorable reception from the standpoint of literary style I may at least do so from an ability to present some hitherto unrecorded events of historic interest and to give some pictures of the frontier where Indians still roved and the last of certain dreaded bands were being rounded up—the chiefs of which we knew, Chief Joseph of the Nez Percé, Geronimo, and other famous warriors. The more peaceful period following their passing was not, however, all one of dress diversion and dancing among brass buttons. It too knew hardship in the slowly vanishing crudities of civilization still lingering in the lesser-known areas where we lived before a turn of the wheel brought us into the brilliant social life of Washington and the large cities. There were also the restraints of rigid army discipline. Looking back I thank God for those regulations. Now it is the fashion to sneer at "red tape" and "regimentation." These brought devotion to something higher than self as the object of life. Without them we children might never have grown up to always put our country first when the choice had to be made, and from this to respect the rights of others.

This chronicle has been written because I have been urged to write it. As my days pass on it has been as a dream dreamed again in colors which have grown more mellow, like the tints of a rainbow in the evening sky.

✷ 1

FORT DODGE, KANSAS

1878–1880

Age Six to Eight Years

THE FIRST scene I can remember on the stage set for my childhood eyes was one of tragedy. It unfolded at Fort Dodge, Kansas, on an evening in September 1878. It was an evening when the sky was full of that vibrant lapis-lazuli blue which arches the western plains after the sun has set. I was standing, a tiny mite of a child, in front of the quarters of our commanding officer, Colonel Lewis. Just why I was there I do not know. It may have been the subconscious prompting induced by some memory of the boxes of candy which used to flow from that house to us children.[1]

The house on this occasion was silent and dark. The shutters were closed and instead of a tall, handsome figure in uniform appearing in the doorway as I probably expected, the door was shut and a group of soldiers stood a little to one side in front, talking in low, subdued voices. On the lawn in front of the porch was spread an army blanket. On it were dark red spots as if something had been spilt upon it.

The soldiers were engrossed in their conversation and entirely oblivious to the little fair-haired child who had stolen up to them.

They were saying something like: "Well, they got him, damn them! We put him on this here blanket and in the morning started to bring him in. We only just got here and he is in there now. He didn't last long after being hit, went out in the night."

There was more I do not remember and did not then comprehend, but I remember one of the men saying, "How did you get here, little one? You are Lieutenant Leefe's little girl, aren't you?" and stooping down and putting his arm around me and drawing me to him. "You better run along home, dearie, they'll be looking for you."

Not till sometime later did I learn what happened, set forth briefly in my father's handwriting on the back of a photograph of Colonel Lewis left me by my father. "Lieutenant Colonel W. B. Lewis, 19th Infantry, killed in action with the Cheyennes at Punished Woman's Fork, 27 Sept. 1878." I remember vividly the scene as it met my eyes but a few hours after a gallant soldier had met his end in one of the many forgotten clashes with the Indians in the yet unconquered frontier. The meaning of it did not come to me till the following day when the silence of the fort was broken by a clear bugle call and a column of troops with arms reversed marching out with a caisson bearing a long box covered with an American flag. Muffled drums beat out a slow, measured cadence as the procession moved out toward the river.

That is the second scene which comes back to me—a bright clear day with white puffy clouds and Lucindy, my nurse, turning aside my question about what it meant by saying, "Oh, just nothin', chile, le's go back and play in the yard."

But I was not satisfied and that afternoon stole away and went again to Colonel Lewis's quarters, not far from our own. It has since come to me that he could not have had any family as the house was still closed with the shades down. I sat on the front steps piecing together what I had seen and heard the night before—the blanket on the ground, the strange talk of the soldiers, the sad expression on the faces of my parents, and, finally, the slow mournful movement of the procession and the silent empty house behind me. Then I knew, the first occasion when the fact of death registered itself in my baby brain as an incident of life to be expected somewhere, sometime, and somehow.

It was not until sometime later that I learned how Colonel Lewis died. As related to us, Colonel Lewis was out in command of a combined force of infantry from our post and cavalry, which I think must have come from Fort Wallace or Fort Lyon, the latter post being the headquarters post of our regiment, the 19th Infantry. I do not recall that we had any cavalry at Fort Dodge. The trifling size of his force is indicated in the last dispatch from Colonel Lewis, received at our post and addressed to my father, in the customary use then of brevet titles in official communications. Preserved in my father's scrapbook it reads:

Camp, 4 miles west of Cimarron
at 11:30 PM Sept. 25th.   Capt. Leefe
                                                                        Post.
Will have to do with what forage we have. Start in the morning early. Sending Capt. Moses' company with broken transportation to Dodge. Let Dept. Headquarters know where we are tonight. I have 5 cos. of Cavalry and one Infantry. Command numbers 220 men.

                                                                        Wm. H. Lewis
                                                                        Lt. Col.

With this force Colonel Lewis intercepted a band of Cheyennes moving north from the Indian Territory some distance northwest of Fort Dodge. Led by Dull Knife and Little Wolf, the Indians, learning of Colonel Lewis's approach, took up position in a ravine, hoping to elude observation or be in a position to repel attack.

Colonel Lewis sent his scouts to reconnoiter the mouth of the ravine. They learned that the Indians had herded all their ponies there in anticipation of an attack at another point. The scouts were sent back with instructions to pick off and destroy the ponies to prevent escape. Meanwhile Colonel Lewis moved up with the cavalry to attack from one side of the ravine, sending his one remaining company of the 19th to attack from the other.

The scouts succeeded in making great havoc with the pony herd, killing at least sixty as the battle joined. Getting into position along his side of the ravine Colonel Lewis, with the cavalry, incautiously exposed himself and was shot down at once.

With their commander killed the cavalry faltered, dismounted, and continued firing on foot until withdrawal was sounded. The troops then went into camp for the night, confident that the destruction of the pony herd would prevent the Indians' escape and that with dawn the attack could be renewed. Some dismay appears to have been occasioned in the cavalry over the course to be pursued. Major [Clarence] Mauck of that arm took over command and established a strong defensive position against a possible counterattack. That night Colonel Lewis died and when Major Mauck moved at dawn he had the mortification of finding the Indians gone. They had gotten away riding double, attacking neighboring settlements which they raided to replenish their diminished pony herd, passing Fort Dodge, scalping and murdering along the way.

Sending the infantry company back to Fort Dodge with the remains of Colonel Lewis, Major Mauck set off in pursuit of the Indians. [He] eventually caught up with them and redeemed his earlier failure by administering a decisive defeat and capture of their leader. Their depredations before capture became known as the Dull Knife Raid.[2]

There is one other first memory—one of my brother seating himself innocently on a nest of stinging ants to watch a corporal put a squad of recruits through the agony of set-up exercises. In a moment the ants were swarming over his entire body as he bawled and yelled in anguish while my sister and I beat and slapped him in the vain hope of extinguishing the source of the misery. The problem was eventually solved by Lucindy catching him up and carrying him, kicking, to the backyard and immersing him in a tub of water.

Fort Dodge was a frontier post established about the middle of the nineteenth century. It played an important part in the campaigns against the Indians and was the headquarters from which set out several historic expeditions under famed commanders.

Originally it was but a collection of adobe huts and dugouts, some of which survived in our day. Several permanent brick buildings, framed barracks, and officers' houses were added shortly before we arrived. It stood about four miles east of what had become Dodge City, Kansas, a town founded but four or five years before we arrived. It consisted in my time of a hotel, several dance halls, and saloons and bore the reputation of a hell center of iniquity. Such was the rate of progress that by the time we moved there it was rapidly assuming the cloak of respectability.[3]

The fort itself by any modern standard would appear a pitiable-looking place. It was surrounded by an ordinary breast-high plank fence and, in one photograph I have of it, looks nothing so much as a shabby section of the Bronx in New York. The quarters had no plumbing, no electric light, and no water supply other than that furnished by outside wells. The roads were plain dirt and I do not recall the presence of any trees. The fort stood on a vast empty plain on which the sun beat down mercilessly in the summer and across which the blizzards howled in winter, burying the fence and roads in deep drifts. We kept warm by stoves and fireplaces going practically in all rooms. I have no recollection of suffering myself to any marked degree, but the suffering among the troops was intense. The year before we came post records showed no less than seventy major amputations for frozen extremities.

All transportation was by horsepower, in escort wagons and ambulances. The latter were passenger vehicles with cross seats, in addition to those designed for hospital purposes. We had one of our own, a handsome vehicle of its kind.

Fort Dodge was an infantry post built in the form of a square, officers' and soldiers' quarters facing each other across the parade ground. At the upper end were the commanding officer's quarters, our quarters, and the administration building. At the lower end were the quartermaster and other service buildings, and beyond these the stables and corrals. Here were kept the many mules and private mounts of the garrison. There were also a number of cows, of which we possessed one. I remember the rich milk she gave us every night for supper. We children went to bed early on the plains.

There were no movies to excite against sweet dreamless sleep and eager early rising.

The army reservation covered a number of square miles outside the fort. A short distance on all four sides the prairie grass was kept mowed down as a precaution against fire and unseen Indian approach. Beyond this mown space the plains began, stretching away endlessly. The Arkansas River flowed from the west a short distance below the fort where there was a ford. I had the feeling in looking at the plains that they stretched away to the end of the world—that they encircled us in a close and, at times, suffocating embrace. Often at night I would get out of bed and steal to the window to gaze at them, knowing that my father, as officer of the day, had gone to inspect the sentries. I would go and sit on the top step of the stairs to await his return.

I remember his asking me once, "Mamie, what are you doing up like this?" And, as my teeth chattered in the chill air, replying, "I was waiting to see you come back." Was it dread? Not for myself I know. Nothing had yet happened to give me fear for myself, it may have been the thought of Colonel Lewis. Whatever the reason, all the time we lived on the plains I felt the urge to get up when I woke in the dark night and gaze out the window. Sometimes the plains lay bathed in tender shimmering moonlight. On other nights, when the moon was hidden, the plains lay dark and brooding in purple stillness. Always there was the feeling of some nameless dread lurking unseen in their vast solitude. It comes in the cry of the coyote, heard often at night, coming from way off where a dim ray of light yet tinged the western sky long after the sun had set. It was like the sound of little children crying and I often got out of bed to go and look and cry silently with them.

Children in an army post were safe in those days. Soldiers were all about and alert in garrison, night or day. Beyond the confines of the post we were forbidden to go without the escort of an older person. We in the garrison were not in danger, but it was not so with those women and children who had to live outside the post in sparsely settled sections where there were no troops stationed.

A few years before we came to Fort Dodge an incident occurred which my father related to us and subsequently recounted in one of the many short stories he wrote for the magazines of the day. This incident I relate to show the conditions prevailing in that part of the country. [This happened at] old Fort Lyon in Colorado, headquarters post of our regiment, some four or five years before my time [there]. The post was then occupied by the cavalry under Custer. To meet the needs of the cavalry several hay farms were established in the rich bottomlands. One of these camps was eighteen miles from Fort Lyon.[4]

One day all the people working it were out in the hayfield except a woman and her infant child, wife of a teamster employed by the quartermaster department. He was on his way back to the house when a band of Cheyennes, renegades from Black Kettle's band, broke out of a patch of woods, killing and scalping another man and attacking the house. Quickly pillaging the place, they carried off the teamster's wife and infant. The poor man at a distance, being unarmed, could do nothing and was an agonized witness of the raid.[5]

An expedition in force was accordingly organized to seek out and bring back the captives, if still alive. The Indians, it should be added, rarely took male prisoners, usually killing and scalping these on the spot, and only carried off women and children. It should be mentioned that all the outrages were not committed by Indians. The whites frequently outraged them with equal ferocity.

Black Kettle, then supreme chief of the Cheyennes, was a well-disposed Indian who strove unremittingly to preserve peace with the whites, but he could not always restrain the evil-doers in his tribe. In recognition of his efforts the federal agency authorities invited him to a conference. It was done in good faith, but before the government emissaries arrived a force of Colorado Volunteer Cavalry swept down on the peaceful, unsuspecting camp and butchered a great number of them. Sadder still to relate, the commanding officer, Colonel J. M. Chivington, was in civil life a regularly ordained minister of the gospel. No force of U.S. regulars ever behaved in this way, but nothing appears ever to have been done about it.[6]

It was some time before the scouts sent out after the hayfield abduction reported the Indians having gone into winter quarters down to the south in the Indian Territory, in the region of the Washita and Canadian Rivers. By this time it was late November. General George Armstrong Custer and the troops, consisting mainly of the 7th Cavalry, forded the Arkansas River at Fort Dodge and headed south on the long march to the Indian Territory. The husband of the woman who had been carried off went along as a teamster. Some days later the force halted and formed a base at what came to be called Fort Supply. From there the column moved south, experiencing many days of frightful cold.

When finally arriving in the vicinity of the Indians' winter camp the expedition stealthily halted and waited through the night, no fires being allowed in the bitter cold. At dawn, with no breakfast, they were in the saddle and attacked. The attack itself was a complete surprise, the trumpet sounding the charge was the first intimation the Indians had of it. Awakened, they rushed from their tepees to be shot down at once as they emerged. Those who did not fall threw up their hands and surrendered. They knew this time they were dealing with U.S. regulars and that as prisoners of war they would be protected and fed and had no need to obey the impulse to fight to the last with no quarter expected. That was the customary course in intertribal conflicts and clashes with bodies of irresponsible state volunteer forces.

Nevertheless the fury of our men was such that the officers had great difficulty in restraining them from proceeding to a general massacre. They had been goaded by their own intense suffering on the way down and knowledge of the deed which brought them there. This was intensified when the woman and child were found in a tepee guarded by some squaws. The teamster had gone in with the charge. The poor woman, crouching in a corner, barely had time to cry out and her husband to answer when the squaws plunged their knives into her breast and she died in his arms at the very moment of rescue. To cap it they disemboweled the child with one stroke and then threw up their hands in tokens of surrender.

General Custer, I am told, in his memoirs speaks only of the disemboweling of the child captive, apparently not deeming the grief of a poor teamster as worth recording. But this may be expected of a man preoccupied mainly with his own glory. In my father's relation [of the story] the poor teamster had to be put away in an institution to preserve his reason.[7]

The attack was all over in a few minutes, Black Kettle himself being among the slain. Custer's loss was some eighteen men, among them the youthful Major Joel H. Elliott, last seen pursuing a small body of fleeing Indians. It is not to Custer's credit that on conclusion of the action he made no effort to find them, simply crossing them off as dead and withdrawing to his base at Fort Supply. Custer's prestige in his regiment and in the army generally was never the same following his abandonment of Major Elliott and his eighteen men.[8]

Other happenings during my father's tour of detached duty in that section show what our troops had to go through in those days, from discarding overcoats for close-hand fighting in a temperature of eighteen below zero to fighting in the same blue woolen uniform in the frightful heat of southwestern deserts. [Once] our forces ran out of water in pursuit of the Indians in the midsummer heat of a desert section in the Panhandle area and the men had to open the veins in their arms and drink their own blood to moisten their swollen tongues and parched throats. Did they turn back? Not a bit of it, they kept right on till the mission was accomplished.[9]

Such an incident might well have brought every man the congressional Medal of Honor, but it did not and these grand old regulars took it all in stride as part of the day's work. Graded decorations were to follow in a later period for varying degrees of heroism. My father in the Civil War had nine promotions, brevets, and citations for gallantry, one before his assembled regiment, but never received or wore an awarded decoration.

But all was not battle, murder, and sudden death in that time. Life had its lighter and more humorous side. A story which had become a classic at Fort Dodge was that of an Indian who came to the fort the year before we arrived. He brought with him five fat dogs and desired to swap these for the attractive wife of one of the lieutenants of the regiment then in garrison. When met with a curt refusal he departed, very wroth, remarking to someone on the way out, "White man fool. No squaw worth more than five dogs." So in that day did the Indians of the plains hold their womankind. They swapped and traded them freely.[10]

I have spoken of the peculiar effect the plains had upon me in their vast endless sweep of waving prairie grass. It always fascinated me, that grass. One day another nurse we had, Celeste, took me to view this close at hand, on the border of the reservation. Beyond the mown space it rose in a solid wall four or five feet high. Gray-green at the base, it graded to lavender, blue, and soft white-gray at the top. I can still see myself, with my arm out, pushing it aside and walking into its soft feathery midst. I can feel again the sense of smothering embrace as it enfolded me—the feeling of mystery and dread I encountered when viewing it from afar at night through the bedroom window. Something of the same effect it must have had on Celeste. I recall how her eyes rolled as she called me back, "Don't go in dere, chile, dey's t'ings in dere," and my running back to her arms in fright. Years later at a woman's garden club I heard a speaker allude to this aspect of it, saying, "Have any of you ever seen the prairie grass? If so, you will know the effect it has on you when first viewing it." I felt like jumping up and saying, "Yes, I have. I know all about it, and about the snakes, gophers, and coyotes too."

Our father, in addition to being a company officer, also functioned as the post quartermaster. He had his office in a building at the other end of the fort from our home and we children often visited him there. One memory comes to me of the enduring bonds of affection we formed with the enlisted men—those grand old frontier types of hard-bitten mature men who formed the rank and file of the old regular army. I was walking one day along the road to the corral when a large army wagon with its billowing hood came suddenly upon me. It was drawn by six mules going at a lively clip. Smith, the driver, was sitting in the high seat, one hand holding the reins and the other on the dashboard.[11]

"Get out of the way, you!" he roared. "Get off the road!"

"I won't!" I yelled back, planting myself squarely in the path of the approaching avalanche.

There was a harsh grinding of brakes and a hoarse "Whoa, whoa!" A moment later I found myself lifted by strong arms and deposited, fuming, in the high driver's seat. The six-mule team dashed on with me behind it and Smith using some words I had never heard before. Then, putting an arm around me and drawing me to him he said, "You just can't keep out of anything, can you, little one?"

It was always that way in all the posts we were stationed—a great bond between us and the enlisted men grew and has never passed. It was so also with my father. He loved his men and, like children, they intuitively knew it. This bond showed itself, strikingly, many years later at a post on the Canadian border which he commanded. The men, when off duty, were free to come and go across the border as they willed, from where they could have snapped their fingers at any effort to bring them back. Yet in the six years we were there not a man deserted from his company. This is a record that, so far as I know, is unmatched by any company in the army.[12]

Many years later I was moved to tears by receipt of a letter from another enlisted man, long out of the army, who had seen the announcement of my marriage in a newspaper. He wrote to know if I was the same Mamie Leefe he had known in her childhood, "daughter of the grandest officer and gentleman he had ever served under."

Army children are taught early to observe the rules of the garrison: not to walk on the grass in certain places; not to "cut corners"; to keep off the parade ground during guard mount and drill. But with other routine work and duty it was different. We children would give all we possessed to ride with Smith, or any other teamster, in various trips around the reservation. Sometimes we rode on dump carts on top of mounds of sweet-smelling mown grass.

Our greatest joy of the whole day was retreat, the hour when the flag comes down, bugles blow, and the evening gun salutes the sinking sun. The flagstaff at Fort Dodge seemed to our young eyes to reach the highest heaven. Every night two soldiers from the guard [detail] took the flag down and carried it away. As the gun fired they were too busy hauling it down to notice four children creeping up on them [to] crouch at the foot of the mound. It was in the days before the elaborate flag etiquette of the present provided that it must never touch the ground. Usually it was allowed to sink there in greater part; our object was to be underneath it when it did. When the unsuspecting soldiers gathered it up we would burst out screaming with glee and scamper off. It was very unmilitary, but I do not recall that we were ever called to time for it. The soldiers simply laughed and, in the spirit of the thing, feigned great astonishment. I have the feeling today that in some way our being enfolded by the flag had a marked influence on our lives. People outside the army may not understand this.

Fort Dodge did not differ very much from any other average small post of the day out there on the plains. The garrison had to make its own entertainment. By this I mean not only its amusement but the general routine of social life and calendar events, winter or summer. Births, marriages, and deaths followed one another and the fort's activities in this respect kept the garrison on its toes, and Dodge City also. The inhabitants of both places were able to forget for the moment the nearness of Indians and the dread they occasioned.

I do not remember how closely following the death of Colonel Lewis at the hands of the Cheyennes, the Utes also went on the warpath. After it was all over and they were being escorted back to their reservation as prisoners of war, they were brought to Fort Dodge by that brave and afterward distinguished soldier, Lieutenant Frank Lawton, and went into camp with the escort directly across the river from Fort Dodge. On Lieutenant Lawton's invitation practically the entire fort went over to visit the Indians. The fact that we children were to be included sent galloping shivers down our spines.[13]

Nevertheless we greeted the prospect with ecstatic shouts of anticipation. Imagine what it meant to small children who had heard of the massacre of whites and killing of soldiers and officers of their own garrison. Now we were to see these terrible foes at first hand! I look back and smile at the reaction of our elders. We children must all have our hair cut close lest some among the captive warriors be tempted to fall upon and scalp us! I can recall Grandmother Pinckney's vociferous objection to sacrificing my sister Kate's beautiful curls. It was finally compromised by her hair being braided, coiled, and bound tight with a ribbon of the same color. The rest of us were cropped close as billiard balls. This always occurred when large bands of Indians were reported in the neighborhood. It was the custom also of recruiting depots in shipping out to us batches of new recruits. They arrived with shining bald pates. I myself wore a boy's haircut up to my sixteenth birthday.[14]

On the morning we were to visit the Ute camp we children were up before anyone else and of course after that no one else could sleep. After a hearty breakfast preparations were made for the trip. Each of us children were given a small cotton bag filled with marbles, beads, pencils, crayons, a knife or two, and a clay pipe for bubbles. These were for the Indian children, [and] candy was added. Our elders took various presents for the chiefs. Two escort wagons were provided for the officers and members of their families. In these were set benches and stools. Perched on these we could look over the sides of the wagon.

The river was low at this season and the officers and soldiers not riding could wade across without getting too wet. As we forged into deep water the wagons began to sway and the mules felt the water under their bellies. Our excitement was keen but we obeyed the injunction not to show this until at the sides of our wagon suddenly appeared several brown heads emerging from the muddy water. They were followed by more and still more, until the water was swarming with Indian boys swimming around us. They were diving and bringing up mud from the bottom which was smeared over their heads and bodies, their white teeth gleamed, and their shrill cries froze us. We were scared pink, as the saying goes, [but] in truth our little faces were probably a shade whiter than usual. However, we screamed back in friendly greeting and waved our gift bags. In a moment they were swarming up the sides of the wagon, our bags went in no time.

Some bucks had also come down for an early swim. One of these climbed up on the opposite side, attracted by the feathers in my mother's hat, reaching to finger these eagerly. He was put off with a smile, a shake of the head, and "No" uttered emphatically. Disappointed, he dropped back into the water.

As we pulled out and up the steep bank of the opposite bank the Indian boys were swarming ashore to be met by mothers and sisters, squaws of the camp, with their harsh gutturals of inquiry and admonition.

We were guests for luncheon of Lieutenant Lawton, who commanded the escorting detachment. All that remains in my memory from then on was the war dance which took place at night and which we remained to see. It was evidently put on for our benefit. All was blue black around the camp, except where fires were burning among the lodges and the brilliantly lit space around the huge fire where the dance took place. With hordes of Indians standing behind us, we and other spectators formed a big ring encircling the fire. The dance was performed by about two dozen bucks. These young Indian warriors were a deadly, fascinating sight. Their bodies were stripped to only a breechcloth and glistened with grease, paint, and sweat. Their heads were bound with a cloth from which projected a single high-standing feather. I can still see the picture as if it were photographed on my brain in the lurid red glare of that fire, the utter ferocity of their faces and the sinister savagery of their red-and-white painted bodies, no two of which were painted alike.

Whether, despite all precautions, they had gotten hold of some "firewater" and were primed with that, I do not know, but their gestures were very bold and at times threatening. As they danced they would bend low, singing in a staccato guttural which, at times, would rise to a high clear note which only the Indian in his upper register possesses. Their hands beat out the rhythm of their chant. I remember that they frightened me terribly. Every now and then they would break out of line, rush up to the encircling whites, and let out a blood-curdling shriek, thrusting their faces close and baring their teeth in an ugly manner. The fascination was intense and we were tingling all over with excitement, the faces of our elders tense, but calm, and we children too dumb with fear to utter a sound.

When the time came to go we were bundled into our wagon, the restive mules set off at a lively pace, and we plunged into the silent darkened river, crossing back into the cordon of our own sentry lines near the fort. God bless those slowly pacing figures in the dark with bayoneted rifle and crisp alert challenge. Then the comforting welcome of home, a mother's soft breath in the goodnight kiss, and with it the passing of all fear as we dropped off to sleep.

It has taken many years for those of us who were children of the old army to overcome the dread and hatred we had for the Indians of those days. With the threat of terrible outbreaks and the death and torture of our loved ones hovering at the back of our minds, it is not so surprising that we did feel so and failed perhaps to appreciate the flagrant injustices perpetrated on the Indians by our own government in the betrayal of many promises. Yet, in the army, there was a certain friendly feeling intermixed, as we understood the Indian better than those on the outside. The Indians themselves had more respect for the army than for the civilian population and [they] honored the wearers of Uncle Sam's uniform. A soldier was a warrior, like themselves, and usually a fair one. They would salute often when meeting one.

Today the Indian is a very different person, often indistinguishable in dress and occupation from other rural folk. As I write, over thirty thousand of them are serving loyally in our overseas armed forces. But our feeling toward them as it once was can be understood from what we then had to face.

My mother has told me of a post they once occupied where the officers dwelt only in adobe houses and where the Indians were all about and very, very near. Sometimes a penetrating smell would first betray the presence of one of them and she would look up from her knitting to see the face of an Indian peering at her through the window. Can you imagine what this meant to some woman reared in the tender refinement and security of an eastern home, as many in the old army had been?

Fort Lyon, I think, is the place where my mother first had to face this close, too close, contact with the Indian at unexpected moments. I was but an infant there, [and] it was at this post that my two brothers, both younger than I, were born. From there we moved to Fort Dodge in the later seventies.

There, in the still raw conditions prevailing, my parents and Grandmother Pinckney impressed upon our young minds the traditions we must live up to. Devotion to the flag and the part our forebears on my mother's and grandmother's side played in this respect in our country's history from Plymouth Rock down. Of the heritage of noblesse oblige from the gentry of England where my father was born and, lastly, the honor of the army and esprit de corps of the regiment. We must remember that we were part and parcel of this and must never disgrace it. Our social poise was established early. I do not mean that we were snobbish. We were always able to adjust ourselves in an American way to fit the life of that part of the country in which we might happen to be and to look for the good in it as it might be found there.

2

DIVERSIONS AT FORT DODGE

AS A FAMILY we were very musical. My mother and grand-mother both had very lovely singing voices. My mother might well have become a grand opera singer if she had not married early a poor junior army officer. She it was who bequeathed to me the talent which set my foot in later life upon the path of a professional concert singer. My two brothers also sang well, eventually. The elder, Fred, who for some reason we called Dick, was usually a bit off key but later developed a baritone voice of great accuracy, beauty, and pathos. The younger brother, Sydney, also developed a fine baritone but found no corresponding inspiration for its further development. Absence at college and marriage removed them both from our daily lives when still young. Kate developed a bent for instrumental music rather than singing and became an accomplished pianist. I was always singing, almost from the time I can first remember. Our house overflowed with song from dawn to sunset and sometimes later.

There came to Dodge City while we were there that beautiful singer, Christine Neilson, "The Swedish Nightingale." My mother was thrilled at the chance to hear again some beautiful professional singing after a long time away from the big cities. She told me of the evening concert she attended in Dodge City arranged in that wild place where nothing of the kind had before happened.

The hall was filled to capacity with an audience of the kind I will venture to say Miss Neilson had not before faced. Cowboys from adjacent ranges came in, some in "store clothes" and others in their usual attire. During Miss Neilson's singing the silence of these men was very marked. These strong wild-drinking men, who usually sat down only at a faro table and would not hesitate to take the life of anyone who cheated, sat still as death as her voice filled the air.

Then, as her last note fell off in tender sweetness, the storm of their tribute broke. They leaped to their feet with hats waving, their yells and "yippees" shook the house. They would not sit down and encore after encore had to follow until Miss Neilson, exhausted and overwhelmed, retired with her handkerchief before her eyes. Nowhere in the cultural centers of the East had she received such a tribute. Hers were not the only moist eyes in the house when she finally was dragged forth again to sing "Home Sweet Home."

Of the cowboys much has been written which does not need repeating here. We children, brought up with them and knowing nothing of that side of their character which has been described as "seamy," soon learned to love them for that side which we saw, the fundamental good and worth which was there. They were part of the landscape all about us, in their colorful garb, going usually at a gallop. It is the reason why in later life I still love their unmusical whining songs.

In the army we always had a retinue of servants, some from the enlisted ranks and some from the outside. In our own family there were Johnson, our colored cook who was from Dodge City, and Lucindy, the housemaid and for some time our nurse, followed later by Celeste. Frank, a Hollander whose last name sounded something like Dudu, was an enlisted man who served as our striker. A striker in the army was an enlisted man who performed, voluntarily, the function of general handyman for an officer's family, for a consideration. Frank also acted as our coachman and took care of our cow. He blackened boots and kept all lamps trimmed and filled and fires going in winter. His mother, wife, and children lived on a farm of their own near Dodge City.[1]

The days when Frank invited us children to visit there with him were red-letter days for us. Frank would drive us there in our own ambulance. This vehicle was of dark polished wood resembling ebony and was handsomely upholstered in blue broadcloth. It had a back seat, with another facing it, and a front seat for the driver. Under the cushion was a lid covering a hole for the benefit of anyone, especially children, who just "couldn't wait" in a protracted trip. Many changes of station were effected in those days by animal-drawn transportation, and this feature was indispensable. One of my girl friends, an army child, was born in one of these vehicles during a change of station. War Department orders did not envision contentment of mind for anxious husbands and postpone or time troop movements accordingly. For our use horses were always available from the garrison stables. We used two jet black ones, and the appearance of our equipage, with shining harness and steel trimmings burnished to shine like polished silver, was very handsome.

To sit with Frank as he drove was the greatest thrill we could have. Frank and his family were of thrifty Dutch stock. They had a fine prosperous farm. Enlisted men sometimes were well fixed through some such connection. They were usually local enlistments, not depot recruits. Generally enlisted men fared very well in the matter of food. Each post had its own garden worked by the men and furnishing edibles not drawn on the government ration. Their meals were hearty and pleasantly varied.[2]

The table at Frank's farm was always well supplied. On the days we were there we hardly could see across the table for the heaps of good things—chicken, potatoes, corn, and other fresh vegetables, interspersed with bowls of rich gravy, bread, butter, and usually two kinds of jelly. Of course we stuffed and after eating I usually went to sleep in Grandmother Dudu's ample lap. Others of us curled up on the couch.

One day, however, we did not. It was very hot and Frank decided to [take] off his woolen uniform and lay down in his underclothing on a bed in a room off the living room which, fortunately, had a door leading directly outside. This opened on a sloping roadway beside the house where Frank had parked the ambulance after unhitching the horses. He had left it with the brake on to prevent its rolling back down the drive. This terminated in a solid brick wall about eight feet high, put up as a snow shield against northern blizzards in winter.

On this day, dinner being over, it was suggested that we play out-of-doors so that Frank might sleep undisturbed. We bounded out with a shout and after playing around a bit concentrated our activities on the ambulance, climbing in and out. In some way one of us must have loosened the brake by playing with it. The ambulance began to move. Climbing on the pole to play "horsey back" we shouted "giddap" and thoughtlessly accelerated the movement with our feet. Opposite Frank's window the ambulance began to gather speed and we became alarmed. Our shouts and the crunching of wheels on gravel must have apprised Frank of what was happening. He came bounding out the side door in time to see the ambulance receding down the slope at a fast pace.

I remember a frantic shout, "The kits! They will all be kilt!" and [him] starting down the hill after us. Then the ambulance hit the wall with terrific force. Kate, who was inside, had opened the side door to jump out and was thrown violently to the ground. Those of us on the pole were spilled all over the driveway. Kate was the only casualty. She suffered a severe injury to her arm, a fracture I think, from the treatment given by the doctor at the fort when we got home. "There's a little heroine for you," he remarked as he bound her up. "You're a soldier's daughter all right." She had not whimpered a bit during his ministrations nor on the drive home, although in great pain.

I should add that the ambulance, strangely enough, was not damaged a bit, landing stern first against the wall and rebounding. So ended that memorable day at Frank's hospitable farm. Many more such visits were to follow before we left Fort Dodge. It was all part of that feeling of intimate family relationship which prevailed in that day among the occupants of far-flung isolated posts with such small garrisons, officers and men alike. Nor did this intimacy lead to regrettable consequences in discipline among the sober-minded mature men of the time, hard as they might be and exhibiting the weaknesses to which all men are subject. In all my army experience we never encountered personal disrespect from any of them. It was always "Miss Mamie," "Miss Katie" from all of them.

The inner life of a post is something the public never sees. It sees, from the outside, post police details forcibly herding back men who "have had too much" in some red-light district, or some man carried, kicking, to the guardhouse, [or] groups of prisoners under armed guard cutting grass and cleaning up roads. From this they may conclude that living among such men cannot be pleasant. But we who dwelt among them knew the gold in human character to be found among them under human failings and, with this outlook, could dwell among them happily.

Especially at Christmastime was this family feeling evident, thrown together as we were, alone, in that far-off plains post. Christmas was the outstanding event of the year. In our family it was, first and foremost, the birthday of our Lord, Jesus Christ.

Weeks before the event our household was in a great state of excitement. Mysterious packages coming from a distance were stored away in a closet by Grandma Pinckney and Daddy went about the house with a smile and a subtle twinkle in his eye. When the great night arrived we were all grouped about the piano to sing the old sweet chorals, ending with "Silent Night," a reverent hush following. The entire house was lit up with candles in every window. Excitement knew no bounds when the hour arrived for the garrison Christmas tree party in the administration building. This was an occasion when the entire garrison, excepting officers and men on guard or other outside duty, gathered with the members of their families in the large hall where the tree had been erected.

The preliminaries to be gone through in our case whetted impatient anticipation. The boys were washed "behind the ears" and told to sit down with a book to keep them off the floor. My sister dressed in all white with a blue sash having a big bow in the back. I too was in white, but with pink ribbons and sash. My father wore a tight fitting uniform and a pair of black boots we had never seen before and which later came to be detected on Santa Claus. The two boys were in black velvet suits and white collars.

Our parlor [had] tambour lace curtains, wine-colored velvet drapes, a rug to match, and the white mantel with a vase or two on it, and, of course, the piano. So would our Christmas Eve begin. Then, for safety, the candles in the windows were extinguished and we all repaired to the administration building. The great tree, brilliantly lit with real candles and carefully watched by two enlisted men, stood upon the stage at one end. It seemed to our young eyes at least fifteen feet tall. The hall was painted white and lit by many kerosene lamps on brackets and central fixtures. It was festooned with garlands of evergreen and filled with the odor of burning wax candles. An orchestra of enlisted men furnished the music for dancing which was to follow the distribution of gifts. These were grouped about the tree and along the walls of the stage. There were dolls, Noah's arks, animals, and every conceivable kind of toy for the kids, brought from afar on orders placed weeks before. But many of the toys were made by women of the fort [such as] dolls in complete costume, even to coats and hats. They had been made from dainty bits in the clothing of officers' and soldiers' wives. It is doubtful if any children of today get any greater thrill from their expensive mechanical toys than came to the tots on that far-off plain from something that had been made by the wife of Captain This or Sergeant That.

Some of the little boys and girls who danced that night on the plains were in after years to dance to the music of the Marine Band in the White House in more distinguished company and luxurious surroundings. But no later thrill coming to me in that way exceeded the one I felt as a child on that wonderful night in the plain white painted hall of Fort Dodge.

What excitement when Santa Claus came in from a side door on the stage to distribute the gifts! I was so overcome with awe that

I ran and hid behind the big bass viol. One of the musicians bid me not to be afraid and go up and get my gifts. I edged timidly up to Santa Claus. There was something funny about his eyes, they looked just like my daddy's. I was no longer afraid.[3]

When the presents had all been distributed and Santa had retired, chorals were sung and the floor cleared for dancing. I ran to my mother with my presents and looked 'round for my daddy. He was nowhere to be seen, but shortly came out the side door through which Santa had disappeared. The children sat along the walls and watched the dancing begun by their elders. First, the commanding officer and his lady, then the other officers present, in order of rank, with their partners, followed by the noncommissioned officers in the same order down to and including the many private soldiers present, till the floor was filled. The children had their chance in an interlude, during which they were also treated to refreshments—popcorn, cake, and ice cream.

We were bundled up to be taken home. Those among the elders who had no children and who so desired remained to pursue the dancing to a later hour. Outside all was still and the stars shone as they only can on a clear winter night on the plains. Someone struck up "Silent Night" and the various groups diverging on the paths leading to the officers' and married soldiers' quarters joined in, filling the stillness of the night with this sweet melody. Thus would pass our Christmas Eve, the memory of which has remained undimmed through all these years.

The sense of being one family in the life of our post extended as well to our servants. Johnson, our colored cook, we adored. He had the same feeling toward us. From the moment my mother engaged him he exhibited toward her devotion and respect. If he failed to scrub the kitchen floor, following a night out and the loss of his wages in a crap game at Dodge City, my mother had only to walk across the floor, lifting her skirt slightly and giving him a meaningful look. Then out would come the pail and scrubbing brush and he would "fall to" lustily.

We children were never so happy as when allowed to visit his quarters in an outbuilding in our backyard. It was next to the chicken coop. Johnson's great purpose in life, after being a good cook, was to assist little baby chicks into the world and see that they attained chickenhood safely.

Whenever we were invited by him to "come see de new nest" we were eager to go. Entering his own hut we became aware of baby chicks everywhere—hats full of them. He must have collected for the purpose from everyone. The hats often held as many as six chicks, little feathery things with staring black eyes and yellow beaks. Going from one to another we would squeal with delight when he put one in our hand.

But they were not always inside. One day I came upon him in the yard. He had on an enormous straw hat, which was bobbing up and down strangely. To my wonder at this he replied, "Jus' chicks, chile, jus' chicks, only jus' born."

Johnson was a character, a bit of the old South and of a type I fear has gone, never to return.

The day the traveling photographer came to Dodge City and the fort was a red-letter day in both places. Word went like wildfire through the town and post. Soon there were enough men, women, and children to keep him busy for days. When he came to the fort we were dressed in our best and ready. He set up his tent at a point assigned to him and his waiting subjects formed in a line. I do not remember if our elders in the Leefe family were all photographed but we children were, with Grandma Pinckney's lap acting as the throne and her hands as instruments for assuring perfect stillness. Kate made a beautiful picture with her curls and fawnlike eyes. I, in my rabbit skin coat, and not much bigger than a rabbit, was photographed successfully along with the younger of my two brothers.

When it came to Dick's turn he simply would not behave. He kicked and yelled and bawled to be let down. Finally the photographer, to hold his attention, lit a bunch of newspapers and held these in one hand while he took off the camera cap with the other. The stratagem worked until the flame burned his hand and he dropped the blazing paper to the ground. It promptly set fire to the dry grass inside the tent and a wild scramble to get out ensued.

The blaze was extinguished before much damage was done and the picture, a tintype, when developed turned out perfectly.

This custom of traveling photographers was a quaint feature of the day on the western plains. It included in this instance hauling along an organ on wheels and combining the work of photographer with preaching the Gospel.

Another event before we left Fort Dodge was the baptism of my two brothers by that beloved figure, Bishop LaTourette. We lost touch with the LaTourettes when leaving the plains but years later in Washington were reunited with them in the persons of three daughters who had married army officers. The baptism took place in the Episcopal church which, by that time, had come into being in Dodge City. Dick again furnished some excitement by asking on that occasion, "Why does that man wear a nightgown in the day-time?"[4]

These are among my last memories of Fort Dodge. The move we were about to make was to Fort Leavenworth. As each day brought us nearer to departure we saw the various rooms in our house stripped of their furnishings until at last we were surrounded by only bare walls. The night before our departure we slept on borrowed cots. Our household effects had practically all gone the day before, only our trunks and valises remaining. Nowadays, I am told, the government provides basic furniture which remains in the house for succeeding occupants, but in our day everything was packed and shipped at government expense. Transportation was not provided for domestic servants. These usually remained to be engaged by newly arriving officers' families. So it was to be with those dearly loved servitors and friends, Johnson, Lucindy, and Celeste. Gathered in the apelike arms of Johnson and to the smelly bosoms of the other two I cried bitterly and their tears mingled with mine. The last we saw of them was as they stood in front of the house waving to us as we drove off.[5]

Everything being in readiness, we climbed into the ambulance. Hark! The bugle! There, swinging down the road from the barracks came the battalion, arms at right shoulder and the bugles sounding a lively quickstep. They marched the four miles to the station, their baggage following in wagons.

Many friends were at the station to see us off. As our train pulled slowly out, with the men of several companies waving from the windows, we were followed on the road running along beside the track by cowboys on their beautiful mounts, friendly Indians on their swiftly racing ponies shrilling to us in parting whoops, and a whole cavalcade of wagons lashed to a gallop with people running alongside.

These were left behind as the train gathered headway and passed the fort in a rush. Then it was gone and none among our family but myself ever saw it again.[6]

Years later, when a married woman with my young son, then a child of eight, I accompanied my husband on a lecture tour across the country to the Pacific Coast. As night was falling on the Kansas plains the train came slowly to a stop at a local station. Glancing through the window of our compartment there, on the side of the station, was a sign, "Dodge City, Kan." With one bound I was in the aisle, racing to the platform where the conductor stood.

"Conductor," I gasped, "how long does the train stop here?"

"Exactly three minutes, ma'am," he answered.

"Then I am going to set my foot on that ground again if I never do another thing."

And I did. I stood for a minute in the fading light and looked about. A few buildings I did not recognize stood beyond the station. A few men lounged about in front of them. Could this really be the place? Far off to the southeast a few lights began to twinkle. Could they be the fort? Did it still stand? There was nobody at hand to ask. Then, running along beside the track was a road I knew—and I was a child again. From far off where the lights twinkled against the rose and lavender of the eastern sky there seemed to float to me the sweet clear notes of my mother's voice, coming through the open windows of a house on a corner behind a rough board fence and an outside well. She was singing "Seeing Nellie Home." I could see the pacing sentry pausing to listen as other passers would.

Then—"All aboard!" As the train pulled out I was standing on the observation platform, my eyes, through their tears, fastened on the distant horizon where I pictured the fort might still stand with the flag flying and the bugles blowing as the sun went down.

Not until many years later did I learn that as the train pulled away the fort was but a tint on the rainbow of my memory and that it had been abandoned in 1882.

3

FORT LEAVENWORTH, KANSAS

1880–1881

Age Eight to Nine Years

THE DAY which followed our departure from Fort Dodge is a bit hazy in my recollection. I recall the excitement of being on a train and all the new things to be seen from the car windows, hasty meals at the eating counters in one or two stations, and the wonder of our seats being made into berths by porters with shining black faces and bright smiles for us children. There is the memory of being awakened the next morning by the bump of recoupling in the outskirts of a large smoky city, which must have been Kansas City, then more things to be seen out the windows as the train speeded north to Leavenworth.

We were met by two officers coming forward to meet us on the platform, old friends of my father. I remember the battalion detraining and lining up beside the cars, the men of several companies barking, "Here," as the roll was called and then marching off into the fort to the "west end" where the infantry barracks were located.[1]

We and the other officers' families were entertained at breakfast by the families of officers stationed at the post. Then came the selection of quarters, which were assigned according to rank. This was a custom which sometimes involved unwelcome removal by occupants to accommodate higher-ups to whom the more desirable houses would go.[2]

Our assigned quarters were in a block at the west end and contained features not familiar in the simpler accommodations at Fort Dodge. They were frame houses and, I suppose, might be considered primitive compared with what may stand there now.[3]

"We like this place," was our immediate verdict. Yet at night, when tucked away in our beds, our minds would drift off to Fort Dodge, the tall waving prairie grass and scenes and faces we were to see no more. There was a certain sadness over leaving the small post on the western plains tinging the joyous anticipation with which we looked forward to life in the new post where we were to spend two enchanted years.[4]

Fort Leavenworth was a post which, when once lived in, was never to be forgotten. Situated on the eastern border of Kansas on a high bank overlooking the Missouri River, it was imposing and beautiful in its setting. One could gaze down from its heights on the river's swirling and usually muddy water flowing between shores where quicksands were an ever-present threat to the unwary foot. We children were commanded strictly never to descend to the shoreline under any circumstances. While we were at Leavenworth two soldiers were lost while swimming there and we were careful to view the spot only from a distance.

The military reservation then covered some twelve square miles. It was the headquarters of a district and was garrisoned by infantry, artillery, engineers, and other special troops and was the site of a large military prison. Many officers of various arms and their families were stationed there. Staff headquarters were on the main parade ground. My memory of compass points is not very distinct but, as I recall, there was a large arsenal to the north and quartermaster and commissary department buildings overlooking the river.[5]

Military regulations, routine procedure, and formality were more strictly observed in this big post and there seemed less of the intimate family spirit prevailing than in the smaller garrison at Fort Dodge. This was natural, there being so many more officers of high rank and so many more troops of diverse arms. There was also less of the dread induced by the nearness of the Indians, a dread ever present in the smaller posts farther west.

The things to be seen and wondered at in this post were something to fill the minds of children with excited interest—the bigness of the fort, particularly. One large area, when explored, merged into another equally large. The main parade ground was the biggest we had ever seen. We could see it from our porch and it held a never-ending interest when resounding to the "hep-hep-hep" of drilling exercises and when large bodies of troops swung by in parade with bugles blowing, drums, and the band alternating with bursts of martial music. I can never feel as some civilians do that this atmosphere of military life fostered the desire to kill for killing's sake. Our home training took care of that in the ideas instilled by our parents and my observation in later years was that this was true among army children generally. We were all fighters, it was true, and at each post where we went, we, girls included, had to fight the boys who lived in the post when we arrived. It was so at Fort Leavenworth, but we never failed to earn our right to be tolerated among them and to develop lasting friendships.

Of army children it has been said that none of them are angels and most are devils. If so, many of the most honored names in our history came from that tribe. To the credit of army children, they may be "little devils" like other good healthy specimens of childhood, but they observe the rules of life laid down for them in the garrison and this training led them to observe the rights of others. There was no wanton destruction of others' property in all the mischief they were constantly up to—and that was plenty. It was not only the teaching in our case within our own family but the general disciplinary conduct among all, old and young, which was imbibed as the natural way of life. I cannot see that this deprived any of us of that initiative and individuality which is supposed to depart in any regimentation.

[At Fort Leavenworth] we children fell into a new routine. It usually began each day with a walk down a path bordering one side of the main parade ground. We had been instructed to go no farther than a certain point when alone and to these instructions we adhered. I do not think we children ever disobeyed these commands willfully; possibly my two brothers may have stretched a point occasionally, as boys growing up will do. In time they had walked over the entire reservation.

Army children as a rule had only such facilities for formal education as post schools offered. These were far from the best. At Leavenworth we attended a Catholic parochial school outside the post. We were not Catholics but Episcopalians and although the post school may have been good, the parochial school was preferred as better and many from the fort attended it. We never regretted it. It gave us good schooling, including one in manners and while we had this at home, we were thrown into contact with children from outside the service and in that way learned to have respect for these. We never developed that narrow spirit which occasionally led some army folk to speak of those outside as "damn civilians." Similarly, in the respect we developed for those of differing religious faith. In later life we had many friends among the Catholic clergy — dear friends of high minds and noble outlook.[6]

The day we were told we were to attend real dancing school was a day of joy to my sister and self, but to the boys it was a day of woe. "We are not sissies. We want to play ball," they wailed. Later when the ice was broken they learned to dance beautifully. We had a good dancing master, a Frenchman, M. Lanier, also a good orchestra. The annual children's ball at the end of the season was quite an event. Our dear daddy soon after their marriage had given our mother yards of the most heavenly blue silk. This had been made up into a ball gown for mother, trimmed with real Valenciennes lace. It had not been worn for years and Grandma Pinckney had put it away after having the lace cleaned, for Kate's and my benefit when older. It had gone out of style and as the ball approached it was gotten out and cut up for us. It was made up into little tight bodices and full skirts with lace on the sleeves and around the neck. White stockings, sashes, and black French sandals completed the costume. Our hair was done up with colored bows.

All the families in the garrison attended the ball. I mean, of course, those having children. A collation of ice cream, colored lemonade, and cake was served. The dancing hall was large. During a pause in the program M. Lanier came forward on the stage where the orchestra sat and made a speech congratulating the class.

"And now," he said, "we have the pleasure of presenting this medal to the one who has become the best dancer in our class. Will Miss Kate Leefe please come forward?"

How I jumped, clapping with joy and pride as Kate, a rosy red, mounted the steps. Since that day I have attended many brilliant functions but never with more pride than on that night when he pinned that medal on my dearly loved sister.

The many attractions to young and old at Leavenworth were a continuing source of happiness during our stay. The "grown ups" were very gay. Dances, card parties, balls, theatricals, and formal and informal calls succeeded each other through the winter season. My father, mother, and even Grandma Pinckney were still young, full of life, and very popular, both in the garrison and the neighboring city of Leavenworth. My father and mother both were beautiful dancers. I even became so in later life when I had outgrown my early tomboy look—at least I have been told. Up to that time I was known in army circles as "Legs."

But life at Fort Leavenworth also had a more serious side for us. We were in no danger of Indian attack and I do not recall that troops from the fort were called upon to take any action against them. We did have as a prisoner of war the famous Chief Joseph of the Nez Percé tribe. As a prisoner of war he was kept in the guardhouse and not in the prison, which was for military convicts. I can recall him sitting on the upper balcony of the guardhouse looking down on the groups from outside the fort who came for a glimpse of this great warrior. I don't doubt that secretly he was inclined to spit at them; Indians were inclined to express their contempt that way. We children were cautioned not to go too close to him when encountered walking about as he was allowed to do occasionally under guard. The reason was, we were told, that he "had crawling things on him." This kept us away from him as nothing else might have done.

One day my father, then a first lieutenant in actual rank, although addressed as captain from a regular service brevet, had been detailed to escort Chief Joseph to a reservation in the Indian Territory to which his tribe had previously been sent. He was to have a squad of soldiers as escort.[7]

The day he left we children wept. Our dear daddy was going to where he might be scalped, especially as he refused our plea to have cropped the luxuriant black hair which he wore long in the custom of the day. When, afterward, he came back to us safely and told us the story of the trip, we never ceased talking of it. As a bit of authentic history not appearing elsewhere, to my knowledge, I here set it down.

The trip was made in a day coach especially set apart. The squad of four soldiers was divided into watches, two remaining awake while the others slept. My father himself, being responsible, slept also in the day coach with his revolver on. I should add that Chief Joseph was told that at last he was to return to his tribe. The only sign of emotion he gave, and a strange one for an Indian, was a deep flush of color suffusing his handsome swarthy countenance. His only comment was a short "Ugh!"

They left on an early train and when night fell they made themselves as comfortable as one could in a day coach with ordinary plush seats. My father slept at intervals while the soldiers kept watch in relays. Toward morning my father was awakened by a strange humming noise blending with the roar of the train. Sitting up, his eyes were greeted with a strange sight. The two soldiers on guard were standing up looking at Chief Joseph. Joseph had mounted his seat and was sitting on its back, his feet on the seat, chanting some sort of song in a low voice. The great chief made no movement and my father and the two soldiers remained watching him until the chant ended and he dropped down again into his seat. The song lasted a long time and it was nearly daybreak before it ceased and sleep could be resumed, with the soldiers changing watch. What the chant may have been my father did not know—whether it was a war chant or one in celebration of his return to his tribe. The tribal sentiment was very strong among the Indians.

For some time the graduates of the Indian School at Carlisle, Pennsylvania, on returning to their reservation, promptly discarded their school clothes and resumed the dress and speech of their tribe. My husband has told me of an instance of this related by an artist friend who spent some time painting among them. He tried to obtain a photograph of a beautiful Indian girl when a buck in full war dress galloped up and said in perfect English, "Stop that! You can't photograph that woman, she is my wife."

"All right," said the artist, "but tell me this, how and where did you learn to speak English like that?"

"Carlisle," said the Indian as he galloped off.[8]

My father had a certain admiration for Chief Joseph, as indeed did all the army of the day. He was said to be among the noblest of the Indian chiefs and an outstanding strategist, comparable as a cavalry leader to Sheridan. Before his capture he had conducted his tribe on a two-thousand-mile march from Idaho, ancestral home of the tribe, to a point fifty miles south of the Canadian border where he surrendered. His march has been compared by military men to the march of Xenophon's Ten Thousand.[9]

It was occasioned by his refusal to yield peacefully to an ultimatum to surrender their existing lands in Idaho for white settlement and accept another reservation in the Indian Territory. They would find their home elsewhere [and] the whole tribe set out on this migration, striking north and east. It included young and old, the infirm and the dying. Every foot of the thousand miles Joseph had to fight three armies assailing him from both flanks and rear under Colonel Nelson A. Miles, General O. O. Howard, and Colonel Samuel A. Sturgis. When finally capitulating he is said to have pointed to the sun with the dramatic gesture for which the Indian orator is noted, and said, "From where the sun now stand I will fight no more forever." The officers were so imbued with admiration of him that they made generous terms of capitulation which the civil government at Washington ratified, I think, and then shamelessly broke. The indignation of the officers at this was profound and bitter.

Arriving at the reservation in the Indian Territory, my father delivered his prisoner to the agency authorities on hand to receive him. The last my father saw of Chief Joseph was his erect and stately moving form receding in the distance where his assembled people stood waiting. It was almost, to my father, like the passing of Arthur in Tennyson, or of some other legendary hero to the shores of Valhalla.

As one season merged into another at Fort Leavenworth, as in autumn and spring, the changes were heralded by severe and sometimes disastrous storms. The rain fell in torrents and the wind tossed everything about. Chimneys usually suffered, sometime torn off the roofs. I can recall the sound of bricks from our own chimney bumping down the roof and plopping off onto the ground.

I think it was at Leavenworth, although it may have been Fort Gibson, [when] awakened by noise and being a bit frightened, I got out of bed and went into the hall, running against something soft as I did so.

"Hush," said a voice. "Did you hear that?"

It was Grandma Pinckney crouching at the head of the stair. Below, a window or door was being forced open. Then a stealthy step could be heard at the foot of the stair. Grandma raised her arm and hurled some heavy object down the stair toward it. It was a big water pitcher she had grabbed from her washstand. There was a crash and a cry and the sound of someone stumbling around at the foot of the steps, then the front door was jerked open and the figure of a man could be seen vanishing into the night. Grandma promptly ran down after him and out onto the porch. She said afterward that it looked like a big black man but she could not be sure in the dark. Who it was we never knew. It may have been a convict escaped from the prison or a marauder from outside who had sneaked by the guard lines. Our house was in a block at the west end not far from a patch of woods, from which access to the fort undetected would have been easy in the dark. My father was away in the West on another mission when this happened and

Grandma Pinckney, who had the indomitable fighting spirit of a pioneer woman, assumed the role of man of the house on this occasion.[10]

Though we remained at Leavenworth but two years, these years were so packed with interest and variety that we never had a dull moment. I must except the period when we went through the measles there. Which brings me to the untiring work of the Medical Corps, the doctors who took care of us at Fort Leavenworth, of the doctors we knew at this and other posts. First, and in fond memory, is Dr. William C. Gorgas, who in later years was to achieve world fame in connection with the Panama Canal. He was a dear sweet friend. During the First World War, my husband, as a major in the army, met him. He was then a major general and surgeon general of the army. It is among my prideful memories that upon my husband mentioning the family he spoke of me as "a sort of godchild of his." There were other doctors I recall who gave their best to the people of various garrisons.[11]

One amusing incident I recall happening at another post. A doctor was routed out of bed one cold night by an excited lieutenant who exclaimed when the door opened, "Doctor, sorry to disturb you, but I have just made a dreadful mistake. Instead of taking the medicine you gave me I have swallowed some of the baby's eyewater."

"Humpf!" replied the doctor. "Well, go back and swallow the rest of it, and if you don't feel better in an hour come back and let me know."

These army doctors were great men and, in addition to their usual practice, had to bring into the world the babies of officers and soldiers alike, working generally without most of the modern equipment the profession now has.

As our days at Leavenworth lengthened into the succeeding year we found never-ending pleasure in wandering about the huge post. We were growing up, and the scope of our permitted wandering was increasing. We had come to regard the post as our very own and wept when told we were to leave soon.

Such is the army—a short time only, as a rule, at any one post and then on to some other. At some we found the stay too long, but not at Leavenworth. It was the same with our elders. There was so much going on that could not be enjoyed at other posts. The round of receptions, dinners, and other events was endless. Of course we children did not participate in any of these diversions of our elders. But my mother has told me of fifteen-course dinners given by the commanding general and his wife, two very wonderful persons, and others. I can still see my mother dressed for one of those in a gown of black satin and jet passementerie with Duchesse lace, pink roses in her low bodice, and her dark hair low on the neck with a curl over the forehead. Those knowing her only late in life when she had grown stouter could not suspect the beauty that was hers in her younger days.

Our attendance at the Catholic parochial school did not interfere with regular attendance at our own church, the Episcopal. The Episcopal has been our church ever since my mother and grandmother lived in Tennessee, from which they went to live in Arkansas. My mother was born in the North, but spent most of her girlhood in the South. Fort Smith, Arkansas, was the first post lived in by my mother and father after they were married and the little Episcopal church there was the first they attended together. Incidentally, that post was where my sister Kate was born. I was born afterward at Baton Rouge, Louisiana, where my father was also stationed.

So we went regularly to our own church, the Episcopal. The one at Leavenworth was a simple little one in the traditional English architecture. We loved it and its surroundings. On a later visit to Leavenworth I sang in this little church. I had come, a young society bud, to spend two delightful months as the guest of friends stationed there. By that time I was counted as having a beautiful voice, the church was filled, and I received many compliments. They came to me from the general commanding the artillery there and others of rank, down to the private soldier from the band who played the violin obligato to my solo. Twice I sang there and I remember seeing again the same general present. He came up and introduced himself, [saying], "I don't usually come to these things, but I wanted to hear you sing again."[12]

It was one of the things which encouraged me later to go on and become a professional concert singer.

In family procedure our departure from Leavenworth did not differ materially from that of Dodge. There was the same packing and similar parting from servants to whom we children had become attached. I do not recall that any considerable part of the regiment accompanied us on this move. Probably it was one of those instances of detached service to which my father was occasionally assigned. Of course at this time there was not the same accompaniment of cowboys and Indians racing along beside the train with shrill parting whoops. We were given a more stately send-off in a quiet way.[13]

✳ 4

FORT GIBSON, INDIAN TERRITORY
1881

Age Nine to Ten Years

THE POST to which we were going was a small one, Fort Gibson, in what was then the Indian Territory, now Oklahoma. We did not look forward with any eagerness to what lay ahead of us in renewed contact with the Indians in more primitive surroundings. Leavenworth had spoiled us for that.

But the disappointments of childhood are not of long duration. As the train sped south curiosity again preoccupied us with what we might find when we got there. My father had been there once in earlier days when carrying dispatches and the post had played an important part in the exciting events of the time. Perhaps there would yet be some compensation in what we would encounter there. The stories which had reached us suggested that. One of these related to us by my father was one of a wild night ride in a storm when he experienced the strange illusion of being accompanied by a galloping escort of cavalry.

Our journey southward from Fort Leavenworth remains in my memory as continuing an interlude in our frontier life which was broken by two glorious years at that post. It seems fitting that I should give here some things told us by our parents and Grandma Pinckney during the trip to while away the tedium of inaction.

My father, John George Leefe, was born in London and came to America with his parents when four years of age. They were from an old Yorkshire family, partly Scottish in ancestry. In our later life particulars of descent were contained in parish records sent my father by his first cousin, Major General John B. Leefe, Royal Marines, with whom he regularly corresponded. These parish records went back to the fifteenth century. I mention them here because they indicate the hold which tradition had in our family. Not that we were snobbish, but it did operate in our having a sense of something to live up to in our conduct.

Nor was there ever any hyphen in my father's sense of allegiance. He was always intensely American and among the earliest volunteers to fight for the Union, where he rose from lieutenant to be an adjutant general of a division. He came into the regular service from the volunteers in 1865 when he was offered and accepted a lieutenancy in the 19th Infantry Regiment. From then until the age of retirement he continued in the service, reaching, finally, in the slow process of seniority advancement, the grade of lieutenant colonel, the same rank he had attained as a young man in but three years of the Civil War. People may wonder how a man of any ambition or "get up and go" would be content to bury himself in a lifetime of subsequent service with no great prospective reward in money and the material things in life. The answer is that my father loved the military service as a doctor loves his profession, [as] a minister loves his religious service, and was not interested simply in making money and leading a life of luxury.

Most of his service was in the 19th Infantry, in which he became a major, passing as a lieutenant colonel to the 30th Infantry before retirement. In these minor ranks, however, he was to fulfill many high responsibilities in the Spanish-American War and the Philippine Insurrection, where a large territorial area became subject to his military rule.

In appearance and manners my father was always the "grand seigneur" and a handsome military figure. In early life, with his jet black hair he wore a mustache and goatee, which went well with the jaunty French military cap worn by the army in those days. Later he wore a beard, and under the later full dress helmet with its white flowing plume, he looked somewhat like a Russian grand duke. His men adored him, which was no wonder. He was quiet and firm with them and always in a way which preserved their self-respect—the secret of true leadership.

Our mother was born in Vernon, New York. Her mother, Grandmother Pinckney, was a Keene, from the family after which Keene, New Hampshire, was named. She was a descendant of Mary and John White of Plymouth Colony and of Peregrine White, the first child born in the colony. She married Charles Clarence Pinckney, of Manchester, England. A branch of the family in very early days emigrated to the colonies, settling in South Carolina.

Charles Clarence Pinckney came himself, however, directly from England before the Civil War and settled in Tennessee, where he had an estate and held slaves. He never liked the system and became an abolitionist, freeing his slaves and, when feeling rose against him, sold out and went north to Michigan.

There, later, he joined the Union army, going to the Civil War as a captain and quartermaster of the 1st Michigan Infantry under Colonel Russell Alger, afterward secretary of war. At the close of the war he acquired an estate in Arkansas on the Arkansas River near the towns of Van Buren and Fort Smith. The estate was near Fort Smith and officers of the garrison were frequent visitors. It was in the course of one of these visits that my father and mother first met.[1]

The estate was very large, in the foothills of the Ozarks, and located upon a bayou bearing the ugly name of Frog Bayou. There was a large southern mansion with many cabins for negro servants and the hands working the plantation on which tobacco was grown. Grandfather also had a special hunter who, in coonskin cap, kept the table supplied with game of all kinds. There was a steamboat landing at the bend of the river and every few days a boat tied up to be loaded with bales of tobacco and other produce for distant markets. My mother has told me of the excitement this always occasioned and her little negro handmaid rushing up to her breathless, exclaiming, "She's coming, Miss Mollie, she's coming now!"

She has also told me of the songs the negroes used to sing while loading the boat and afterward at night, in their cabins. These were real negro spirituals sung in their original way and not as many of the modern versions give them. She used to steal out at night and listen to them as they sang in the moonlight before their cabins.

They sang best when alone and not conscious of the presence of "white folks." Their songs included "When You Wants to Be Dah," "Go Down the Hill and Pray," and the present well-known "Nobody Knows the Trouble I've Seen," "Swing Low, Sweet Chariot," and "Li'l Nigger Baby."

My mother taught me to sing these songs in the original "darkie" way and I sang them all through my childhood. I also sang them in later life to a woman's club, adhering to the original way and wording, and it made a great hit. Most of these songs have been modernized into a more classic form and are today being sung by many who never heard them as done by old-time negroes in their cabins.

There were unique characters among these negroes. Most of them were jolly and easy to manage when intelligently and humanely treated. From old "Uncle Allen" and his coonskin cap with its tail to a tall, lanky negress, they had a real affection for members of the family, especially for "Mis' Emily" as they called Grandma. The lanky negress had the inspiring name of America North Carolina South Carolina Johnson.

Of us children it is not necessary to speak at length. [My older sister] Kate reigned as the elder and the beauty in the growing generation. I was never jealous of this supremacy and of the attention and admiration she received. I have never had any use for that feminine trait which shows itself in narrow slanting glances and curled lip when another is praised. Nor in the absence of praise for another which indicates that feeling. Later in life I could never abide the showing of that spirit by others. Perhaps by then I may have become myself a bit over-solicitous about my own appearance and dress (what woman isn't?) but nothing beyond that.

Of Grandma Pinckney a word should be said. In early life she was a beautiful woman with a slender graceful figure which she kept to the end. She had deep blue eyes and brown hair with a glint of copper which she wore in a coronet braid with wavy curls hanging down at the side.

She was a woman of decided force of character. Her son, my mother's brother Henry, enlisted in the army at the age of fifteen and came home in uniform to announce it, with a tintype of himself taken on the way. She promptly grabbed him by the collar and literally dragged him back to the recruiting office, demanding that they take that uniform off him at once, flaying the recruiting officer unmercifully. Henry had misstated his age as eighteen, which he was large enough to look, and was released at once. But Uncle Henry went to war nevertheless. Grandfather took him with him as headquarters clerk in which position he was fairly safe from Confederate bullets.

Both my brothers rounded out the irregular education they had received at army schools by attending the University of Michigan, at Ann Arbor, graduating and carrying through life the marks of the fine training they received there. I never knew either of the boys to exhibit a mean or cowardly trait. The elder became a civil engineer with important authority in engineering work around Pittsburgh and later on the Bonneville Dam in Oregon. He had married Miss Lida Austin and now lies buried at Morrice, Michigan. My other brother also went into engineering work and later served in the marines. He died in a hospital as the result of an illness of the brain brought about by a sunstroke in the tropics and now rests peacefully in Arlington National Cemetery.[2]

Because the boys departed from the course followed by many army boys, that of following their fathers into the army and perpetuating the name in the Officers' List, the name Leefe no longer appeared there after my father's death in 1903.

The military tradition, however, has been a continuing one in our family. My sister married a titled former officer of the old

German army, Baron Albert von Mangelsdorf, whose father was an aide to the king of Saxony. Albert had come to America after resigning his commission in the artillery and became an engineer in the [Great] Lakes Survey of our government. A beautiful daughter, Mary Emilie, is the result of this union.[3]

As for myself, I followed a European custom and sometime after my army life married a cousin, Frederick Sturgis Laurence. Although a civilian by occupation he served as a major in the army during the First World War and for a year thereafter. As I write these lines our son John is serving overseas in our military forces as a private first class. I am proud of the fact that, notwithstanding defective eyesight, which barred him from receiving a commission offered him by the navy and from corresponding rank in the army, he chose to throw in his lot with the "common soldiers" as a voluntary inductee. I have always loved them and always shall.

From this digression I return to the life of my childhood and our arrival at Fort Gibson. Fort Gibson was in the northeast part of the Indian Territory on a river which flowed into the Arkansas River at a point nearby. The buildings still stand, but as a military post it is not [now] occupied. It was a very small post compared with Leavenworth.[4]

Arriving at the station at Muskogee we found an ambulance and escort wagon waiting. The former was for our family of seven. The escort wagon was for our household effects. When the escort wagon had been loaded we started off for the fort. After leaving the station we traveled a mile or two until we came to a ford. This was the only way then of getting to the military reservation on which Fort Gibson stood. Muskogee was then the only town nearby to supply its needs and furnish social diversion for those stationed there. The small river I have mentioned flowed between the town and the fort.

Arriving at the ford we were ferried across on a huge raft propelled by two men—Choctaws or negroes. The ambulance filled the raft so the escort wagon had to follow on the next trip. Our ambulance was drawn by four mules and as we descended the steep bank of dark red clay to the raft we were somewhat fearful lest the mules take us into the river.

As I remembered the raft did not need much propelling. There was a swift current and it had only to be steered with an occasional push to get across. This mode of travel was new to us and we certainly got a kick out of it. We children were allowed to get out and stand close to our father's side and watch the little eddies and whirlpools as we passed them in succession. On the other side the mules took the steep ascent up the bank steadily and I can remember being fascinated with the straining muscles of their legs as they pulled up the bank. They were going at a lively trot through the brisk clear air of an autumn morning. We arrived at Fort Gibson in time for luncheon.[5]

As we drove up to our future home I was awed by the appearance of a tall imposing southern house—basement and upper verandas in an overgrown garden. We all disembarked and ascended the long flight of steps to the upper veranda. Here we were met by Captain and Mrs. Alexander M. Wetherill and ushered into the large parlor where a fire was roaring in the huge fireplace. There were bright autumn flowers everywhere, a thoughtful touch which the captain and his lady had provided before turning over the quarters to us and saying good-bye. These flowers were on the mantel and in the openings of the big windows.[6]

Of course we inherited his servants in line with the custom when these were locally hired and had families in the vicinity. While our things were being brought in and unpacked and the servants preparing some hurried luncheon, we set about inspecting the layout of the home in which we were to spend the next six strange months of our young lives. We were strictly impressed with the usual rule—when arriving at a new post do not go anywhere alone. I remember even our new maid adding to this injunction, "You young uns keep out dose woods. Dey's tings in dere!"

One day, however, I strayed from the path of strict obedience. We were growing up and felt a bit more on our own. The path of departure I chose was the path leading to my father's office in the large building housing provisions for maintenance of the garrison, the commissary department, and household goods, uniforms, and equipment, quartermaster stores as these were called. The path was really a dirt road shaded on either side by live oak, persimmon, and other large trees. The woods beyond were closely planted by years of nature's deposits of seeds and richly fertilized by a natural humus from dead leaves.

On this lovely morning I walked down the straight road, looking right and left for explanation of the various little sounds and scents that came from the shrubbery. Nothing to be afraid of! I hummed a tune to keep my courage up. Several times I heard what seemed like branches crackling and then I hummed a little louder. At last I saw ahead the building to which I was going and quickened my pace, landing in Daddy's office somewhat out of breath.

I can recall the severe note in his voice as he said, "You children have been told not to come away from home by yourselves. Now you just run back as fast as you can. There will be no visit to Sergeant Smith and the sugar barrel for you. Now run along."

This was the first time in my life I had disobeyed my father and the first time I saw a different light in his eyes. It was a kind of light we later called "the candle" and knew to be a warning sign. It came only at rare intervals.

So I ran off to the house, to encounter a scolding from my two brothers with thumps on my back. It was never a practice of my parents to frighten us with bugaboos to procure obedience, and the reason for the restricted freedom at Fort Gibson must have been because we were in the Indian Territory and again surrounded by Indians on every hand. These were Choctaws, Kickapoos, Creeks, and several other tribes while farther off, in the southwestern part of the territory, were the Comanches, fiercer and more warlike, and the much-dreaded Apaches.

But how I wanted to be free of the restraint imposed on us. The smell of the outdoors was always an invitation hard to resist. I can still see myself going out on the porch in the early morning, opening my mouth and gulping great draughts of air ladened with the sweet smells of the garden and nearby woods. The first smells

I remember were the hunger-provoking ones from Frank Dudu's farm kitchen at Fort Dodge, the "Indian smell" which no one can ever forget, and the sweet smell of a vegetable wagon which I first recognized at Fort Gibson. It came from a wagon with big white horses driven by a very large woman, a nearby farmer's wife in a dress of light lavender. She herself had a combined smell of lettuce, radishes, onions, and soap—not a bad combination. A vegetable wagon has never had the same smell to me since.

A child of the open spaces is a rare thing apart these days, so many of them being brought up in the cramped districts of large cities. They do not know the joy of lying stretched out on a bough in a tree high above the ground, the leaves stirred by a gentle breeze and a bird perched on a swaying branch looking at you with startled eyes and then flying away in fright to call back at you in defiance from a neighboring tree. Then to scramble down to cries of triumph from your companions who have found you out, while you stake out your claim to that tree by carving your name on it. Such was the life of an army child in the West in those far-off days. It was a healthy and beautiful life.

We children did get a lot of fun out of Fort Gibson in spite of the restrictions laid on us. Mama and Daddy made many friends in Muskogee and we were invited many places. Grandma Pinckney was a great standby for us and she found so much for us to do that was pleasant and benefiting. There was our schooling, sewing, fancy work, and, on rainy days, candy pulls and other amusements [such as] stories of life on Grandmother's plantation, giving a picture of a yet unvanished time.

Always we were read to, mostly historical things by Daddy and Mama; Dickens, Thackeray, Bulwer[-Lytton], etc. Among the stories which come back to me from our dinner table talk were of Charles Dickens being entertained during Daddy's own childhood at his father's residence in New York during the famous author's visit to America.[7]

One incident at Fort Gibson connected with our church life comes back to me. My mother announced one Sunday morning that she could not accompany us to church but that Henry, our striker, would take us and bring us back. Our way to the church led down a road through fields of early primrose and violets and trees with feathery tendrils, a lovely scene which still stands out in my memory. The little church itself, about fifty by twenty-five feet, [was] painted white with windows low enough for the people in the pews to see the church ground outside. Arriving at the church we found our seats to be well up front under the very nose of the preacher. He was of a denomination and type which expounded hellfire and brimstone, but no kinder man ever breathed. His sermon was a hot one—something about three men in a fiery furnace.

Henry had the unpleasant habit of chewing tobacco and on this morning his quid was carried to church and I recall his Adam's apple moving up and down as he swallowed the juice. He could not of course get rid of it otherwise. It was a hot day and toward the end of the sermon he began to get pale, but everything held until after the blessing and we were on the way home. Then he let everything go at the side of the road. I do not know who felt sicker, Henry or I.

The only incident I recall connected with the Indians during our short stay of six months at Fort Gibson was about a large swivel chair my father wished to get rid of with some other things. Among the customers who came to look at it was a chief of the Choctaws. "How much?" he asked. "One dollar," answered my father. "I bring him tomorrow. You keep for me?" Yes, my father would keep it for him.

The next day he came, bringing not a silver dollar but a gold one. "I got him long time," he said as he unwrapped a red handkerchief. It was a bright coin with the date 1852 on it and we kept it for many years, making it into a bangle for a bracelet.

Handing the dollar to my mother the chief did as he had done before, [sitting] down in the chair and swinging back and forth for some time, making happy noises in his throat and beaming genially to Mama as if he had never known happiness before. After all the Indians then were but big overgrown children underneath all their cruelty and savagery. Much bloodshed might have been avoided if they had been handled from that standpoint more intelligently. They were often very good to those who understood them.

I recall an instance which illustrates this. My husband had a friend, an artist, who was stone deaf and who spent several years living alone among several of the fiercest tribes, painting their chiefs' portraits. The Indians regarded a deaf person as one who had been touched by the finger of God, the "Great Spirit." On many occasions among a drink-maddened crowd of them dancing round a fire he would withdraw, wrap himself inside a blanket, and lie down to sleep. They carefully abstained from molesting him and saw that nobody else did so.

After six months at this remote post of Fort Gibson my father was ordered to Fort Slocum, Long Island.[8] This post, close to New Rochelle, New York, was at that time a recruiting center and known as David's Island. It was directly across the Sound from Port Washington and Sands Point, on the Long Island side, which became my home in the later years of my married life.

Imagine the excitement when we were first told we were going to a place where there were boats, plenty of boats! Our parents had lived in New York in earlier years and looked forward to renewing old friendships and associations. We had heard much of it and now we were to go there.

So we bade good-bye to our friends in Muskogee and the old fort and got into the ambulance and were ferried across the river again and driven to the small railroad station from which our household effects had departed the day before. Our father looked so different in civilian dress, a long dark coat and trousers to match, with a small soft cap with upturned brim, which we found to be entirely out of style when we got to New York. I can remember the train as it came in, grinding to a stop, hissing, an old-fashioned engine with the smokestack shaped like a huge inverted cone belching great clouds of black smoke. I remember my desire to run forward and put my hands in the grease of the great wheels, but of course I did not.

On the train a great cry immediately arose for something to eat. In those days few trains had a dining car and lunch was eaten from a basket, . . . dinner at station restaurants along the way. Poor father! With a family of seven and sometimes a nursemaid, no wonder we were poor. Still, we never knew in those days the extremes of economy and even hunger we were to know later in twentieth-century life. We children were always comfortably dressed and well-shod.

5

DAVID'S ISLAND, NEW YORK

1881–1882

Age Ten to Eleven Years

HAD IT not been for the rushing in and out of towns and the great variety of scenery encountered we never could have been content to remain on the train during our long journey north. At last it was over and we arrived in New York one morning and I then experienced a new smell—the smell of New York. We had plenty of coal gas on the train from the engine. In the city it seemed like a mixture of this and a strange aroma, new to my nostrils, given off by hot pavements and people in crowds. It is hard to describe how it seemed to our young senses, fresh from the wide open spaces where the air had always been fresh and pure. It had the fascination of something novel while repellent. I have since heard that today the smell coming up to aviators flying over the city is something awful.

We spent a couple of days at the home of my aunt, my father's sister, while Daddy reported to David's Island and arranged for our quarters and the installing of our effects. My aunt and Uncle Ed then had a small brownstone house on East 64th Street near Madison Avenue, having just moved there from a large house on Murray

Hill, which was one of the show houses of New York at the time. East 64th Street at that time had not been fully built up, there were vacant lots nearby in which goats roamed. The streets were all paved with cobblestones and the noise made by iron tires and horses' hoofs was terrific. Sparrows were legion and came down in flocks. We could not sleep for the racket, which began at daybreak from passing carts and the jangling of streetcar bells on Madison Avenue.

Among the other memories of our two-day stay was that of my brothers wandering off by themselves over to Central Park, getting lost, and being brought home by a gray-coated policeman. These police, separate from the regular blue-coated force, were known as "sparrow cops."

The day we left this hospitable home for our "dear island," as we came to call it, was a beautiful one of sunshine. We went by train to New Rochelle where, at a dock, the government launch lay rocking gently as we went aboard. I shall never forget the thrill of this experience. It was the first time we had seen "blue water." River water in our experience had been mainly the color of coffee with cream. That between New Rochelle and the island and the sound beyond was deep blue. We stood near the bow of the launch and could scarcely restrain our impatience as it drew up to the dock. Had it gone near the beach I am sure we might have jumped overboard to wade ashore. As it was we were herded up the gangplank to be met by a lieutenant and his lady who walked with us to our quarters. Arriving there they left us, with an invitation to luncheon.[1]

The lovely cottage which was to be our new home was of wood painted buff and white and had a porch with large windows. It stood not far from the dock on a sloping bit of ground which ran down to the beach on the side of the island facing New Rochelle. When we entered we found that our dear daddy, who had unpacked some of our things while we remained in New York, had placed flowers all about in vases and pitchers to welcome us. We loved the place at once, and all during our stay on the island were happy and content with it.

After our experience with the muddy waters of the western rivers the island appeared to our young eyes like a gem set in a pool of emerald and sapphire. It faced directly on Long Island Sound and on the landward side where we lived the ascent from the pebbly beach was gradual, while on the southern, or sound side, it terminated in more abrupt banks above a beach strewn with boulders. The enlisted men's barracks ran along this side of the island. The main parade ground lay between these and officers' row on the other side. There were many trees; pine, spruce, oak, and fruit trees. Also at that time [were] scrubby growths of bushes bearing many kinds of berries.

Our great delight in living there was in the ever-changing scene in land, sky, and water under changes of weather and season. I loved to stand at a window and watch the great rollers sent to our beach by passing steamers and when storms lashed the waters in the narrow stretch lying between the island and the mainland. The turbulent waves left foam which looked like white lace spread on blue silk. We children were never afraid of storms, no matter how hard it blew or rained or snowed. When we had to leave all this and go down to the hot dry plains of the Texas border we used to long for them; they were preferable to the tornadoes and twisters we sometimes got there.

Little did I know then that when I next saw David's Island and its storms I would be a married woman living directly across the water from it at Port Washington on the Long Island shore. When I went with my husband to call on the daughter of General Adna Chaffe, an old family friend, all the old frame houses were gone and in place were the brick structures which stand there now.[2]

David's Island got its name from Thaddeus Davids, a descendent of Admiral Lord St. Davids of the British navy in colonial times. Thaddeus Davids, born in 1810, planned to make the island his country seat but relinquished it to the government for use as a hospital during the Civil War. The post in our time consisted of a headquarters, staff, and recruiting force of officers, noncommissioned officers, and enlisted men assigned to this duty, with a large body of newly enlisted recruits who were assembled for dispatch to the various posts throughout the country. While a good many were thus crowded into a small space, there was plenty of room to get a lot of joy out of life. For one thing, there was the big city near at hand with relatives in it and our mother used to go in and come back with lovely things for us all.[3]

I should say it was there that I first met the man who was many years afterward to become my dear and devoted husband—the little boy cousin I was to see several times afterward without having ever suspected this ultimate outcome. It was by no means a childhood romance such as we read about in books. In fact, my husband has confessed to me that in childhood I was his pet detestation. I was always sneaking up behind him and pinching him and he didn't like it. My own feeling, as I recall, was one of indifference. Little did we suspect the wonderful love and mutual devotion that would come to us in later life when the romanticism of early youth gave way to the mutual appraisal of mature years. I was to know other passing attachments first and so was he.

All larger posts of the army are given to some form and here was plenty. The routine of guard mounts, drills, parades, band concerts, receptions, dinners, and dances made up our days, to say nothing of the bathing hour, and the joy of swimming in salt water. All the garrison not on duty turned out, the officers and their families on one side of the island, the enlisted men on the other.

One amusing incident I recall did not take place at the bathing hour. A well-known writer and musical composer of the day was an occasional visitor. His name was Stephen Massett, a most eccentric man and altogether unpredictable in his actions. He had a shock of white curly hair of which he was inordinately proud, and a heavy white mustache. He was so proud of his hair that on entering a streetcar or bus he immediately would remove his hat so that the occupants might admire it. There was enough about him to attract attention without that. Winter or summer he went about in a long blue cape with a velvet collar. When he began making faces at children among the passengers the whole car or bus would be thrown into gales of laughter.[4]

One day when visiting us, not having brought a bathing suit

and desiring a swim, he stole away at the afternoon band concert hour for a swim au naturel on the enlisted men's side of the island. The orders were very strict about anyone bathing without a suit and a sentry was posted there to enforce this. Getting behind a boulder Mr. Massett undressed and got into the water without the sentry seeing him. Only his head then showed, bobbing about. There was nothing unusual in someone swimming at odd hours and the sentry paid no attention. But the band struck up one of our visitor's own compositions. He stood up, the water not reaching his middle, clapping vigorously and shouting "Bravo! Bravo!" which of course the band could not hear. This brought the sentry up on the run yelling lustily for the corporal of the guard, [and] adding his post number.

"Get down under that water at once and stay there until you're told to come out! Who the devil are you anyway and what do you mean by going in without a suit?"

"Why, my good man, they are playing my piece, don't you hear, they are playing my piece!"

"I don't give a damn about that!" yelled the sentry. "The orders are that no one can bathe here without a suit. Now you get down in that water as you're told and stay there!"

The dialogue which ensued when the corporal came up and they got him out and behind the boulder was related to us afterward by our outraged guest, who insisted that he had been grossly insulted and that something should be done about it. But of course nothing was done, as the sentry was only doing his duty. After getting him dressed and upon his identifying himself as the guest of Captain Leefe they let him go with a warning.

Other amusing things about our guest furnished us children with things to talk about for years afterward. He had a horror of firearms and when the evening gun went off he would run into the house and stop his ears. Which reminds me of another incident related to us which happened elsewhere. Mr. Massett had gone to stay over the Fourth of July with some friends to avoid the noise. Someone let off a giant firecracker in the yard as he was saying his prayers when getting into bed.

"There!" he exclaimed, "I always said it and now I know it! The Bible was written by a set of lunatics. I prayed for quiet and got that! I'll never pray again, so help me God!"

Because of the bathing incident and his relating to us the firecracker episode in the presence of us children, my father felt impelled to ask him on leaving to forbear further visits. This notwithstanding his being quite a celebrated and popular figure of the day in the New York world. He was a brilliant poet and composer of music, some of his compositions having become hits. But no eminence counted with my father if it carried the prospect of affecting the religious and moral upbringing of his children. Although of English birth and deeply aristocratic in social tradition he would have put the king of England out of the house, if he sensed such influence. It was this loyalty and regard for those under his care, including the soldiers under him, which inspired us as it did them, never to do anything to bring discredit on him.

The religious side of our life was pursued in the post's little chapel. Here my mother's singing often inspired some young recruit to drop into a back seat and listen. She sang there often as well as at home. As at other posts she became an outstanding figure in its social and cultural activities. Our house became a center of gaiety and her influence extended also to the life of the enlisted men of the garrison.

I do not know whether today in our huge army the influence of officers' wives can have anything like the success in creating esteem between officers and men which existed in the old army of only twenty-five thousand men, with the now outworn concept existing then of social class status.

This existed well up to the First World War, when it began to disintegrate. It seems to have exploded in some bitter feeling, I am told, in the Second World War, as in the first, so many men of high social standing in civil life wore the rank of private soldiers. Even in the First World War my husband's chauffeur, a corporal, was a millionaire in civil life. Today I think no one regards an enlisted man as a socially inferior being, unless he is personally.

In our family, even in those early days, nobody in the ranks was made to feel that we so regarded them. I can recall noncoms and private soldiers being introduced to visitors at the post by my father with all the grace and courtesy he would have observed had these soldiers been commissioned officers. This courtesy had an immense effect when he came to preside in summary courts-[martial] and he was called upon to inflict punishments. The sentences were accepted without bad feeling. Culprits would back out with a salute on the way to the guardhouse.

The two years we passed at David's Island added much to our stature as growing children, physically and mentally. In some ways the older posts seemed to offer much latitude for individual home life. My father, for instance, had the post carpenter at David's Island build my brothers a little workshop back of our house. It was about ten feet square. My brothers had quite an accumulation of tools given them from time to time, and a workbench was provided under the window.

Pelham Priory on the mainland was among the spots we visited in our outdoor existence at David's Island. I believe it is now some kind of a public show place maintained as a historic landmark, but I recall it as a spot in a beautiful setting of family life. I remember going with others of our family to call on the family then living there. These elegant ladies always served tea, and after stuffing ourselves with cookies, we children were released from the apron strings and allowed to wander about the place. I can remember the thrill and shudder I experienced when walking down a corridor and coming suddenly upon a suit of armor standing like a man before one of the panels and looking as if to say, "Get by me if you can." I knew he couldn't move but felt goose pimples all over my body and would not go too close to him.

We went to Pelham Priory a number of times by way of New Rochelle. There we would be met by the priory surrey or coach, the latter a very dark affair with glass windows and two big horses. We enjoyed these visits hugely.[5]

As the time approached for our departure from David's Island we felt great sorrow at leaving the little house and rooms in which we had spent two happy years and the always enchanting scene of blue water and white sails decking the sound in the golden after-noon sunlight. I remember little of our actual departure, simply a dim recollection of our father, as usual, keeping his small brood intact as we bade good-bye to friends in the garrison and went aboard the launch. As on former occasions, our good-byes included the servants as well, who remained to serve others.

The launch chugged away. In New York we were accompanied to the train by my Aunt Kate, for whom my sister was named, and by Uncle Ed. Then began the long journey southward, which was to terminate at Fort Ringgold on the Mexican border in Texas, where my father had been ordered to rejoin his company and that part of our regiment which had moved there. This constant shifting of environment was one of the things which made life in the army a thing apart from civilian society. We were thrown back on our-selves for that sense of continuity of interest which would sustain us in the life we led.[6]

I cannot close reference to David's Island without mentioning something unusual in army records. Among my dearest treasures is a bit of yellowed paper bearing, in handsomely engraved form, the following message to my mother from the enlisted men of the permanent garrison:

TESTIMONIAL

to

Mrs. J. G. Leefe

"In view of the departure from our midst of one who has contributed so much to our benefit and happiness; who has, re-gardless of personal interest and comfort, unselfishly devoted her time and talents to the edification and amusement of the enlisted men of the Island, we, members of the Depot Detachment, as a body, feel bound to extend to you our heartfelt thanks for your disinterested kindness, feeling however that so feeble a tribute but poorly pays the debt we owe. However, in contemplation of the long monotonous evenings that loom up before us, we can but deeply lament your absence and sigh for the days of 'Auld Lang

Syne.' And trusting that your mortal journey may be fraught with safety and comfort, and that your Heavenly and immortal journey may be assured, and that we shall all meet as here to sing eternal praise, we again say, Thank You."

DEPOT DETACHMENT
David's Island, New York Harbor
December 19th, 1882

6

FORT RINGGOLD, TEXAS

1883–1886

Age Eleven to Fourteen Years

LEAVING David's Island we were very sad. The two years spent there were a golden dream to us young children and we were almost heartbroken at leaving. Our sorrow was tempered only by the prospect of being able to ride a bronco. Of course to us this was almost the greatest opportunity that might be open to any child. In this way our long journey southward was made bearable by dreams of days to come.

Our destination was Fort Ringgold on the Rio Grande between Brownsville and Laredo on the Mexican border. It was one of the oldest forts, being established in 1848, and named for old General Ringgold.[1]

We left the train ninety miles from Fort Ringgold and made the rest of the trip in an army ambulance and escort wagon across a vast expanse of sand, cactus, scrub oak, and mesquite before achieving our journey's end. This and other features of our trip are so well described in a letter from Grandma Pinckney to Cousin Mary Virginia Keene that I cannot do better than quote from this letter retained in remnants of family correspondence:

"The weather was delightful when we passed through the Indian Territory, but at two o'clock we were struck by a 'Norther.' At one PM we were switched off on a side track and remained until eleven at night, the cold wind taking all the heat out of the sleeper. We had quite a pleasant party on board, four children besides ours and a youth from Newport R.I. who sails around David's Island in his yacht every summer. He gave a dinner to all the children and they had a jolly time.

"The next morning we got to San Antonio, the air full of frozen fog. We then changed cars and went to [Fort] McIntosh where we were received very kindly by both infantry and cavalry. Company F of our regiment is stationed there. We were taken right in. They would not let us go to the hotel. Major Sumner, son of Gen'l Sumner, and wife did all in their power to make us comfortable. Made us stay over Sunday and rest.[2]

"Monday morning we went sixty miles on a branch of a railroad, where government and baggage wagons had been waiting for us three days, very cold riding all afternoon. Pitched our tent. Ate our supper—made our beds, shivered all night, cold until noon, when it grew warm. The escort killed quail and deer. We had quail on toast for supper and venison steaks for breakfast.

"We were fortunate in getting a colored cook at McIntosh so we did not suffer as far as food was concerned, but it was fearfully hot when we got here at five PM. The thermometer stood at 97° in the shade. We all had very bad colds and I was so sick after the first day I had to go to bed. I came very near having pneumonia. Mrs. Liscom insisted on my having the doctor. I was sick for nearly a week and that is my excuse for not writing you sooner. This is the first letter I have answered since I came to this disgusting place.[3]

"The thermometer was up to 99° yesterday and the signal officer telegraphed us that we would have a 'norther' during the night so I got blankets ready for the beds, had to put flannel underclothing on all this morning after taking it off. The snow flew for a few minutes this morning, the first Mexicans in Rio Grande City, a place right in sight of the post, had ever seen in their lives.[4]

"We have two rooms upstairs larger than the parlor at David's

Island and a large hall, no closets nor cupboards. I have a stove in one room but I have not been able to get the old shell warm today. The sand has been blowing for two days and everything in the room is covered with it. There are quite a quantity of trees planted all over the post—they are about the size of apple trees. The parade [ground] is covered with crows, jackdaws, and ravens. The water is so full of alkali that it makes us sick to drink it. No ice, and worse, No Beer! Jack has been sorry ever since he brought us down that he did not leave us at New Rochelle so the children could go to school. There is one here but the Mexicans use such bad language that we have concluded to teach them at home. I teach them all but music. Jack will teach them drawing and French.[5]

"There! I have been to the stove and got my ear thawed out and will try to finish this long scrawl. All of our things came safely except my machine which was pretty badly smashed and the children's bedsteads, also Mary's piano came alright. They got her in the choir already. We have got pretty well settled. Mary has a parlor below and a bedroom the same size with folding doors and a long closet on each side of the door. Mary has her raw silk curtains between the parlor and bedroom also at the door leading into the hall. Large hall, then a room with a safe for food, then a dining room about the size of the one at 'Dear old David's Island,' then a cook's room, then the kitchen, most of it lattice work. A very good range. Beef very tough but cheap—5 cents per lb., chicken 25 cents apiece, no milk fit for use.

"By the time I write again it will be warm enough for mosquitos, scorpions, centipedes, tarantulas, and other dear little creatures. Mary and Jack and myself were invited to a Spanish, Mexican wedding tonight but politely declined. I had a ticket presented to me while in McIntosh to attend a 'Bull Fight'; it being Sunday I could not attend, much as I would have liked to witness the pleasant pastime."[6]

Our first impression of the Rio Grande was in the dry season. Fort Ringgold was just outside Rio Grande City, a small place at the time, and across the river at some distance was the town of Camargo in Mexico.

After living at David's Island from where the vast expanse of Long Island Sound could be seen, the river seemed to our eyes a very small thing in the way of water. Seeing it in the dry season, it certainly was a very narrow stream. Our first trip across was in an army ambulance and Arnold, our teamster, drove us very carefully down the steep bank on our side and as we crossed the hubs of our wheels did not even get wet.

When we were across on the other side we all exclaimed, "Pshaw! That wasn't anything." Dick, my brother, added, "I could wade across."

"Just wait till the floods come," said Arnold. "Then you'll see something."

"What?" we asked. "Alligators?"

"No, dead horses, trees, houses, and things like that."

We were incredulous and thought he was fooling us. But see these things we did, later. I recall the scene perfectly. My mother, one evening when the moon was full and the river roaring at full flood, gave us permission to go down to the river with a young lieutenant who promised to shepherd us there carefully and bring us safely back. Instead of the narrow stream winding like a snake in the center of the broad space between two banks, [there] was a raging torrent overflowing to a great width on each side. The chocolate-colored water looked at night to be blue black except where a floating object was turned to silver in the moon's rays. The water was racing by and a log bathed in the moonlight looked like a long silver bullet shooting past in the swirling current.

"What is that out there in the middle?" we cried.

"Dead horse," answered Lieutenant Smith. "There she comes!"

It was a small cabin whirling by and followed by a crowd of men, women, and children running along the water's edge on our side shouting excitedly. Whether there was anyone in the cabin I do not know.

Poor Ed Smith. We did not dream then that years afterward he was to be killed in the Philippines heroically holding off single-handed twelve Filipinos and killing many of them before they got him. At the time we knew him at Fort Ringgold he was a second lieutenant of Company B, which was the company my father commanded in the 19th Infantry.[7]

Ed Smith's mother had known George Eliot, having first encountered her in Germany, and was a very brilliant woman. Some years after we left Ringgold, Kate and I called at Fort Mackinac and sat very stiff in our chairs while she talked to us. Ed was always very kind to us children at Ringgold and on another moonlight night sent chills down our spines by telling us the story of a huge snake, a rattler, the skin of which hung suspended from the ceiling of his porch, the rattles reaching nearly to the floor. Ed had gotten into bed when his foot touched something cold which moved. Springing up he threw down the covers and there was this big snake which uncoiled and slithered down to the floor. How we shivered as he told this! Then it coiled, holding its head high and Ed, grabbing his army Colt, fired at it but missed.

"Then," said Ed, "he put his head down and stayed there long enough for me to fire again. He must have been frightened by the report of my gun. This time I got him and there he is hanging up there."

This story illustrates one of the things in those days which people living on the border had to be on guard against. I have never gotten over my horror of snakes and years later when my husband brought home from San Antonio a snake skin he had purchased there, nearly as long as the one on Ed Smith's porch, I refused to have it in the house. He gave it to our son, who at that time was in college, to hang in his room, and when he did, the woman cleaner there refused to enter his room until it was removed. It was wrapped up and finally sold.

There were other precautions we had to take besides turning down the bedclothes before getting into bed, to be sure it was safe. I have never gotten over that habit to this day. Other women look under the bed, not in it! We had, among other things, to keep the legs of our icebox standing in pans of water as a precaution against ants and other voracious insects from outside. Ice was a great luxury when finally obtained, which was once a week, when a steamer

brought it up the river. Butter usually had to be kept in tins, un-
opened, until the hour of eating and then eaten at once. Daddy said
it should be put on bread with a paint brush. Water was kept in
suspended earthen pots where it remained fairly cool.[8]

But everything during our stay at Fort Ringgold was not
snakes, centipedes, bugs, and discomforts such as I have mentioned.
Life there had its lovely side too. The Decker family in Rio Grande
City were cultured people with a beautiful home where we used to
visit. It had an enclosed court with palms and a fountain in the
center, and parrots. With our mother we two girls spent many
happy hours there on hot afternoons with these lovely ladies. There
were two brothers and two sisters. Always lemonade for us young
ones and wine or something else for the grownups. Mr. Decker, the
younger brother, was most gallant and played the piano beautifully.[9]

Our home life also continued to have its beautiful side. Here
Mama pursued her custom of reading to us two girls, which lasted
for many years wherever we went. I shall never forget her reading
Barnaby Rudge and *The Old Curiosity Shop*, also the works of many
other great authors. Much of my education came this way. I never
had any schooling such as civilian children get, most of it being at
army post schools of varying degrees of merit, and sometimes by
private tutoring. One such tutor was an enlisted man who taught
us grammar and mathematics. He was a highly educated and very
handsome man who came from an English family of high station.
His name was Moncrieff. My father had a high admiration for him
and backed him [in] an application he later made for a commission.
We also had a French tutor, but our private tutoring came in the
main from our parents and Grandma Pinckney, until she took sick
and had to be sent north.

This occurred while we were at Ringgold and my father took
her to New York for treatment. The trip to the train was by ambulance, ninety miles over hot plains. Then the train they took was
derailed, the car in which Grandma and Daddy were being the only
one which remained on the track. On arriving in New York
Grandma was taken to St. Luke's Hospital, where she died. At the

time the hospital occupied some dingy old buildings on Fifth Avenue, not the fine present structure uptown.[10]

Such were some of the vicissitudes army people at remote posts had to face in those days. Poor dear heroic Grandma. She had the courage, fighting spirit, and faith which our legends give only to the pioneer women of a day earlier than hers.

My memory of my mother's reading to us is varied with that of the musical evenings we had at our quarters twice a week, violin and piano, Lieutenant Roberts, "Polly" as we called him, playing the violin, Mama at the piano. Her lovely voice floated through the house while we children, awakened, lay in our beds and eagerly listened. One piece they played was a rhythmic thing woven about *A Tale of Two Cities,* which our father had related to us, and I was transported to France with Sydney Carton and the great beautiful sacrifice he made for others.[11]

There were numerous incidents of an amusing character to enliven our stay at Ringgold. It was while there that the garrison had an official visit from General O. O. Howard of Civil War fame. It is related that at the Battle of Fair Oaks, having his arm shattered, he rode over to a first aid station, had it cut off, and then rode back into action again. I don't know if the story is true, but it was current and I do know, as a bit of unwritten history, that my husband's father, then a major, was in command of the right of Howard's line when he was hit, was wounded himself, and received a glowing tribute from General Howard for his gallantry in leading the countercharge.

When the general came to Ringgold the troops of the garrison were turned out for maneuvers and one of the general's two sons, who was an officer, was present—I think as an aide to his father, but as he was of our regiment, he may have been stationed there. Anyway he served as an aide on this occasion and the general sent him with a message to the officer in command of the reserve, a crusty old veteran who was a stickler for the proprieties. Running up to this officer the aide said, "Papa says to come forward now." The old veteran glared at him and said icily, "Who the hell is Papa?" This story went the rounds of the 19th for years.[12]

Other humorous incidents enlivened our stay. One of them was a famous fight between Mrs. Gazelle and Mrs. Truan of "Laundress Row," as the row of married enlisted quarters was called. It took place in an "over the fence" exchange between the two women, terminating in a fight with brooms and mud swept up from puddles after a rainstorm. It went on to the accompaniment of encouraging shouts from bystanders to "Go it, Mary!" "Give it to her, Norah!" An effeminate little man from my father's company rushed in and dragged off Mrs. Gazelle, while others took care of mud-spattered Mrs. Truan.[13]

The sequel was that some time afterward Mrs. Gazelle became a widow and was faced with the prospect of relinquishing her domicile. She then proposed to this same little man, who was known throughout the garrison as "Lady Smith," because of his ways. Soldiers wishing to marry must first have the permission of their company commander. Lady Smith asked this of my father and was given an emphatic "No!" Notwithstanding, he went off and married the lady—or perhaps I should say she married him. There was a great ado about it and a summary court-martial, after which Lady Smith was put in the guardhouse. But Mrs. Gazelle, now Mrs. Smith, saved her home and they were allowed to live together in Laundress Row afterward.

Then there was the incident of a Captain Ropes of the cavalry detachment, who was the unhappy possessor of a set of false teeth which did not fit. All army posts were subject to a visit from the inspector general at least once a year. When the IG came to Fort Ringgold the troops were turned out for inspection, passing in review afterward. Captain Ropes rode a particularly hard trotter and in wheeling his troop his teeth came loose and he could not give a second command necessary to bring them properly into line for the march past. The result was [that] the cavalry got into a jam. Captain Ropes, in trying to readjust his teeth with his bridle hand, the other holding his sabre, fumbled and dropped his teeth, and his lieutenant had to take over and straighten out the mess. The rest of the troops did well and received high praise, but the poor cavalry troop, through no fault of its own, was in disgrace.[14]

I should explain that in some border and western posts where complete regiments were not stationed, there was sometimes a mixed force of one or two companies of infantry or cavalry and a detachment of some other arm. This was the case at Ringgold when we were there.

About this time we became the owners of a pony, Prince, a roan color, gentle but swift, and a good trotter. Now began fights, and how! If one child had the pony the other three wanted it. I was an eager rider, afraid of no horse on four legs, and was on him a good deal, galloping about the post "astride," in a way then considered in the East at least to be highly improper for anyone of the female gender. I was not allowed to go outside the post, but my two brothers sometimes were allowed to go as far as five miles beyond.[15]

By way of amusement, there came to the fort a circus which was allowed to pitch its tents outside the enlisted men's barracks, and from there, on one of the upper balconies, the officers and their families had a place from which to view the goings-on. It gave us a grand view of the performance. This was preceded by a parade led by the local band of Rio Grande City, mainly Mexicans. They marched the whole way out, about a mile I think, and then into the fort, playing "La Golondrina," that beautiful melody which is almost the national air of Mexico. No one who has not heard a Mexican band or orchestra play this can appreciate its full beauty. Mexican musicians seem to put their whole soul into it and it is like the soul of Mexico speaking. Few American orchestras which I have heard ever do it justice.

[The circus] had an immediate reflection in the establishment of a circus of our own, with all the attributes except lions, tigers, and elephants. We performed all sorts of stunts on a trapeze with bad falls and risky bareback riding of horses, of which there were plenty available. The toughening influence of this culminated in all sorts of fights, in which I never hesitated to "sic" my brothers on and join in to help out when other boys were too many for them. But fight as we did among ourselves, we were always one when anyone came at us from outside. That was an unwritten code. Kate, who was older than I, was brave, but more dignified and ladylike, and rarely participated in our fist brawls, confining herself to a pacifying role.

Other events also enlivened our stay, some musical. One of which I recall, organized by my mother, was attended by practically the whole garrison, the enlisted force—those not on duty—attending in a body. My mother sang, and at the conclusion of the program when they stood up to march out, my mother struck up at the piano and started to sing, "Tramp, Tramp, Tramp, the Boys Are Marching," and the hall echoed to the chorus, the men joining in as they marched out.[16]

Patriotism was not something taught us then, it simply filtered into us with every breath we drew, as something natural. It was not much more than fifteen years after the close of the Civil War and the old marching songs of that day were still popular.

Life at Fort Ringgold is remembered as midstream in my childhood years. If asked why I should spend so much time recording childhood happenings of little interest to older folk, my answer is that this chronicle is written in the hope it may carry some interest and benefit for the younger reader in the rising generation, as well as the parents responsible for the upbringing of children under conditions much more favorable in some respects than we enjoyed. I know of no chronicle of child life in the old army and picturing it may help understand many historic figures who have emerged in our national life who were subject to the same formative influences.

Thus there emerges the figure of Custer, living and active in the days of Fort Dodge. At Ringgold there rises the figure of Robert E. Lee, who was a junior officer before the Civil War and occupied the house at the other end of the officers' line, and whose quarters at old Fort Duncan we later occupied. At Fort Clark we encountered Sheridan. In essence they embodied nobility in varying convictions of rightful courses. In the vast increase of our armed forces today I can only wonder how much of the binding code of officer conduct may have survived in the "customs of the service."[17]

Our school at Fort Ringgold would have amused modern educational authorities. It resembled the typical small red country schoolhouse with its paddle-wielding testy old civilian schoolmaster. Officers' and soldiers' children of all ages and sizes were mixed together in one group with no grade distinction. It was quite a letdown from the well-organized private school we had attended at Fort Leavenworth and the fairly civilized counterpart we enjoyed at David's Island. We were far south on the Mexican border with such instructions as were available there.[18]

In procedure it ran something like this: assembly at ringing of the school bell; a scuffling pushing line of robust youngsters with Mr. Anderson, the instructor, reducing to some sort of order by stern injunctions to "Stop that and get into line. I'll have no fighting here! Now go in and take your seat quietly—quietly I say!"

Then would begin a spelling lesson, characterized by all sorts of variants and exasperated corrections until the right version had been given. Then an incursion into the field of geography with a bit better result as more interesting, particularly about the adjoining country of Mexico, what kind of people dwell there, and the historical relation of Texas. Recess and home for lunch. In the afternoon it was worse. Drawing at the blackboard, followed by some singing in which Kate and Mamie Leefe come off at the top. In recitation the younger of my brothers also leads, reciting "Old Ironsides" with much fervor and dramatic pointing. At the end he suddenly yells out. Someone has stuck a pin in him from behind.

"Charles, you come here!" Mr. Anderson, laying him over a knee, proceeded to warm him in the same place, good and proper. School dismissed, we file out and thus ends another miserable day for poor Mr. Anderson. For the agony we children must have caused him may his shade in heaven forgive us. He did his best, according to his lights, but is it any wonder that I never learned to spell?

Of course every school in the army was not like this. We were far down on the Mexican border and had to do with such teaching talent as was available there at the time. It was supplemented by the more effective and better-liked instruction of Private Moncrieff, and by our parents' home teaching. Otherwise I fear we never would have gotten through this particular period with much benefit.

One day we received an invitation to attend a fiesta in Camargo in Mexico, across the river from Rio Grande City. It was to be a Christmas Eve celebration with a pageant depicting the Flight into Egypt. Christmas Eve on the Mexican border, at least that far south, is not a time of crisp cold with snow on the ground. Winter was something when the thermometer did not usually stand over one hundred degrees.

Camargo was some five miles beyond the river and the trip there was made in a sort of open barouche. It was drawn by a mangy-looking horse and a mule and was furnished by our Mexican host who went by the name of don Caesar. By means of much urging with the whip and shouts from the Mexican driver the team was lashed to something resembling a gallop for nearly the entire distance. Then as we came upon a line of grass-grown earthworks at the edge of town [the horse] dropped down into a walk. Passing up a broad unpaved avenue we arrived in the plaza where there was an old mission-looking church of Spanish architecture and some surrounding buildings. A soldier guard was there, consisting of a coffee-colored lieutenant and ten men. They were in white cotton uniforms with enormous shakos resembling an inverted coffeepot with a pom-pom projecting out the bottom in front. They were not at all the smart-looking soldiers I am told can be seen in Mexico today, but could do their forty or even sixty miles a day in their bare feet if they had to.

The don's abode was a handsome brick house with a gateway of gilded ornamental iron giving access to a patio. The interior of the house was handsome and luxurious. We were received with much ceremonious formality. There were a number of pretty señoritas standing about who could not speak English. Some of these accompanied us to the casa of another don, a prominent personage of the town. There the pageant was to be presented.

It began with a blare of music from a Mexican band or orchestra, which is always musical when playing any of the native Mexican airs. Then, from a side door of the patio emerged a column of damsels, each carrying a lighted candle. They were singing beautifully. We recognized among them the señoritas who had accompanied us from the first house visited. By this time night had fallen and the effect under the luminous Mexican sky with its bright stars was very striking.

At the head of the procession was a donkey, or burro, led by two diminutive Mexican boys. On the burro sat the most extraordinary personification of Joseph imaginable. A shock of black hair done up in a point like an Ashanti towered above a saddle-leather countenance. Possibly some thought of Egypt as a place of pyramids inspired the conception. But, most extraordinary, was a pair of gauze wings protruding from his shoulders. He had on some kind of white sheet or shawl falling away and exposing a pair of brown legs clad only to the knee in short white drill pants. Behind him sat Mary, holding the Christ Child, a somewhat tawdry doll.

Shades of Madonna! If Raphael, Fra Angelico, or Fra Lippi could have seen what their immortal conceptions had inspired in that little city of Mexico in 1884. Mary's hair was done up in equally bizarre fashion, but in plaits hanging down with bangles on them. Her spangled blue gown was sleeveless and beneath it protruded two legs in crinkly white stockings which suggested the absence of garters. The saddle of her spouse swayed and her seat on the burro's rump was none too steady.[19]

The animal was not happy under this double weight and constantly sought to pay off to one side and go back. Our host would then run out, seize him by the head, and, with the help of the two Mexican boys, swing him back into line. In this fashion the procession made the rounds of the large patio to the reverent applause of the spectators, who evidently were greatly impressed by the spectacle.

At its conclusion everyone knelt on the cool brick pavement while Ave Maria was sung. The evident piety and sincerity could not fail to impress, and stilled any tendency we might have to laugh. Of course in no event would any of us have been guilty of this discourtesy, but I suspect that for a time our elders had to exercise considerable self-mastery.

We got back to the fort after this glimpse of something in the life of Mexico which, I dare say, is only to be seen, if at all today, in some remote inland Indian community far from the Rio Grande.

The great event of our lives at this time was when we were ordered to Fort Duncan, farther up the river near Eagle Pass, beyond Laredo.[20]

7

FORT DUNCAN, TEXAS

1886

Age Fourteen Years

THE JOURNEY [from Fort Ringgold] had to be made in an ambulance and escort wagon, there being no train connection. The distance was something like four hundred miles, going by way of Laredo and camping out at night on the plain and sleeping in a tent.

To us children it was a great experience all through the first night to be awakened by the stamping feet and deep booming snorting of bulls and hear a fast-moving mass of cattle swinging by our tent. There must have been a cattle range near or else they were being taken somewhere. We had a double-spring [bed] which was carried in the escort wagon and unloaded and set up each night for my mother and one girl—usually my sister. This spring sat on legs about two feet above the ground. I slept on a cot at the side of the bed about two feet away.

I remember waking sometime after twelve to see my father standing near the door of our tent and holding in one hand a bottle and in the other his sword. The sword was the fine narrow straight one, almost like a fencing rapier, which dismounted officers carried, mounted officers carrying a saber. On the tip of his sword was a huge black spiderlike thing with wriggling legs. The bottle was a squat one of the type used for pickles and had a large neck. Setting this on the ground he jammed the spider into it and quickly clapped on the big cork.

It was a tarantula! On my asking what he was doing he simply replied, "Go to sleep, dear." Which I did in a twinkling, not knowing the peril which had been avoided, for these things jump, I was told, and their bite usually means death. As I afterward learned, our dear father remained awake the rest of the night, alternating between our tent and the one where the boys and he slept, watching out for the mate of the one he killed, but it did not appear.

In the morning we went on. I must say a word about Arnold, the enlisted man who was our teamster. Arnold was a character. Tall and thin, he had a high-pitched voice which, when he was excited, went up the scale until it almost broke.

"Miss Mamie," he said to me one day as we were passing a range of hills, "see that mount way over yonder? Well, I was goin' one time with another outfit to Laredo when I see over there settin' right on top of it a big puma—that's a mountain lion—lookin' out over the landscape. Of course he was far enough away not to bother me, but I up with my rifle and took a pop at him and doggone if I didn't hit him right between the eyes."

When I asked how he could tell that far away where he had hit the lion he replied that on the way back he went over there and found him lying dead where he had pitched off the top of the bluff.

"Weren't you afraid?" I asked.

"No, Miss Mamie," he replied, "I fear men more'n I fear beasts."

Our trip to Laredo was to be a prolonged one. When a day's journey from there we ran into a heavy rainstorm. The whole landscape seemed to turn into a broad expanse of water. The road was entirely obliterated, so much so that a small surrey driven by some civilian, which had been going ahead of us, pulled over to the side of what must have been the road and the driver got out in water almost up to his knees.

About a half-hour later we came to a hacienda and made up our minds to go no farther until the water subsided. In answer to our father's knock on the door, it was opened and the faces looking at us from inside were anything but hospitable. But we had no choice; night was coming and we had to stay.

I remember Daddy lifting us children out of the ambulance and carrying us into the large room and placing us on a bed running along one wall, about four feet above the floor. Returning for my mother he carried her to another bed adjoining this and placed her, sitting, on that. In the dim light we could see that the water covered the dirt floor to a depth of about three inches and that boards had been placed on other pieces of wood to walk on. The occupants were three men and a woman, all with bare feet. We were tired and maybe just a bit frightened; the people were not at all anxious for us to stay. We remained in the room about one hour while Daddy went out. When he came back, it was with the welcome news that a short distance away was a piece of rising ground, free of water, and that the tents had been pitched on that, and Eli, our man cook, had started to get some dinner, having got hold of some dry firewood from a shed. The water outside was subsiding, he said, and in a short time we could go over. When we were ready to go, Daddy offered to pay the people, who were Mexicans.

"Oh no, Señor," they said, "you are welcome," which their looks did not indicate. But, they accepted the money all the same. It was now getting dark and a lantern lit in one tent showed us where we were to dine. We were hungry!

To our mother [Daddy] said, "Well, we are here for over Sunday."

"You don't mean we must stay in this awful place until then?" asked Mama.

"Yes," he replied, "the arroyos ahead have all overflowed and we are water-bound until they go down."

Eagle Pass, which was to be our journey's end, was the approach to the post known as Fort Duncan. This was where we were to take up our abode for a few months. The little town of Eagle

Pass was situated on the Rio Grande with a connecting bridge between it and Piedras Negras on the Mexican side.

Our entry was anything but dignified, although we intended it to be just that. Having been on our journey two weeks with only our family and the soldier escort, our ambulance and escort wagon, eight mules, and our pony, Prince, it was a very personal cavalcade. Imagine two wagons filled with human beings and camp equipment creeping along over a land which held only, here and there, a few travelers like ourselves or transplanted Mexican farmers. Picture a few stretches where grass and verdure grew, alternating with sandy wastes dotted with cactus and mesquite. Imagine this traversed only by wagon track roads deep in sand, dried-up stream beds alternating at times with rushing torrents brought by heavy downpours. Picture the ambulance swaying and the mules floundering as they crossed, and the escort wagon being caught in quicksands from which it could only be rescued with great difficulty. There you have a brief picture of what such a journey meant in those days.

All through the trip we counted the days, each of which brought us one day nearer to our destination, the very old post of Fort Duncan. I can never understand its being maintained even then and it was abandoned soon after. But it was a sure thing in the chain of events in our army life.

So, on that beautiful clear morning we made another day of history in this as we approached it. Our dumb animals, the mules, were very sensitive to any unusual occurrence, especially after being away from civilization so long in the empty wilderness. In the interval between our stopover at Laredo and arrival at Eagle Pass, the only sounds usually were our voices, the straining of the mules' harness, and the soft padding of their feet in the sandy roads. When we ascended the height to Eagle Pass and came upon hard-beaten roads the sound of their own hooves must have been a bit stimulating.

The stage was all set for a dignified entry again into civilization. The linen duster which my mother had worn every day was put away that morning, replaced by a lovely blue gown and small flower-trimmed sailor hat. We girls also wore dresses of light color with bright sashes and hair bows. My sash was rose color over a dress of tan chambray. The boys were in short pants and shirtwaists of brown linen. Daddy was also all spruced up and Arnold made his mules look as if they had come from a millionaire's stables.

As we reached the top of the hill we could see two miles off the Stars and Stripes flying over Fort Duncan. It gave us a thrill, as it always did when we first saw the flag flying over a new fort. Our last view of a flag had been the one flying over the garrison at Laredo.

"I see the fort!" we all shouted.

Hardly had the words left when the lead mules, so good and tractable all through the journey, wheeled to the side of the road, the wheel mules following, and all four rushing pell-mell toward the rear of the ambulance. There was a report like a pistol shot and the tongue of the ambulance broke off clean, the front wheels jamming under the body, tilting it. Our father leaped to the ground and yanked open the door for us to get out, Arnold jumping to the other side and into the tangle of snorting, stamping, terrified mules, the man from the escort wagon rushed to his assistance in time to prevent the complete overturn which might have followed if the mules had not been quieted.

We children spilled out and saw our father lifting Mama out of the ambulance and wipe a thread of blood from her forehead. She had been thrown against the door by the sudden stop.

Dickey was the first to detect the cause of our misfortune.

"There he goes!" he shrieked, pointing. It was a pig that had been asleep at the side of the road and evidently, being awakened by the sound of the mules' hooves, had run in front of them, causing their fright.

Mr. Pig was evidently frightened more than any of them. He was making off at top speed down the road into the town street, his terrified squeal followed by the hearty curses of Arnold and our own babble of excited voices.

Piggy's Paul Revere ride down the main street and the uproar we made at its outer end brought out a number of people who gathered round us. Soon we had quite a crowd present. Among these was a tall imposing-looking man dressed all in white. He had no coat and I could see his gray suspenders. I had never seen suspenders before as Daddy always wore his coat and insisted it was bad manners to appear without it when these were worn. But this man, who turned out to be a very fine gentleman, always went about that way in warm weather. Mr. Braddock was one of the finest characters we ever knew, and he and his wife became our very good friends.

Mr. Braddock came up saying, "Captain, can I be of assistance? My house is near here and if you will come down we will make you and your family comfortable until you get straightened out."

So we all went off with Mr. Braddock and were given refreshment while Daddy went back and gave instructions for getting the ambulance in shape to go on to the fort. There it arrived in due season with the escort wagon and after a brief rest at Mr. Braddock's our hosts sent us on to the fort in their own carriage.

Thus was our dignified entry as a caravan upset completely by a pig.

When we finally arrived and descended a winding road in the hills outside the fort, we could see over the bordering treetops the flag flying from a tall flagstaff. Then, as we came into view of the quarters, there was our escort wagon in front of the long rambling house which was to be "Home, Sweet Home" for us after the long journey. A welcome sight it was. From a chimney at the back a tall thin column of smoke rising told us that Eli had already gotten a fire going in preparation for a meal. The army habit, which made this the first order of business when pitching camp, was strong with Eli.

Never shall I forget that desolate fort, a very small post with long rambling one-story quarters. Always on entering a fort we children picked out the best and the worst, but more usually the best spots and, after a closer inspection, we decided this might prove a very interesting place.

The house, after all, was not so bad, a bungalow type built in the form of an "L." The parlor, or living room, was very large and had a huge fireplace. To the left on entering was a large bedroom, connecting with it another large room and a small room. A continuation of the first led onto a porch. The porch ran across the front of these rooms and around the side of the third to a lawn or backyard, forming a sort of court. The dining room was the best spot in the house, directly back of the living room, and led to a pantry from which, down one step, was a large kitchen. This room we made beautiful with its curtained French windows, odd pieces of fine dining room furniture, china, silver, and glass. The lawn was large and beautifully planted with colorful flowers, palms, and shade trees. Our whole life centered around this spot.

Our father and mother were entertained a lot in town and, as my sister was nearing the "coming out" age, she went to a number of little dances there. The remaining three of us were made happy at home and found much to occupy us after study hours. We also played all sorts of games with the other children of the fort under the trees in the side yard where we spent much of our time. There we also read our books and I even played ball. There was no house immediately next to the side yard and this ground was used for our ball games and for running about with our beloved pony and other animals we attached to us—cats, dogs, and eventually a burro.

One day an old Mexican came with the thinnest horse I have ever seen. He would sell it for "cinco pesos"—five dollars. At first our father said no, but finally succumbed to our pleading, "See, Daddy, he is so thin. He needs us to feed him and make him strong."

"Well," said Daddy, "take him then and let him graze in the lot a few days."

Then his searching gaze took in the emaciated form of the old Mexican and he paid him the five dollars. No one ever lied to father when he looked that way.

"Si, Señor, he starve, I too." When he went away he was full of coffee and cornbread.

This pony we named Lazarus because of his bones. He was the same color as our other pony, Prince. He was so thin his hindquarters were dubbed "the hatrack." Very often horses in Texas eat too much mesquite and this results in a condition which makes them very thin. It took us a long time to cure this little fellow but when we did we had a fine horse. As children we always had horses and became fine riders, utterly fearless. All rode bareback but Kate, who rode sidesaddle.

The post had been established in 1849 to guard an important crossing of the Rio Grande, [to protect] the caravans trading with Mexico, also for punitive expeditions against the Lipans, Kickapoos, Comanches, and Apaches. It had long since ceased to serve any of these purposes when we were there. From the manner of our arrival and ultimate departure, I infer now that my father must have been sent there on one of the many detached services to which he was assigned between prescribed periods of duty with troops.[1]

In that day commissions and promotions were within specific regiments, in this case the 19th Infantry, and not generally in the arm of service, the status which came to pass later. He had thus found himself stymied at a relatively junior grade in the 19th for many years and was struggling to get out of the impasse, seeking and obtaining quartermaster assignments, one of which seemingly was the impending disposition of old Fort Duncan, as interim caretaking commander.[2]

I do not recall the presence of any other kind of garrison troops although the post had two battalion barrack buildings and other structures of stone and wood which had been added from time to time. They had served for the accommodation of infantry, cavalry, and artillery at various times, and on one occasion for the Negro troops of the 24th Infantry.

My bareback riding began at Fort Dodge when I was six years old. At Fort Duncan we were older and I rode about as well as the boys. My hair was bobbed like a boy's and my face red with sunburn. I also had freckles, chiefly on my nose. We now had two horses and a burro. Consequently there were not so many fights for privilege. Our great objective was a small mountain or height near the fort but we never got to it, as the going was too rough. My older brother rode Prince, the younger the burro, and I had to be content with the bones of Lazarus.

The little burro stayed behind when we moved to Fort Clark.

We were very fond of him in spite of his bad manners, and visitors made a great pet of him. I don't know just when we came to own him, he just wandered into the post and was allowed to stay and graze with the horses. One night he occasioned considerable excitement and fright, poking his head through a window when Kate was reading to me and hee-hawing loudly with his hot breath on my neck at the climax of a thrilling mystery story.

Another quite similar incident happened at an earlier post, which our burro adventure recalls. This happened in the daytime to Grandma Pinckney [and] it may have been at Fort Dodge. As at all posts in those early days, the "plumbing" was of the outdoor variety, housed in neat little structures not unlike sentry boxes, in some cases camouflaged with plants of climbing roses or honey-suckle to conceal their purpose. They always had a window in back for ventilation.

Grandma was in occupancy that day, indulging in quiet reverie, when a horse poked his nose through the window and neighed in her ear. She came flying out the door and headed for the house without stopping to identify the cause of her discomfiture. It is the one instance we ever heard of when indomitable doughty Grandma succumbed to the panic to which I am told all good soldiers may yield when caught off guard.

[Perhaps] our burro, by some psychic process, caught the spirit of mischief or friendly interest from this earlier animal.

Our days at Fort Duncan were ones of play, alternating with industrious activity, making things of the kind now undertaken so much in our schools as shop practice. All the posts had a post carpenter among the enlisted men, and at Fort Duncan he kept us supplied with scraps of lumber left over from his operations.

Our days there drew to a close after a stay of only a few months. Once again we children paid a last visit to the spots which had become dear to us, our ball ground and grazing pasture, which looked lovely behind the bordering trees in their fall dress. Daddy was for leaving Lazarus behind with the burro as a parting gift to some friends, but we all insisted that Lazarus go with us, so he did, along with Prince.

We children said good-bye to the old fort with the same feeling of sadness with which we had left other posts, even if the feeling was not quite so pronounced. But we had fun there and had come to love it. As we drove off in the ambulance we looked back at the flagstaff whose tip showed over the treetops. The flag was no longer there, the fort had been abandoned.[3]

So I came to another period of life which was that of a young, but no longer very young, child who was leaving behind the thoughts and memories of babyhood years while not yet old enough to see things with the eyes of ripened girlhood and a woman's dawning understanding. I was of the tomboy age and a tomboy I was, close-cropped and skinny, with some freckles on my nose. My sister and brothers were growing up too and beginning to show something of the good looks which were to mark them later in life. And here I should add a word about that period of our life nearing its close when fights were frequent. We children as fighters were more or less indifferent. We never sought a fight with other children, but when one started we usually finished in style. I remember my sister being manhandled by the son of a lieutenant who was hitting her with a mallet. I tore into him with fists and nails, his mother stood by complacent and did nothing to restrain him. I kicked his shins and beat him in the face until he howled.

Years afterward this same boy became my father's lieutenant in the Philippines, and my father said he was a good officer, efficient and very brave.

8

FORT CLARK, TEXAS

1886–1889

Age Fourteen to Seventeen Years

OUR DESTINATION was Fort Clark, a large post about 125 miles west of San Antonio in Texas. There was a railroad running to a point near there from Eagle Pass. We were elated at the prospect of again being on a train, as it was some four years or more since we had left David's Island. It was about nine PM when we arrived at the station nine miles from Fort Clark. There we were met by the post ambulance, taken to the fort, and deposited at a set of quarters. All I remember of our arrival, having been asleep just before, is being led into a brilliantly lighted room and getting off to bed and to sleep again in a twinkling.[1]

Fort Clark was at that time one of the gayest posts in the army and, while not as large as Fort Leavenworth, was larger than either of the border posts from which we had come. The garrison then consisted of seven companies of our regiment, the 19th Infantry, and five troops of the 3rd Cavalry. The commander was Colonel Albert G. Brackett and it was the headquarters post of our regiment, Colonel and Brevet Major General Charles H. Smith, his brevet being a Civil War distinction.[2]

The fort was separated from the town of Brackettville by Las Moras Creek, which wound about it in a serpentine way on three sides. The town and fort were connected by one bridge for traffic, another footbridge, and several fords. The main ford, where the most traffic was, led to the railroad station. We children, as usual, were introduced to these fords, the scene of subsequent adventures, by other children of the garrison.

The formalities of Fort Leavenworth were here on a smaller scale and the routine of the garrison followed the usual fixed form, except where broken by visits from the inspector general, adjutant general, or other such dignitaries. I remember among these a visit from General Philip H. Sheridan. He was a little man, full of fire and brimstone, and had the reputation of being a good drinker. I can recall him in the process of mounting our front steps to call on my father who, he had heard, had been present when he made his famous ride in the Civil War, from Winchester. His visit to us was followed by a light repast at the post commandant's where much champagne was consumed. I noticed some other officers with him who went up the steps in the same way.[3]

These visits from notables outside were occasions of excitement, which broke the routine pleasantly when it tended to become monotonous.

The town of Brackettville was proud of its several main buildings, the town hall, meat market, grocery, and several other stores, its very good public school, and its several churches. The western towns of those days sometimes had their own causes of excitement, but between times were usually asleep and only awoke from their tranquility when something unusual happened, then they did with a snap. Brackettville was no exception.[4]

We children went to school in Brackettville for about two years, and then it became necessary for a few families who could afford it to employ private teachers. We had one, Laura Coleman, who came from Englewood, New Jersey, to teach us and the children of General Smith, in whose quarters she lived. She had black hair and large dark eyes and fine teeth. Of course she was immediately "taken up," and after teaching hours was just like any other young woman guest visiting in the post. I hope the happy time she spent in this way compensated for the awful life she led with us children, the most riotous possible, for we were tough. But while rough in our play, we never did destroy property.[5]

At an early age children sense the difference between the servants in various households with which they have had so much contact. We had brought Eli, our cook, from Fort Duncan and he stayed with us for a time at Fort Clark. He was succeeded by Clarke. Like others of our old-time servants who had black skin, he could not read. One time he made a cake and after dinner my mother asked him, "Clarke, what was the matter with that icing you made for the cake? It was so hard we couldn't bite it, much less eat any of it."

Investigation showed he had gotten hold of a box of plaster of paris and used that. "Thank the Lawd, Mrs. Leefe," said Jenny, the laundress, "that good-for-nothing, he come near pizen you all with that stuff!"

Clarke fled out into the backyard, flinging the box far over the fence. But no one scolded him, he couldn't read, and it looked "jus' like powdered sugar."

Nancy was the name of our housemaid. She was a Seminole and lived in a camp of this tribe a few miles from the fort. The women of this tribe were very pretty, some very fair with a skin of café au lait, others very dark. They had a dialect of their own and beautiful singing and speaking voices. Some of them had intermarried with negroes and their way of speaking and singing [was] a blend of the two. Jenny was a Seminole too and, when dressed up, a beautiful creature. Too beautiful in fact to be around among soldiers, poor girl. She did not stay with us very long. She was fast and knew we knew it, and did not care.[6]

Clarke, in addition to being a fair cook, was a good ventriloquist. He would have made a fortune today with Charley McCarthy. Sometimes my mother, hearing strange voices in the kitchen, would come to the door only to find Clarke alone.

"No ma'am, dey's no one here. Ah'm just talkin' to myself."

After that he would put his head in the wood box to muffle

the sound, having been told he must not make so much noise. On one occasion we drafted him as a feature artist in a minstrel performance given at our home. The guests were officers and their wives and children. Clarke, hidden behind a large draped packing box in our dining room, entertained them with quips and conversations of several unseen men and women before disclosing himself as the sole performer. How the children screamed with wonder and delight at this revelation!

Army children were always hungry from so much outdoor activity, and in our case our mother always had tin boxes of cookies and doughnuts from which we were free to help ourselves. Our meals, however, were very formal. We all sat down at the same time and Emily Post would have gotten an eyeful at the way our meals were conducted. My two brothers sometimes rebelled at having to wash up and get dressed for dinner, especially when they wanted to ride their ponies a little longer.

My riding hour was usually about four in the afternoon when my two brothers were yelling themselves hoarse at baseball. The pony I rode was a veritable bucking bronco when I got on him. Whether he disapproved of girls riding astride in skirts which tickled and showed too much of a pair of skinny legs, I don't know, but he used to bound up and down and do his best to throw me. I would gallop around the square bordering the parade [field] after he found he could not unseat me. In passing the band quarters one day I heard one of the musicians on the porch say, "That beast she rides is a devil." Later someone overheard another musician say, "That kid sings like an angel and rides like a devil." He had heard me piping in church, I suppose.

On some occasions, however, I was thrown, sometimes in front of the barracks, but always got on again. The particular experience of this kind I recall best was when a certain Billy Lane of New York was visiting at the post.

"Miss Mamie," he said to me one day, "will you take a ride with me outside the post?"

"Certainly," I replied. Billy loved to ride but only had a chance when visiting his sister, wife of the ranking surgeon, and was never very comfortable sitting down after riding.

"What horse are you riding?" he asked.

"The Brute," I answered.

"Aren't you afraid of him? He's pretty mean."

"Not so he'll know it," I answered.

So off we went. I did not often get the chance to go outside the fort and could only do so when accompanied by someone older. So, on this day I was full of joyful anticipation. We rode out, crossed one of the smaller fords, and reached a winding road traversing a lovely stretch of woods on which we continued for about two miles, reaching another ford much larger than the first and at some distance from the fort.

As we waded in, Billy in the lead, I sensed a quivering in the body of my mount as he lifted one forefoot after another in the deepening water. This should have been a warning to me but I was enjoying it all too much to pay heed. The water was up to our horses' bellies.

"It's getting deeper," a slight uneasiness in his voice. Billy had not had much experience in crossing streams and was evidently a bit apprehensive.

"If you are afraid, go back," I said. "I'm not!"

Just then, as if to spite me, the devil I was riding took it into his head to lie down and roll over. I yanked on the bit trying to get his head around and force him to rise up but to no avail, and over we both went. I disappeared completely. As I went under I knew I must get my skirt off the pommel and my feet free of the stirrups. This I was able to do except my skirt, which tore off at the band, leaving me in my short "undies." The devil, having got rid of me, promptly scrambled to his feet and ran up the bank where Billy seized his bridle, calling to me, "Want any help?"

I was too angry to reply and, with tears of mortification and rage, stood there, waist deep, sputtering and wiping water from my eyes. Billy, I am bound to say, showed more presence of mind, first taking turns around a small tree with the horses' reins to prevent

1 Mary Leefe Laurence, portrait, circa 1930, by an
unidentified artist. Courtesy John F. Laurence.

2 Mary Leefe Laurence, age eighteen, in *The Mikado* at Fort Brady, Michigan, circa 1890. Amateur theatrical performances were a common form of entertainment in the nineteenth-century U.S. Army. Courtesy John F. Laurence.

3 Leefe quarters, Fort Dodge, Kansas, circa 1879. This photo was taken just after the Leefes left the post. In her scrapbook Mary Leefe Laurence marks the frame house on the left of the picture as "our quarters." The view is looking south at the back end of officers' row. The stone building in the center was the commanding officer's quarters, and the stone structure on the right was the post hospital. Outside the fence in the right foreground is a roofed water well. Courtesy Kansas State Soldiers Home, Fort Dodge, Kansas.

4 Leefe quarters, Fort Leavenworth, Kansas, circa 1880. The fifth building from the right, 43 West End Parade Field, was the Leefe quarters from 1880 to 1881, according to the post directory. This row of officer duplexes on present Kearney Avenue was torn down in 1902–3 to make way for the construction of the artillery barracks. Courtesy Frontier Army Museum, Fort Leavenworth, Kansas, photo number 6003.63(2).

5 Leefe quarters, Fort Gibson, Oklahoma, circa 1934. In the Laurence family scrapbook this photograph is identified as their quarters while at the post in 1881. The building is currently a private residence. This photograph was taken in March 1934 by Fred Q. Casler as part of the Historic American Building Survey. Courtesy The Library of Congress, photo number HABS, OK, 51-FoGib, 1B-3.

6 David's Island, New York, circa 1890. The post appears much as it
would have when the Leefes were stationed there in 1881 to 1882, when
the fort was a recruiting depot. This image shows half of the island,
looking north across part of Long Island Sound toward New Rochelle,
New York, in the background. In the foreground a group of soldiers,
with a few children looking on, apparently have interrupted a game of
baseball to watch the photographer. The building in the foreground was
the depot detachment barracks. Officers' row runs along the shore in the
left of the picture. Courtesy National Archives and Records Service,
Washington DC, negative number 92-F-19–2.

7 Fort Clark, Texas, circa 1892. This U.S. Army Signal Corps photograph was taken about 1892, two years after the Leefe family departed
from the post. The view is from the northwest corner of the post with
the satellite town of Brackettville in the background. The small bridge
in the right center of the photograph crosses Las Moras Creek. The
building in the upper left foreground surrounded by a high curtain
fence appears to be a soldiers' bathhouse. Courtesy National Archives
and Records Service, Washington DC, negative number 111-SC-97900.

8 Company B, Nineteenth Infantry, at Fort Clark, Texas, 1888. Armed with the single shot "Trapdoor" Springfield rifle, the company is in the dress uniform of the period. Captain John G. Leefe is at the extreme left. The other two officers are identified on the photograph as Lieutenants Theodore H. Eckerson and Arthur B. Foster. The company is assembled in front of a typical company barracks of the period. Courtesy John F. Laurence.

9   Leefe family in quarters, Mount Vernon Barracks, Alabama, circa 1890. On the porch to the left are Captain and Mrs. Leefe. To the far right is Cindy, the cook. Courtesy John F. Laurence.

10   Opposite page. Lawn tennis at Fort Clark, Texas, circa 1889. Mary Leefe Laurence noted on the photograph, "This was the net over which I leaped, occasioning the order against tennis playing during guard mount." Tennis was a popular sport among the officer caste by the last decade of the nineteenth century. The ladies played in long dresses, as the photo illustrates. Identified left to right are Lieutenant Wilder, Willie Jordon, Mary Leefe, Sax Pope, Chuck Leefe, Will Washington (in tree), Issa Jordon, Miss Purington, Miss McKee, Dr. Rafferty. In the background are officers' quarters. Courtesy John F. Laurence.

11 Apache leaders at Mount Vernon Barracks, Alabama, circa 1893. From left to right, Chihuahua, Naiche, Loco, Nana, and Geronimo. Mary Leefe Laurence came to know these Chiricahua and Warms Springs Apache prisoners of war during 1889–90 when her father's infantry company was detailed as their guard force. She liked Chief Chihuahua, admired Naiche, but remained apprehensive of Geronimo, about whom she wrote, "We children were afraid of him and took care to heed him whenever he spoke to any of us." Courtesy National Archives and Records Service, Washington DC, negative number 111-SC-94845.

12 Apache families at Mount Vernon Barracks, Alabama, circa 1887–1894.
When Mary Leefe Laurence arrived in May 1889 there were 380
Apache prisoners present. The death rate was about 24 percent, pri-
marily among the women and children. "One day we hated them," she
recalled, "and the next day were sorry for them and wanted to help."
Courtesy Alabama Department of Archives and History, Montgomery,
Alabama, negative number PN6438.

13 Fort Brady, Michigan, parade ground, circa 1911. Mary Leefe Laurence lived at this extreme northern border post in the period 1890 to 1896. Courtesy John F. Laurence.

14 Company B, Nineteenth Infantry, at Chicago, 1894. Deployed to stem violence from urban labor strikes, the company is in field uniform with cartridge belts and bayonets. Major John G. Leefe (with the beard) is in the center. His hands are resting on his sword. Courtesy John F. Laurence.

their getting away, and then coming down to the bank to give me a hand. I was safe and could see he wanted to laugh.

"Do it!" I screamed at him. "Go ahead and laugh if you want!" Then I slapped his face.

He promptly retaliated with a smart box on my ears which I deserved. I was so astonished and shocked that I lost control and, throwing myself on the ground, gave way to angry tears. I guess I must have howled and when I next heard his voice it was very tender, "Darling child, don't cry. I'm so sorry."

I sat up and looked at his red, mud-streaked face where I had slapped him and burst into laughter. Then he did the same. I must have been a spectacle, in my short undies and skinny legs, all wet and smeared with mud.

What to do next? Billy stood up and looked around.

"There's a house!" he exclaimed.

When we appeared at the door and explained our plight, the astonished woman who answered our knock very kindly asked us to come right in, but Billy stayed outside while I went in to clean up and dry out. The first hint I had of anything like a romantic feeling on his part, and certainly on my part toward anyone of the opposite sex, was when he put his arm around me and kissed me on the forehead.

Me! Skinny, freckled, tomboy me! I had seen evidence of tender feeling toward my sister, young as she still was, by one or two officers at the fort, but she was beautiful and I took it as a matter of course that this should occur with her. But Billy and me! It was too strange, and me looking such a fright.

When I emerged an hour later it was to present Billy with an even stranger sight, which should have cured any romantic feeling. The kind German woman had outfitted me with a complete set of her own clothing—clean white underwear, much too large, a white skirt with embroidery, reaching almost to my ankles, a black bodice miles too big, and a long black outer skirt which had to be pinned in at the waist to keep it on. White stockings and black shoes completed a costume in which I was to ride Devil back to the fort astride.

I was really a sight and Billy agreed to my insistence that we take a back way into the fort and our quarters, not the main entrance. We were now on the same side of the stream as the fort, with no more fords to cross, fortunately. After assuring our good Samaritan that her things would be sent back to her promptly, we set out.

To get back in the fort without recrossing the ford we [had to] go by the soldiers' quarters. It was almost the hour of retreat. When we got there the men were beginning to line up in front, waiting for the command to snap to attention, come to "parade rest," and listen to the bugles and the booming of the evening gun.

"Make it quick," I urged Billy, hoping to get by without notice, giving Devil a good cut with the whip. He gave one snort and broke into a gallop and by we went, Billy a bit behind, but soon catching up. Just as we got in front of the barracks my voluminous skirt blew up, almost enveloping me and showing the long white drawers which encased my skinny legs. I tried to hold the skirt down, gathering it in one hand to the pommel and holding it there to keep myself on in case Devil tried any of his tricks. We went by full tilt to roars of laughter from the crowded porches.

When we got to our quarters and came in the back service way the family were about to sit down to dinner. "Great Scott!" exclaimed my father, while my brothers shrieked with mirth. Only my mother, sensing something had happened, took me to her arms with a little quick cry of relief. She had been growing anxious. Just then Falkenberg, our striker, put his head in the door and asked, "What shall I do with your horse, Miss Mamie?"

"Take him out and shoot him!" I snapped. "I don't care what you do with him."

Father asked Mr. Lane, somewhat stiffly, to stay for dinner, which he did, and of course the whole story had to be related, all but the tender parts. I told these to my mother afterward. We never had any secrets of the heart from her, nor from Daddy, but I knew that I would have to stand from my brothers and, besides, Mr. Lane was present. That aspect of it came to nothing and I was to have another affair of puppy sentiment with someone else later.

At this time I was constantly outraging the decorum of post life with tomboy antics. For one thing, I played tennis a great deal, and a fast game at that, with anyone I could induce to join me. My favorite trick, after a victorious set, was to jump over the net in a wild kick-up leap. This I did one morning during guard mount while the guard was passing in review near the net, to the amusement of said guard, which passed with smirks on their faces. This resulted in an order, in the usual printed form, to the effect that hereafter there would be no more tennis playing during guard mount or evening parade.

Years afterward at a reception at the vice president's house in Washington I met a major who asked me, "Are you the Miss Leefe who was responsible for that order about tennis playing at Fort Clark?" I admitted that I was. He turned to his wife and said, "Here she is. You remember that, when we relieved the 19th at Fort Clark, we couldn't play tennis except at certain hours." The order evidently stood after we had left, and the cause of it had become a tradition.

Other misdeeds of ours, or our household pets, led to similar restrictions. In our menagerie we had a goat, dubbed by my father Wilhelmus Capricornus. My father's scrapbook contains the original of a printed order issued from there in consequence of the goat's behavior:

"No goats will be permitted to remain in the garrison, they having already done considerable damage to the ornamental shade trees. Horses, and animals, liable to injure the shade trees and grass will not be permitted to enter or graze in the front yards of officers' quarters at this post."[7]

While this may have been one phase of our goat's behavior, the real reason [for the regulation] could not be given with dignity in an official order. One evening there was a formal parade. The troops were drawn up in line and the adjutant about to report to the colonel who was standing stiffly and full of dignity out in front. Wilhelmus Capricornus, tethered on our lawn, broke loose and trotted onto the parade. He made a beeline for the colonel and before anyone could stop him, biff! just where the colonel's coattails hung down. The effect was electric. A wave of laughter swept the ranks as the colonel, propelled several steps forward, faced about and dodged a second onslaught. Someone from the spectators, an officer from the headquarters staff, ran out and grabbed the offending beast by the horns, dragging him off. Meanwhile the officers with the lined-up troops, themselves convulsed, were bawling at the men, "Cut that out! Stop that laughing instantly!"

So, Wilhelmus Capricornus had to go.

Another order of a similar kind was issued about the same period. I was doing a circus stunt with one of the officers, a lieutenant, who afterward became a high-ranking general. The horse was a stallion and dangerous. We were on him bareback, I standing up behind the lieutenant and holding on to his shoulders and letting out shrill Indian whoops as we pranced and cantered down the line in front of the officers' quarters. After this grand finale, we went to our quarters to gulp lemonade and eat cookies, accompanied by a few others who had gathered as an impromptu audience. The next day out came an order forbidding any more bareback riding on the front line. My escapades certainly kept the headquarters' press working.

I am not certain that the so-called damage to the ornamental shade trees in "the goat order" may not have been occasioned really by our practice of climbing into these to hide after some disturbing trick which sent an orderly from headquarters looking for us. On one occasion General Smith, whom we called the "Generalissimo," passed directly under the tree in which I was hiding and in my fright I nearly let go my hold.[8]

Other diversions which worried our parents, if not headquarters, were when we went down to Las Moras Creek to play. This had its source in a spring which spread out into a small lake or pond before narrowing down to form the stream. It was a lovely spot. The banks of the stream had gradually sloping sides on which grew gorgeous ferns and tall trees in which birds made their nests, filling the air with their song. Moss covered the trees at their foot and sweet flowers of brilliant hue grew all about.

The creek was safe but the pool very deep. On this lake there was a boat or two and we children loved to paddle about, [the boat] filled with as many of the fort's children as we could squeeze in. This was not safe, but we had only one spill. We loved to look over the sides with our faces close to the water to see the cool green depths where fish swam. One day I must have leaned too far, or the others did, for the boat seemed to slide and dump us all in the water. It was deep and we had to cling, and did we cling! It was way over our heads. Fortunately my brother Dick, in the other boat, came to the rescue and got us all ashore, looking like drowned rats. When dry we hated to go home and have to tell, as we feared it would mean the end of our going there. As it was we waited until retreat when everyone at the fort would have their attention occupied with that, and sneaked in by a back way.

On another occasion we had a picnic with some of the grown-ups at another lovely spot some distance from the fort, where there was a pool, and found this to be filled with water moccasins, a deadly snake. They fascinated us, swimming about with their heads above water, literally in droves, but it spoiled our afternoon.

Another pest, and a smelly one, was the skunk or "prairie queen." The evening breeze used to waft their aroma to us, and murderous traps were set for them in the back lines to get rid of them.

Which recalls a story my mother told me of a certain distinguished foreign officer visiting at another post where these beasts were also in evidence. As I have said, our mother was very beautiful, and this officer, Baron somebody-or-other, very gallant in the European manner, said to her, "Ah, Madame, you are, what shall I say, as beautiful as a prairie queen!" It was with great gusto that we children used to twit her about "the man who called her a skunk."

About this time I was asked to sing in the choir at the church as the soprano. I loved nothing more than singing, having begun early and being considered something of a prodigy in this line. I was now growing up, had let my hair grow, and was wearing it usually in pigtails. In the choir we had two soldiers as the male voices, my mother being the other female voice. The tenor had a gorgeous voice and the basso was fair. But it was over the basso that I got the blind staggers in my first real experience of what we call, in the case of men, puppy love. I adored him. He was an enlisted man and very handsome, educated, and with fine manners.

Of relations with the enlisted men—the friendly intimacy which we developed with many was a phase of our early childhood when, as mere kids, we were out-of-doors so much and necessarily more in contact with them and treated by them as pets. Soldiers love pets and were always very kind to us and we grew to love many of them—Dudu and Smith at Fort Dodge, Arnold at Ringgold, and later at Forts Brady and Wayne "Seechy" as we called him. Grand old rugged veterans these, with whom we could have trusted ourselves anywhere and to whose arms we would have flown had we needed protection or sympathy any time. These old types are mostly gone from the army in this day, when the call appears to be chiefly for eighteen year olds. Let me say on behalf of the grand old regulars, they could stand any amount of hardship and ex-hausting tests of endurance in grilling campaigns against a crafty and treacherous foe as well as any group of youngsters could have done. They are sublime, as we all know, but also were the tough older men of the old army amongst whom we lived.

I was growing up and reaching the age when that bar between the enlisted men and officers had to come down for us children. My developing a case of puppy love for anyone "in the ranks" was not to be spoken of, at least publicly. From my mother I had no secrets and can remember her saying, about my sense of guilt in caring for an enlisted man, "You have nothing to be ashamed of. He is a gentleman from a fine family and if he has paid you the compliment of his affection it is an honor, I am sure. But," and she went on to caution me that I was still too young and that time would have to tell whether it could go further when his enlistment was up and if both he and I would feel the same way then. Mean-while to say nothing about it and be circumspect, as an officer's daughter should, for his sake as well as mine. If only mothers would give their children such advice in cases where artificial class dis-tinctions interpose a bar to attachments from the standpoint of what is wise for happiness. I heeded it, as I did through life while she lived.

Once, crossing the bridge to the fort on my way back from town, I met him and he spoke to me. I brought my horse to a halt and he said, "Miss Mamie, excuse me, but I wanted to tell you how much the men liked your singing. I do too, you have a beautiful voice."

"Oh, thank you," I stuttered.

"I wanted to ask you," he went on, "if you would accept this little pin from me as a token?" Pulling a velvet case out of his pocket he took out a little pin in the shape of a beautiful little sword with an ivory hilt, which I have to this day. I fancied as I rode on that he must have known my feeling for him.

At another time while my two brothers were standing at our gate he rode up on a sorrel pony and handed them a gorgeous bunch of wild blossoms and rode away. When I went out to see what it was all about my brothers handed them to me. I seized them and ran into the house, to encounter my mother, who had a questioning look on her face, but only said, "Put them in your room."

I was a bit uneasy about this, fancying that others in the fort would become wise to this romance between a soldier and a tomboy girl of the officer set who was just becoming conscious of the fact that she might be something else, and as a matter of fact I think a few were. That afternoon the wife of a lieutenant of the cavalry called me onto her porch. She was a beautiful woman but considered a bit gay and was not liked by the other women in the post.

"Mamie," she said, "you seem a bit interested in Sergeant T——." (I don't know if he is alive and as this is a bit intimate I will not give his name.)

As I started to deny, she said, "You can trust me, child, I know how it is and will say nothing to anybody."

"My mother knows all about it," I exclaimed. "I have no secrets from her."

"But I wanted to tell you about Sergeant T——," she went on. "He is no common man. He is a gentleman from a fine old

Virginia family. During the campaign against the Indians in Arizona," she continued, "George, my husband, was the lieutenant of the troop in which at that time T—— was a private. T—— had just come before an examining board for a commission. He passed successfully but something happened to prevent his getting it, just what I do not know. Hostilities broke out with the Indians and George and his troop with two others went out against them. There was a bad fight and our men were badly cut up. Only a ragged remnant of our men came back but later they were victorious.

"At first, as I say, they had to retreat but came back and wiped the band out before they got through. During the retreat George was shot and left for dead but T—— saw him and fell out of line and rode back and grabbed him and put him on his horse and got back with him to the troop. When night came they were able to camp and were not molested. For twenty-four hours George was fighting to live and T—— stayed by his side all this time until the reinforcements they had sent for arrived and the attack was renewed. Then they could not leave the wounded and these had to go forward with them. They had an ambulance brought up for them with the reinforcements and George and one or two others were placed in this.

"T—— got permission to stay with him and rode on the ambulance, watching over my husband and ready with a loaded pistol in case any further defeat meant loss of the ambulance and a last stand for those in it. During all this time T—— had no sleep and when they got back to the post he was all in and had to go to the hospital along with George.

"George was there two weeks and when he came out it was with a weak back which lasted a long time. T—— was decorated in the presence of the entire garrison for what he did. This is the kind of man he is, Mamie, and you needn't be ashamed of liking him. George and I both love him."[9]

"And so do I," I exclaimed. "I don't care if you do know it."

"Oh, well, you'll get over it in a little time," she replied. "I only wanted to tell you about him in case anyone ever says anything to you which might make you ashamed. But I'll never tell anyone," she added.

I have never told this story, [but] it adds one more glimpse of what our army was doing in those days with pitifully small forces of but a few men which were sent against vastly superior numbers of Indians, a page of heroism which is all but forgotten today.

The end of this little romance for me was to come as predicted, and the last scene of it was when we left Fort Clark. Our days there were drawing to a close. Rumors were in circulation that two companies of our regiment were to be detached and sent to Mount Vernon Barracks in Alabama.

When the order came and the two companies were designated, one of them proving to be our own Company B, there was the same feeling of regret and sorrow as we looked back over the four happy years we had spent at Fort Clark. In my case they were mixed with the keener anguish of seeing no more the handsome young soldier who had captured my youthful heart.

Looking back I can see that, in sensing my feeling for him, he had responded in a kindly tolerant way and out of a sense of gratitude to an officer's daughter who paid him the compliment of bridging the social gap which separated us. He was much older than I and must have decided to play along in this way until events separated us. He was of the cavalry and hence did not go with us to Mount Vernon Barracks.

When the time came to leave and the ambulance bore us out of the fort we looked back sorrowfully over the long sweep of the parade with its rows of trees, officers' quarters, and soldiers' barracks, and to me there came the vague sense as these passed from view that I was leaving my childhood behind.[10]

The troops had an hour's start of us and we only caught up with them as they reached the train which was to take us to Mount Vernon Barracks, thirty miles from Mobile. The troops had fallen out and were all over the place loading their equipment on the cars. They were given, as in other instances, a special train and we were assigned to a car and put aboard. We had left our servants at Fort Clark and were inheriting the servants of the officers' families who were leaving [Mount Vernon] Barracks with the troops we were to relieve.

I went out onto the platform of our car and was watching the men of our company putting their barracks bags and other equipment aboard the cars designated for them. I had seen nothing of T—— before leaving and was reconciling myself to the thought of giving him up forever when someone hopped up onto the platform from the other side of the train and a voice said, "Good-bye, Miss Mamie."

It was he. He had gotten a pass and had ridden down to the train to see us off. "You don't mind my coming, do you?" he said. "I felt I had to see you before you went and tell you how much knowing you and singing in the choir with you has meant to me. It is hard sometimes to be so close to people of your own kind and not be able to see more of them in a social way. You've been so sweet and kind to me I'll never forget it. Keep this to remember me with."

He pulled out of his pocket a little red book and handed it to me. It was an autograph album and on the first page he had written, "May your heart's desire be with you, T—— T——."

I could only say, "Thank you. I knew you'd come."

I can smile today, looking back on this bit of sentimental byplay and whatever may have been meant by the words he had written. But at the time the pull on my heartstrings was intense in this, the first romance of my budding girlhood. It was very real to me and is a cherished memory today. My mind was then in too much of a whirl to remember what more he said as he lifted his cap and walked away down the track, his head held up high as became a true gentleman of Virginia.

This he was in all respects in his conduct toward me. Never once did he overstep the bounds of respectful deference. Why he should have chosen me, an unattractive and sometimes wild-acting tomboy of a girl with pigtails, as the special object of his, I never could guess. But this I knew, the tribute of a man's respect is the finest compliment any girl or woman can receive.

As the train pulled out for our new station I cried my sorrow out in my mother's understanding arms, with her words and sympathy soothing me to a tranquil state. Little did she know that in later life I was to comfort and soothe her in a grief far more great than mine in the loss of our dear daddy, who paid her the tribute of his deep respect all through their married life, and that I was to be her sole companion for many years. Her other daughter, [Kate,] in the not too distant future, was to marry a baron, leaving our home nest to be entertained for a time brilliantly by his family in the old Germany which has passed, and returning to live outside the army in a home of her own. I, far from marrying my soldier love or any other later admirer, was to go on to comparative old-maidhood before taking a corresponding step and bringing [Mother] to pass her remaining years in a little home of my own.

There is one other aspect of our life at Fort Clark which I would speak about because the tribute does not apply to me but to my dear father and mother. It came from more than one source, but mostly from humble people, servants and soldiers of the garrison, in things said to us when leaving and which came to us afterward. It was that we were missed more than any other family on post. I suppose this was because we were kind to them.

My father and mother both had a very strong sense of class, inherited and apt to be impressed upon us, from an ancestry in which they took pride. My father especially was careful to impress upon us that we must never do anything to hurt the feelings and the self-respect of anyone beneath us in the social scale, particularly the soldiers. "Remember," he said, "they cannot strike back." Thus it was unchivalrous and cowardly to take advantage of this. Never did I know him to strike a soldier or curse him, even under the severest provocation when he had to put men in the guardhouse or send them to severe punishment elsewhere.

There was plenty of swearing by officers at drill when stupidity provoked it, but it was always "Damn it," not "Damn you." Nor did I ever hear of any officer striking a man in those days, and it was a day of severe punishments, when the ball and chain were among the penalties. Such was the "officer code."

9

MOUNT VERNON BARRACKS, ALABAMA

1889—1890

Age Seventeen to Eighteen Years

THE REGRET we all felt at leaving a large post to occupy another with only two companies of infantry was indeed keen and was further intensified when we arrived at the small station some couple of miles from Mount Vernon Barracks and were driven there in a buckboard and ambulance. Our two companies had been sent there to act as guard over a concentration camp of some 398 Apache prisoners of war who had been transferred there from Fort Lauderdale. They had been rounded up following a series of outbreaks which left no alternative but to break up the tribe and remove the troublemakers from their reservation.[1]

Of all the Indians they [the Apache] were perhaps the most savage, ferocious, and cruel in their warfare. Stories had come to us of how their favorite fiendish act was to take any of our men they captured, or other white captives, and bury them in the desert sand with only their heads above ground. Then they cut off their eyelids and left the sun to scorch their bare eyeballs and the flies and insects to torture them until they died.[2]

Was it any wonder that our hearts stopped a beat when we first saw them? An Indian was at best something to be dreaded, but these! And we were to live next to them with less than half their number of our soldiers to guard them. Some few of them were allowed out and were hanging around the station when we arrived.[3]

Their appearance surprised us. They were not in the traditional Indian costume, but in dark trousers and coats with bright red or blue bandannas tied around their heads. The women wore dresses of black or blue with ruffled skirts, each ruffle being of a different color. Their hair was jet black in two braids hanging down over each shoulder. Some had their hair parted in the middle and cut short below the lobe of each ear.

As we left the station and drove toward the Barracks, our disagreeable impressions were relieved somewhat by the beauty of the foliage and the crisp autumn air. The women and children, there were not many besides ourselves, drove through the sally port ahead of the officers and men who marched in, glad of the short hike after being cooped up so long in the cars.

After leading such a free life at Fort Clark, where in time we were allowed to go all over the place by ourselves, even to the extent of riding horseback outside, imagine how we felt on being told we could not go outside the Barracks alone. The Barracks were encircled by a wall which seemed about twenty feet high and almost three feet thick. The main gate was a sally port and the lower gate gave egress to the Indian camp. Adjoining the Barracks were some sutler's stores, a few homes of white citizens, and some negro cabins. There were also between the main sally port and the railroad station a few houses occupied by noncommissioned officers' families, schoolteachers, and the nurse provided by the government for the Indians, also the post hospital. These precincts were considered as virtually part of the post and guarded as such.[4]

The broad road of red clay through this settlement was bordered by huge live oak trees, the long rambling hospital being on one side of the road and the teachers' home on the other. We were allowed to go there and to the railroad station, when accompanied, and to the store, but never to the Indian camp unless with an officer or soldier escort.

The usual feeling on entering a new post was a strange mixture of unhappiness at having to part from the older post, mingled with a certain happy expectancy of new interests and adventure to be met in the new. But here it was different. There was the uneasy dread at being at such close quarters with so many of these particularly primitive and cruel Indians. We would often be awakened at night by hearing some buck who had smuggled in some firewater giving vent to piercing yells of drunken fury or delight. There were, I regret to say, many whites who would pander to the Indians' worst instincts by secretly selling them bootleg whiskey for the profit they could make. Our rests would also be broken at times by wailing chants over the body of some dead child.

These people were so ignorant and primitive that they would cover the head of a dying person with a cushion or blanket and sit upon it in the belief that if they could keep the breath in his body he would live. It can be imagined that life with such neighbors was not a very happy one. One day we hated them and the next day were sorry for them and wanted to help.

Geronimo, pronounced "Heronimo," was chief of the tribe at the time but had become so only by superior power and might. Naiche, the hereditary chief, was not in power then and Geronimo reigned supreme. To my eyes the tall graceful Naiche was all that an Indian should be in appearance. He had a clear light complexion without that red look and with fine clear-cut features, piercing black eyes, and, with his erect carriage, he was a striking figure. Geronimo, on the other hand, was short and stocky, with short black hair and a dark muddy reddish complexion. He had a big firm jaw and cruel mouth. We children were afraid of him and took care to heed him whenever he spoke to any of us.[5]

He was allowed sometimes to walk about in the fort unattended. On one occasion he came up to our porch when my mother was there alone. What he wanted my mother did not know but she was badly frightened, although taking care not to show it. Possibly he thought that as she was a squaw and a white one at that he could frighten some gift out of her. But he met his match. Drawing herself up to her full height and pointing with her arm she uttered one word only, "Begone!"

Geronimo looked at her a moment and then gave her the military salute. "Brave lady," he said and went away.

Afterward he was a bit more friendly and I still have the little buckskin wampum pouch with its jingling metal cone fringe which he gave me before we left. It was generally thus with the Indians. They might admire anyone who might show that he or she was unafraid and always had more respect for the soldier than they did for the civilian. They were always proud to wear a discarded military uniform, which the law at the time permitted.

An amusing instance of this was the case of another chief there, Chihuahua. He was very indignant when obliged to discard his Indian dress and assume the coat and trousers which were issued to these Indian War prisoners. A gray felt hat in winter and a straw one in summer completed the costume they had to wear.

One day while passing the quarters of a lieutenant of artillery who had been assigned to the post for some special duty, Chihuahua saw the lieutenant busy on his porch with a box of clothing. The lieutenant was a bit of a dandy and was sorting out the too-many garments he had for disposal.

"What you make?" inquired Chihuahua.

"Oh, I get rid of some things, I give them away."

"You give me?" asked the chief.

"Sure, you can have what's in the box over there."

Going to the box the chief took out an old artillery officer's blouse and trousers with their red stripe down the side. The next thing he took out was a high silk top hat.

When Chihuahua next appeared he was wearing the discarded uniform with the stovepipe hat on his head. There were some other things he took, including a lady's parasol and other bits of feminine finery discarded by the lieutenant's wife. He was particularly intrigued by the parasol, the use of which was explained to him, and he went away beaming, never suspecting that it was an item of squaw apparel. The next day it rained and he went by our quarters in his uniform and stovepipe hat, holding the parasol over it.

Loco was another chieftain. "Loco" means crazy. I never knew his real name. He got it in council, wherein he strongly urged his tribe not to go to war against the whites. They shouted at him, "Loco! Loco!" and the name stuck to him. The next day they took the warpath and wiped out a town. Before they were rounded up and put under guard they had ravaged the entire border and some parts of Mexico. What provocation they may have had I do not know.[6]

Their taking the warpath has been laid to the evil influence of Geronimo. He had not the character and high-mindedness of Chief Joseph, but the leader qualities of a bandit. His terrible eyes haunted my dreams and I would often wake in the night shivering with fright. This continued with me all the time we were there. It was not so with the other chiefs I knew.

At Mount Vernon Barracks the Indians were put in log cabins and some of the squaws kept these very neat and clean. Old Chief Chihuahua used to sit by the door of his cabin smoking his pipe and reflecting on the folly of his tribe in going to war with the white man. Most of his tribe I think agreed with him. He was a very old man and they seemed to respect him. Many snapshots of him in uniform were taken by tourists. His youngest squaw used to put this uniform away between layers of paper with bergamot leaves. He prized it so greatly that before donning it he would follow the unusual course for an Indian of sitting for an hour in a sweat bath to make sure he was clean before he would trust his person to it.

Not all of the Indians were free to come and go as they pleased. The chiefs had some liberty but a careful eye was kept on them. On one occasion Geronimo came and stood at the back of a hall which served as the schoolroom to listen to the children sing. I was playing the little melodeon and after some popular songs, they were to sing "Jesus Loves Me, This I Know." The children sang through their teeth instead of opening their mouths, giving a sort of shishing lisp to their words, while Miss Sophie Shepherd, their teacher, kept gesticulating in an effort to get them to sing out.

Geronimo stood this as long as he could, then strode a few steps forward and shouted to the children, "Open mouths! Zing!"

What Miss Shepherd couldn't accomplish Geronimo did. The terrified youngsters opened their mouths and bawled the notes out lustily. After that there was never any difficulty getting them to sing out, they had only to be reminded of what Geronimo had said to them. They stood in mortal terror of him and would have done anything he commanded.[7]

Two teachers had been sent by the government to try to give some education to the Indians in a schoolroom in the camp, one to teach the men and women, and Miss Shepherd to teach the children. The latter was a southerner and lived in Mobile after the burning of her father's home some miles from the post.[8]

One day Miss Shepherd went for a ride with my mother, Kate, and myself out to the spot where her home had stood. All that was left was the skeleton of a very fine old southern mansion. The high porch across the front and around the sides was still fairly intact. The grille between the pillars had been gleaned from the old Creole section of New Orleans and looked like lovely old black Spanish lace.

"How did it come to burn down?" I asked and she told us.

The family was away for the afternoon and some pigs, which had been let out of their pen to root, had strayed on to the lawn and one of the small colored boys from the negro servants' quarters started to chase them back. They ran under the porch, which was very close to the ground, and nothing could induce them to come out. Old "Uncle Dan'l," one of the hands who came to his assistance, sent for a box of matches and being unable to poke the pigs out, attempted to smoke them out with a smudge of dry grass and green stuff pushed in.

It succeeded and the pigs came out, but it also set fire to something in there and the fire ran along the porch beams and into the house, getting into the walls, and soon the whole place was ablaze. There was nothing they could do to stop it, and when other help came from the negro quarters all they could do was carry out as much of the furniture as possible through the back way and then stand around and watch it. When the family finally returned the place had been gutted.

A heavy downpour of rain, she told us, put out the smouldering remains of the fire. Such rain occurred almost every afternoon at four o'clock while we were there. It was one of the things responsible for the heavy verdure which grew all about the post. I never saw such a variety anywhere else, flowers of every hue of glowing color. The thunderstorms were awful but I really loved them.

Sometimes, standing on the porch with my father during these storms, there would be a flash and a violent gust and we would hear a crashing moaning sound and know that a tree had given its life somewhere and was prone. This always left a pain in my heart. I never could bear to see a tree cut down.

The roses at Mount Vernon were very large and fragrant, La France, Mareschal Niel, and other varieties. They were not mere bushes but trees and those of the climbing variety sent their blossoms into your window to greet you in the early morning with the dew still on them—a lovely sight.

Our life at Mount Vernon was unfolding every day and in this we were making rapid strides away from our childhood. We were so confined to life in the Barracks that we had to make our own entertainment very largely. But we grew, and in the one year we spent in this lovely but somewhat terrifying spot, we experienced at least three years of mental development.

There is one aspect of this I recall very clearly, our visit to the camp of the Mobile Rifles, a crack militia outfit, composed, rank and file, of the best blood of Alabama. They held their annual summer encampment at a place called Frascatti on the shore of Mobile Bay and my father was invited to inspect and review them there. We all went and I remember the drive there was along the shore for miles on a shell road. Kate was just blooming out into a beautiful attractive young girl and the young lieutenants of the Rifles were much smitten. Needless to say, she enjoyed all this and had a very happy time with the young fry of the regiment. During our stay we were always surrounded by gallant young officers and some visiting civilians and were feted all the time. The officers entertaining us had their tents arranged in military style in a spot shaded by tall oak trees and there much hospitality was dispensed. Several of the officers of the Rifles had homes in the vicinity, and we were invited to stay at the home of the adjutant, Captain Wilkinson, and his sister.[9]

At night the streets of the camp were brilliantly lit by electric arc lamps. This was our first view of electric lighting and it was hard for me to get over the fact that I was not looking at so many moons and walking about in unusually bright moonlight. We children by this time were well able to take care of ourselves and behave becomingly in social relations and our parents were free to accept much entertainment in the city as well as at the camp. We were well taken care of by all the men in camp, officers and soldiers alike coming from the same walk of life. I was escorted by a big private and Kate had a number waiting in line, so to speak, for the same privilege. I was not yet near enough to the "coming out" age and most of the time just floated around. My tomboy proclivities were not yet over although I can see now that they had gotten their death blow at Fort Clark when I parted from my soldier flame on the platform of the train there.

When the time came to go back to Mount Vernon Barracks I felt like weeping. There it was just "Indians and no place to go." The night of our leaving the train was to go at midnight. On arriving at the station someone of the party from the Barracks was missing. In fact, almost nobody was there, all arriving late, and the train left without us.

So back we go to the home of the adjutant and spent the hours till nine the following morning trying to sleep. Although the house was very large there were seven of us to be put up. My sister and I slept in one room with a lady on a mattress laid out on the floor and on which we three slept crosswise. She was the wife of a captain in our regiment, senior to Daddy, being post commander, so we felt some tact necessary in dealing with her. She was a light sleeper and kept us awake by constantly wakening herself up and everybody else when she turned over. Added to that, a whistling noise when she did sleep. This went on all night and when she woke herself up she would lay us out for disturbing her.

In the morning we were awakened from what little sleep we did get by the sound of church bells, and after a hasty breakfast, were in time to catch the only train leaving which would get us back in the desired time. This was a freight train with a caboose and after some negotiations we were allowed to make the trip back in that, as a concession to "military necessity." The train took twice the time of a passenger train, stopping at every little station to put off or take on freight. We younger ones tried to get a little sleep on some of the caboose bunks, but were jolted out of this every now and then by a terrific bump in stopping and the pull of the engine when going ahead again. I am afraid our parents had to put up with the worse in having to stand the bad temper of the wife of my father's superior officer due to her loss of sleep. Normally she was a very kind-hearted woman.

When we finally pulled into the station and saw old Chief Chihuahua in his red-striped artillery trousers and stovepipe hat, we were really glad to get back and begged permission to walk home. This was given while our elders remained at the station waiting for the buckboard. We started off and had the thrill of being accompanied by the old chief who walked with us, keeping up an unbroken conversation in his broken Indian-English. When we were opposite the hospital the buckboard passed us and we yelled out a salute, Chihuahua joining in. Just then an officer came out on the balcony of the hospital and called out something we didn't catch. Chihuahua stopped, took off his precious plug hat with one hand, and with the other made several quick gestures, finally spitting fiercely in the direction of the lieutenant. Then, putting on his hat, raised the parasol to hide his face and said to us, "Come! Him crazy." When we reached the sally port he grunted and said, "Good-bye."

"I like him," said my younger brother.

"Me too," said Dick.

An incident of our visit to the Rifles' camp at Mobile concerned our bugler, whom my father had taken with him at a request from the Rifles. I do not think they had any bugler of their own, but at any rate he went. He was a fine-looking fellow with black hair and the calls on his bugle were so beautiful and clear that everyone was delighted. Each company had a bugler, and his fame had gone through the entire regiment. A month after returning to the Barracks there came another request for him, this time to blow taps at the funeral of Jefferson Davis, who died about that time. I don't know where he is buried, but the Rifles were to go and they telegraphed for our bugler.[10]

The request was refused, but the bugler went without permission, and there was a to-do about it afterward. I don't remember how long he was AWOL or whether or not he was court-martialed. He probably was, especially as the feeling in the army was still strong against the leader of the Confederacy. Today permission would probably have been granted, but it was different then.

As elsewhere in the South our negro servants at Mount Vernon Barracks included several old-time southern darkies. One of them who worked for us from time to time was old Uncle Allen. One day I overheard him in the kitchen recounting the following occurrence which proved to be a fact.

"You know dat fool Tom Johnson? Well he done throwed his jaw out of joint laughin' too hard. Fact. It was this way: I was polin' the raft across the fode when Willie Thompson come down the bank and hollers, 'Hi, Tom, I got some news fer you. Your wife's jus' had twins!'

" 'Fo' de Lawd's sake!' says Tom and throws his head back laughin' fit to kill. An' then his jaw pops out, and stays out and nothin' he could do would make it go back.

"I hollers to Willie to come across an' help. We got Tom on the mule and they bofe started back across the ford ridin' double. The idea was to get him to the doctah but right in the middle of the stream the mule lays down and dumps 'em bofe off in the water.

"Then who should come ridin' by but the doctah himself. De doctah grabs Tom by the haid wif bofe hands bendin' him way over an' puttin' bofe thumbs in his mouf an' whack! Back goes de jaw an' de doctah yells, 'Leggo my thumbs!'

"Tom did and de doctah asks, 'How you come to throw your jaw out anyway?'

"Tom tells him an de doctah says, 'I know all 'bout it, I jus' come from there and your wife's all right. It ain't twins, it's triplets!'"

Uncle Allen's wife, Aunt Cindy, short for Lucinda, was our cook. She was a light negro, about five feet seven inches tall, rather stout, weighing about one hundred sixty-five pounds. Her costume was plain blue with a checked or white apron. On special days she changed to white, and her usual red bandanna was changed to one of light blue. She had a sweet kind face except when she gave orders to her husband or became angry at someone. Uncle Allen was deathly afraid of her, for one day she had come upon him with a "yaller gal," as she told Mama, and "I jus' grabbed him by his fool froat and I tol' him, 'If I ever catch you wif dat girl again I'll cut yuh froat.' I had a knife an' he knew I meant it."

Aunt Cindy's granddaughter, Jane, was our housemaid. She was a tall strapping girl, very dark, very pious, and "an upholder of the church." She was the mother of a small daughter, rather light with great eyes which she knew how to roll when she wanted to be ornery. She was called Lemon, or "Lem," for short. She also was deathly afraid of Aunt Cindy, but with it all, she, her mother, and Aunt Cindy lived happily together and loved each other, between occasional stormy spells.

One day Lemon was being taken care of by Aunt Cindy. Mama, coming into the kitchen, found Aunt Cindy with Lemon across her knee, laying it on vigorously, but with a barrel stave instead of her hand. Lemon was not crying but making awful sounds in her throat. Cindy was livid with anger and oblivious to everything but the punishment she was inflicting.

Mama rushed upon her, yanked the barrel stave out of her hand, and in a shrill voice, unlike her usual sweet one, screamed at her, "Cindy, if I ever catch you using this on Lemon again I will send you right out of my house."

Cindy began to weep, begging Mama not to do that, but Mama repeated she would and stooping, gathered little Lemon up in her arms and took her out of the kitchen, taking care of her herself until Jane returned. She did not go near the kitchen again for twenty-four hours. Cindy was very contrite and sought to make overtures, but Mama would have nothing to say to her.

I recall a visit I made to the kitchen one day when I was initiated into the mysteries of pie making by Aunt Cindy. I had always wanted to make a pie, but it was not pie making that day which came to occupy the center of my mind. It was a sinister aspect of life in the South which was revealed to me, and one which added needlessly to the unfortunate race problem which is felt so acutely by those who dwell there. How much fault we ourselves, who pride ourselves on the superiority of race and culture, must admit, in meeting many of the problems which vex us. Glimpses of this in relations of the whites with the Indians had begun to penetrate the veil of prejudice we imbibed from early days in the army. It was now to become evident to me in the relations of whites and negroes.

I was expressing my delight in the making of my first pie and little Lemon was sitting on the floor with a dish of spinach and bacon rind, prattling that "She too, make pie." Mama, coming into the kitchen, smiled at her, remarking to Jane, her mother, "How fair she is to be your child. One might almost think she had white blood in her."

"Me white blood, me white blood," squealed Lemon, banging her spoon against the side of her dish. I noticed Aunt Cindy's face go very black and her eyes blaze as she growled to Lemon, "Shut yuh mouf!" Lemon went right on squealing till Jane made a pass at her, when she subsided.

The incident left a vague disquieting feeling, but I did not realize the import until some days later when again in the kitchen at pie making. This time a light-colored negress was sitting there holding in her lap a still lighter-colored baby. She was talking to Aunt Cindy. "Oh, what a darling little baby," I cried, starting to take him up in my arms.

"Miss Mamie!" Aunt Cindy called out sharply. "Doan you touch dat chile. He done got de curse of God on him!"

I was a bit frightened, for her voice rang out so sharp and shrill and stopped so suddenly. "What do you mean?" I asked.

"Come hyar," she said in a quieter voice, moving over to where the mother and child were. "Now you look at him an' tell me what you see."

I drew closer and noticed that the child had clear café au lait skin, blue eyes, and the beginnings of light curly, not kinky, hair.

"Is he white?" I asked.

"No ma'am, he ain't. But he's a white man's child and the girl sittin' in front of you is his mother. She ought to be kilt, bringing shame and disgrace on her kinfolks like dis an' I was tellin' her so when you came in."

Meanwhile the poor baby blinked at us with wondering eyes. I was fascinated by them, light blue with large pupils surrounded by a darker rim, and never still. Out of them seemed to come to me the questioning anguish of a soul facing the agony of an embittered life. It stabbed like a knife and I fled to my mother to ask what it all meant and why it should be so. I was very young and many things heretofore had passed completely over my head. With all the terrible things which had happened in the past with the Indians, life had been so full of beauty and sweetness for me, I could hardly comprehend this. Here was horror, the horror of injustice in a stigma fastened by us on the innocent who had no part in bringing this to pass.

We have had in the army several negro officers, one of whom, a graduate of West Point, was very popular with his class. We also had four colored regiments in the old army, the 24th and 25th Infantry Regiments and the 9th and 10th Cavalry Regiments. They rendered effective service against the Indians who respected them highly. The Indians called them "Buffalo Soldiers," and no Indian was ever known to scalp a negro soldier if killed.[11]

I like to quote a remark attributed to General Eisenhower. [When] asked his attitude on some question affecting the assignment or treatment of "black troops" he is reported to have answered, "I do not know any black soldiers or white soldiers. I know only soldiers." General Eisenhower, I am told, graduated into and served for a time with the 19th Infantry, our regiment, but it was after my time.[12]

One year's stay at Mount Vernon Barracks had come to a close, bringing our departure. Our regiment was under orders for a northern station, the two companies at Mount Vernon Barracks being assigned to old Fort Brady, Michigan, then a two-company post on the northern peninsula near the foot of Lake Superior.

I could never understand why the War Department felt it necessary in changes of station to plunge troops from one extreme of climate to another and do it at seasons when the shock to the system would be severe. It would seem that they could have rotated troops to other stations more gradually in a climatic sense. But no. We had been taken from cool David's Island on Long Island Sound and plunged directly into the terrific heat of the Mexican border at Ringgold, and now were to be taken from Alabama, where it was already hot in April, to one of the most northerly points in the United States, where there was still snow on the ground and ice blocked navigation in Lake Superior.

All our winter things had been put away in mothballs, and the few clothes we could get out and have ready on arrival did not prove nearly warm enough when we arrived there. Our departure from Mount Vernon Barracks followed the usual form in farewells and entertainment. I do not recall just what other troops relieved us and took over guardianship of the Apache or how long they remained in captivity before being sent back to their reservation.[13]

We never saw them again and I assume the present generation of them are respectable inhabitants somewhere in the Southwest. Years later when my husband and I passed through Arizona and New Mexico, I saw only one Indian that I could recognize, selling trinkets at the station in Albuquerque.

* 10

FORT BRADY, MICHIGAN

1890–1896

Age Eighteen to Twenty-four Years

FORT BRADY, when we arrived, was not the fort which stands there now, it was the old fort down by the river in the town of Sault Sainte Marie, commonly called the "Soo." It was at the foot of the rapids which gave the town its name, Rapids of Saint Mary, on the Saint Marys River. The river formed at this point part of the boundary between the United States and Canada. Standing on the parade ground of the old fort one could gaze directly across the deep blue water into the town on the Canadian side, also known as Sault Sainte Marie.[1]

The fort was bordered on three sides by the American town, the fourth or north side being a sort of wharf or quay against which vessels sometimes tied up waiting passage through the locks. On the south side was a street with a trolley car track. The quarters of the officers and soldiers were very, very old, all made of wood. The officers' quarters were a row on the west side of the parade and were of the cottage type, single and double, with a white painted picket fence in front. This picket fence also ran the length of the south side, where the soldiers' barracks stood, backing against the street where the trolley ran. The guardhouse was also on this side. Across the parade on the east end stood the quartermaster and other service buildings. The barracks and officers' quarters were painted light gray with white trim. No one would have ever guessed the place to be a fort but for the presence of the tall flagpole and a single old muzzle-loading field piece standing near it, which was the morning and evening gun. The parade sloped noticeably down to the river. The quarters and barracks closely resembled those at Fort Ringgold when we were there and also those at Fort Clark. The barracks were two-storied with upper and lower balconies.[2]

Our freight and effects were delayed in transit and we could not at once occupy the quarters assigned to us. Instead we put up at the old Chippewa House where we slept under piles of blankets and quilts and ate prodigious quantities of bacon and eggs, wheat cakes, and planked whitefish. Children never forget these things, and in grown-up life they never taste so good.

As to food, we had a great variety in our travels. In Texas we learned to like Mexican food, such as tamales, tortillas, and enchiladas. In Alabama we enjoyed some of the Creole dishes, namely Creole gumbo and ham jambalaya. Another thing we loved, which was certainly not a regional dish, was French toast, which our mother called by the fascinating name, "golden slices for silver children."

When our household effects arrived we did so enjoy fixing up these old houses. Ours was the first in line next to the river. It was a beautiful view which we had from our windows on the porch which ran across the front of the house and around the side facing the river. Our house was divided by a large hall in the middle, with rooms on each side. They were very large rooms and our only heat was from stoves. The "plumbing" was one of the outside variety in an annex reached by a door in the back wall of the kitchen. All light in the house was from kerosene lamps.

Later, toward the end of the stay, we had a much more modern quarters of brick in the new fort built on top of the hill. But at the time of which I write we loved the old fort where we were to spend four happy years. Three of these were in high school. We were just beginning to "look over the top" and see the world in its splendor as more-or-less grown-up persons. There was so much to keep one alert in this Michigan post.

At this spot the great Lake Superior was linked by the Saint Marys River with the lower lakes and through the locks an endless stream of traffic moved in steamers, some as large as ocean liners, constantly passing and repassing. More traffic went through these locks when navigation was open during the summer months than went through the Suez Canal in an entire year. We never tired of watching these ships come and go and the water rising and being let out of the locks in thundering upwellings when the sluices beneath were opened. On some occasions when the locks were blocked for some reason, the line of waiting ships extended for miles above and below the locks.

The rapids too were a fascinating and awe-inspiring spectacle. In these no white person was allowed to fish. The Chippewa Indians, the only Indians we had in that section, had the exclusive right by treaty to fish these rapids, down which tons of whitefish spilled to be caught in nets at the foot.

They also made a good haul, financially, by taking parties of tourists down the rapids in their canoes, which they alone knew how to navigate among the many rocks and whirlpools. We children made the descent on more than one occasion with old Chief John Bouche, a giant old fellow and the only Indian I ever saw with a full beard. He had another Indian to stand in the bow while he steered. The method was to board the canoe in a quiet back eddy and pole up the eddies to the head of the rapids where a great railroad bridge crossed the river to the Canadian shore.

The canoes were great big affairs, as large as a lifeboat and as seaworthy. They had to be, as the waves to be jumped were sometimes over six feet high. The speed was terrific and the thrill intense as we headed straight toward a great boulder, the Indians brandishing their paddles and uttering shrill whoops as we bore down on it, only to be diverted at the very last moment by quick dips of their paddles and shooting by in a narrow sluice and jumping a great wave. This followed by a sickening slump into a hollow and another giant wave and another rock directly in the path and another swerve to avoid it.

On one occasion we had in our canoe an Englishman who was a passenger on a steamer going through the locks, and I remember that he glanced at a book all the way down while being drenched with spray [and] never once looked up. At the end he simply said "Oh." On this same trip I recall we also had with us the boy cousin I was to later marry, who was visiting us and who afterward was always on the river in some kind of boat, trying fruitlessly to pull himself up into the rapids from below, getting only far enough to be swirled around, and coming home with his hands full of blisters.

It was a foretaste of what I was to go through with him afterward in boats on the Long Island Sound. I don't remember much of his other doings at the time as I didn't like him particularly then, but recall that he took my two brothers in a sailboat and sailed with them to the head of Lake Superior and camped for a week on the north shore next to a camp of Indians who had pitched their tepees there to fish. Corporal Chestnut, of my father's company, went along with them and they hunted and fished there for a week, sleeping in a tent. The Indians were Chippewa and peaceful, not molesting them.

Our social life at old Fort Brady was interesting, and although the town at that time was rather rough in outward respects, with deeply rutted muddy streets, we made many lovely friends. Among these was our minister, the Reverend Peter Trimble Rowe, afterward the heroic and famous bishop of Alaska. In after years when he was visiting New York, he baptized our infant son, John, in the Cathedral of St. John the Divine on Morningside Heights, and visited us at our home in Port Washington, Long Island, in 1934. At the time he presided over our little St. James Church at the Soo he wore mutton-chop whiskers and didn't look a bit like the handsome smooth-faced man who later did so much great work in Alaska for the people of that far-off outpost of our country. He was among the greatest figures the Episcopal Church has produced and we loved him dearly.[3]

Another church figure, then eminent, who became, with his

family, very good friends was Archbishop Sullivan of Ontario. We were entertained by him in very hospitable fashion and I can recall his handsome, imposing appearance clad in his clerical knee breeches which, I believe, were part of his Church of England ceremonial dress for social occasions.

And from Canada came an admirer for me, still a skinny little pigtailed girl in her teens. This was a cadet from the Kingston Military Academy, Canada's "West Point." "Little Dumble," as the family dubbed him, graduated to a commission in the King's Own. He used to sit on our porch with me, clad in his summer flannels, which were a kind of uniform with huge brass buttons. My brothers and cousin teased me unmercifully about "sitting out and spooning with him" till all hours—which was not true. Our father sent us all to bed regularly at seasonable hours, unless there was an event on.

This last happened occasionally in private theatricals and other parties in town and when a traveling opera troupe came to the Soo and put on a performance. We also had dances in our own quarters, picnics, and excursions, sometimes as the guests of captains of various government vessels calling at the post or in connection with the locks. We did not have many young officers with us, there being only two companies in our garrison.

Among them, however, was a very brilliant young officer, Lieutenant Frank McIntyre, whom we called "McGinty." He was afterward selected to be a professor of mathematics at West Point and eventually became chief of the Bureau of Insular Affairs in Washington. My mother and I were to meet him again there when she and I went to live in Washington after our dear daddy had gone to his rest.[4]

Another young officer was my father's second lieutenant, Arthur Foster. He was of the typical West Point mold and very efficient.[5]

Another, somewhat older, was Captain Vance's first lieutenant, "Robbie" Guard. He came out of the fighting McCook family, the men of which achieved Civil War fame. Robbie was an inexhaustible fund of anecdote, humor, and good cheer.[6]

All through his service in the regiment he had an orderly who was devoted to him. I understand that when he died, years later as a major, this man was still with him, his devoted servitor and in some respects guardian, and that when he died it was in the arms of this devoted friend, a private soldier. The parting between them was very touching, I am told. Such, as I have said before, was often the feeling between officers and some of their men in the old regulars.

Speaking of this I am reminded of the sad outcome in the case of another private in Daddy's company. This private, N———, who had come to Brady with us, went eventually for a commission and passed the board brilliantly. He was an accomplished, highly educated gentleman from an old English family, in which he was but a younger son and unable to inherit. The case [is] among four I know—men of high station who sought oblivion in the ranks of our old regular army. My father wove the facts [of one] into a wonderful romantic story for *Frank Leslie's Magazine* in 1884, [which] I outline here.

Shortly after Custer's attack on the Indian village—the Battle of the Washita, in 1868—my father, who was then in the vicinity, fell in with a man who had taken his discharge from Custer's regiment, and together they journeyed to Fort Gibson where my father was carrying dispatches. On the way this man told him his life's story. He was a German and had been a lieutenant of Hussars in the king of Saxony's army. He contracted a clandestine marriage with a woman of inferior station who betrayed him in an affair with his orderly.

To spare his family the disgrace of a scandal, he quietly resigned his commission and emigrated, arriving in America in time to participate in the Civil War as a volunteer. He afterward joined the regulars and eventually was sent to join Custer's regiment at Fort Dodge just before the Washita Expedition. Taking part in that, he was also present in the subsequent expedition which found the bodies of Major Joel H. Elliott and his eighteen men. They were from a different troop from his own and had joined the concentration at Fort Dodge when setting out.

Coming on the mutilated bodies of the little party, he recognized among them the body of the man who had been his orderly in Germany, and in a pocketbook lying beside him in the snow was a death notice of the woman who had been his wife and betrayed him. These two men served in the same regiment under Custer without either being aware of the other's presence because they occupied different posts. When my father met him he was on his way back to Germany in the hope of a renewed life there.

Private N——'s case had a less romantic outcome. He had one weakness, and on passing the board went off to celebrate, and so his commission was stopped and denied him. As one officer remarked, "If only he had waited."

It was at Fort Brady that my father's company achieved the remarkable record of not having one case of desertion during the entire time we were there. An astonished inspector general reported on Daddy's company as the best behaved, best disciplined company he had ever inspected. Possibly this was due in part to my father's way of enlisting recruits when applying locally. He had to take such men as the recruiting depots sent him, but they invariably turned out good men. In local enlistments my father, after conducting careful inquiry into the man's background, sent him to dwell with the company a few days that he might see what life was like and afford the sergeant an opportunity to size him up before he was sworn in.[7]

I mention this because so many people have a false idea of the old army. My father used to burn with wrathful indignation when he read in some paper that a judge had suspended the sentence of a criminal on the condition that he enlist in the army. "What does he think we are?" he would exclaim.

Our post commander at that time was an interesting character, Captain Richard Vance. He was a good officer but not very military in appearance. He wore an old loose-fitting blue blouse and a very high white starched collar reaching above it almost to his ears. For a necktie he sometimes wore a piece torn off the foot of a lace curtain and tied in a huge bow, which usually worked to one side almost under his ear. He was senior to Daddy and by virtue of that fact, post commander. He would pitch into "Robbie" about some dissatisfaction with his ways and then go off and have a drink with him at the Chippewa House. Then they would come home together with locked arms.[8]

The climate was terribly severe in winter. Even in the summer the nights were very cool and we could see the northern lights dancing in the sky over Canada. In the winter everything froze up, including ourselves. The sentries were given great bearskin coats and caps and fur gloves. We had one constantly patrolling back of the officers' line, one at the guardhouse on the south side, and another at the east end, back of the storehouse. They had to be visited frequently at all hours. Sometimes the thermometer got down to forty or more below zero.

The performance of routine duties during the long winter months was a severe tax on both officers and men and made the absence of desertion all the more remarkable. Snow drifted into mountainous heaps, burying fences and porches, and clearing these and the walks was a tremendous task. The condition was even worse when we moved into the new fort on top of the hill a mile from town. There we had brick quarters, electric lighting, and central heating, but were never really warm indoors and in getting about had to walk through deep canyons excavated in the snowbanks before the officers' and men's quarters. Getting in and out of town sometimes was a problem because the drifts formed across the roadway and the approaches to the fort.

It had its compensations for healthy youngsters in coasting and sleighing diversions and there was a great thrill in the spring when the ice in Lake Superior broke up and began to move down the river. Then the spectacle at the rapids was worth going to see— great chunks of ice leaping and being tossed into the air and turning over in a roar like continuous cannonading.

It was about this time that Baron Albert von Mangelsdorf began to court Kate. He was then a civil engineer engaged in work on the locks which were being enlarged, and his toiling up to the fort through all this snow in zero weather is one measure of the devotion he showed to Kate at that time and all through their married life. He was a grand man of the old German aristocracy which, in his bringing up, knew nothing of the later arrogant madness which broke out in the First and Second World Wars, the last of which he did not live to see. All through the First World War, while deeply grieved, his loyalty as an American citizen was never questioned and he continued to serve our government in the Lake Survey until his end came. He was an accomplished linguist and musician and it is to him, in our study of German which began about this time, that I owe my ability to speak and sing in German with the right pronunciation. He never let us get by with an error.

Unlike so many European noblemen who marry American girls, he was not a fortune hunter. Kate, [who] hitherto had spent her life mainly in remote army posts in the type of surroundings I have pictured, was a poor girl with no dowry, but shortly after her marriage she and Albert went to Germany to visit his family and she was received with all the honors which could have been showered on an heiress in the brilliant "court life" of the old regime and on his family estate.

There is not much to relate of our life in the new post to which we went toward the end of our stay. The memories I cherish are chiefly those of the old post with its tumbledown buildings and white picket fences, where we spent so many joyous hours. By that time Daddy was in command and I remember that when the time came to leave and go to the new fort on the hill, everything had been packed and was ready but the order had not arrived. We were not supposed to abandon the fort without the official order and on mere forewarning [were] to be prepared to move promptly. It would be absurd, after obeying such an injunction, to undo it all and then sit down and wait for the order to arrive. So Daddy took the bit in his teeth, gave the order, and the companies marched away, bugles blowing, and Daddy at the head on a horse. He was never called to account for it.

So our days began at the new post and continued for the remainder of our stay. Other officers joined us from time to time. There was Lieutenant Eckerson, first lieutenant of my father's company for many years, Lieutenant John Howard, one of the many sons of General O. O. Howard, and others.[9]

It was about this time when part of our regiment, with portions of the 7th, 10th, 12th, and 13th Infantry Regiments, was ordered to Chicago to safeguard the transit of U.S. mail during the great strike of 1894. There had been interference with the mail and President Cleveland, with great courage and decision, and against the protest of incapable local authorities, dispatched federal troops there solely for the purpose of protecting the mail. My father, then senior captain of our regiment, commanded the battalion of the 19th in the absence of the major. This duty was a very disagreeable one, not at all to my father's liking, nor to that of any of us in the family. I am sure the troops felt the same way.[10]

Such was the efficient discharge of this disagreeable strike duty that not a shot had to be fired and the mails moved smoothly after the troops arrived. Despite criticism, the use of federal troops to protect the transit of the U.S. mail without application from the state authorities was upheld as entirely constitutional. It had the merit of avoiding the bloodshed which might have followed if the situation had been left to militia not so well trained and lacking the judgment of seasoned veterans.[11]

The day we left Fort Brady for our new station at Fort Wayne, Detroit, was in the early fall, cold even for September. Mother and I were down in the town when the troops evacuated the post and we walked to the top of Ashmun Street to see them come swing down the road with bugles blowing a quickstep and the colors flying. There was a smile on their faces. Years of shoveling snow and other hard labor were behind them. For the troops relieving them they left signs pinned on the barrack walls: "Get out and shovel snow," "Try sentry duty at forty below," "Can you cut grass?" and finally, "Walk a mile to town—and then what?"

The boys in blue had that sense of humor which sustains the soldier, and particularly the American soldier, in the performance of all kinds of drab and arduous duty. When I think of all they had to do I wonder sometimes that the desertion rate in our army was no higher. There was the carting away of huge quantities of garbage, sometimes to be buried; the cleaning out of old-fashioned latrines in the early posts; stable work and the care of horses, mules, and cattle; working vegetable gardens and other forms of manual labor; drill, continual rifle practice, the policing or care of parade grounds and the cleaning of barracks, and kitchen duty. It was not a lazy life as the public supposes.

But as our boys came swinging down they were looking forward to a warmer climate in the lower peninsula with the attractions of a great city, and no wonder they were glad. At the head of the column was our handsome daddy and other officers in command, also looking forward to a change from the six long years we had spent in the north at a time when the Soo was not the fine modern city it now is. But I loved it as it was and even the old fort, and look back on the Soo as the place where my childhood finally left me and where there began an attachment to last later for some time to a man I thought I loved and was going to marry. "Raymond" is a name I can look back on with sweet affection and respect but he too was to find eventually, as I did, that the love of a lifetime was elsewhere.[12]

* 11

FORT WAYNE, MICHIGAN

1896–1898

Age Twenty-four to Twenty-six Years

FORT WAYNE was a battalion post when we first came to it and later a military museum. It is on the Detroit River across from but slightly below Windsor in Ontario. Although an old post, the quarters had modern conveniences and were comfortable. Life there with the big city of Detroit to draw on for social pleasure was a continual round of dinners, dances, and other diversions inside and outside the post.[1]

Then there was the funny incident of the man from Daddy's company who broke the nondesertion record of six years and who wrote a letter to Daddy voicing his regret and esteem with all sorts of messages to all in our family, which he begged Daddy to transmit. We all roared with laughter as Daddy read them to us.

Of Wayne there is little to recount of the routine picture of later years elsewhere in my army life. In the north we had white instead of colored servants and a much-loved striker named Egmond, a Scandinavian and a quaint character who alternately exasperated and convulsed us by his habit of doing everything wrong. Poor Egmond had his arm blown off firing a salute with the old-fashioned muzzle-loading cannon. Since that occurred as the troops were leaving for the Spanish-American War, he may be counted as the first American casualty.

The event most worthy of recording was when our regiment left for the Spanish-American War. Have you ever seen a regiment leave its home station for the front? If so, you will never forget it. The departure of our battalion did not differ, I imagine, from that of other battalions elsewhere. In the drafted citizen army partings are individual, as sons leave for induction posts. Parents do not usually see a regiment march away. But in a military post it is different.[2]

Many enlisted men, as well as officers, had wives and children living there or nearby. Not many outsiders are present and there was no cheering or flag waving. But as the column comes swinging down the road to the gate there go the wives and children of many enlisted men walking beside them. A wife clings to the arm of a husband, bravely trying not to cry. A boy walks beside his father, holding on to his haversack, trying to keep up. Here and there a man hands his rifle to the man next to him and a little child is lifted into his daddy's arms. All along the column the scene is repeated and officers look the other way. The impression is that something is being torn loose, and any impulse you have to cheer is stifled.

When our battalion left my father was with them. He had reached the age when he could legally retire, but would he apply? Not he. When urged by friends, he replied, "All these years the country has supported me. Now when it needs my services again, would you have me refuse?"

And he went, first to Puerto Rico and afterward to the Philippines, where in both cases as a major of the 19th he was in command of the 19th, becoming finally lieutenant colonel of the 30th Infantry. On returning he was retired.

With our arrival at Fort Wayne, Detroit, I draw near the end of these memoirs. My childhood had been left behind and, like the butterfly emerging from its chrysalis, I was to flutter about for a time as a society belle. It is not my purpose to write about this phase of my life, when, no longer a plain skinny tomboy, I had developed into some measure of girlhood beauty and found myself much sought after in the younger set of Detroit society and able to plume myself on having in my turn a train of admirers.

I have alluded to our dancing together. Daddy would ask, "Will you favor an old fellow like me with a dance?" Off we would go to one of Strauss's matchless waltzes. It was the same later in New York, with all the cotillions and balls I attended there, I never got over the pleasure of dancing with my father. He was a superb dancer and we would polish off the boards in this way on many occasions. Sometimes the other dancers would draw to one side with admiring comment. It was not jitterbugging in those days, but the poetry of graceful movement.

The last time my father danced with me was at the 7th Regiment Armory in New York where there had been a full dress parade of the regiment, followed by a dance. Daddy, as a guest, was in full dress uniform and looked very handsome. I can still see us swaying to the lovely waltz the band was playing and the gaiety of the scene with so many handsome men in striking uniforms.

This was the last memory in the joy of that period that was to end so soon. A few weeks later Daddy contracted pneumonia and passed away. We were planning to return to Detroit when it happened but instead, afterward, my mother and I went permanently to reside in Washington. The two boys were married and living elsewhere and Kate and her husband were at their home in Detroit.

After the military funeral in New York, with troops from Governors Island, my father's remains were placed temporarily in a cemetery in Brooklyn and then sent on to be buried in Arlington National Cemetery where he and my mother now lie and where, later, one of my two brothers was also buried. The elder brother is buried in Morrice, Michigan.

The years which followed were to be of study and struggle to achieve a professional position and recognition as a concert singer. In all this time I was to receive the encouragement and uplift of my mother's dear companionship and her faith in my ultimate success. It came, and the grand ballroom of the Willard was to know my voice and, later, Constitution Hall where I was the first guest artist to sing for the Daughters of the American Revolution, with the Marine Band. There were to follow other engagements and the round of brilliant receptions and dances at the White House and various legations to which my mother and myself were invited. The administrations of Theodore Roosevelt and of President Taft were in office during this period and we met and knew many distinguished national and international figures, among them General Wang, at that time the generalissimo of the Manchurian Army, who was the guest of our government and who became a close and dear friend.

But it is not my purpose to write at length of this period of my life and the rich years to follow, nor yet again of the deep happiness found later in life with my dearly beloved husband and among the many wonderful friends in Port Washington, [New York,] the town where most of our married life has passed and where I now live. This period did not differ much from that of any other girl. It formed no part of my army life, even when my husband wore the leaves of a major in the First World War and our son wore the uniform of a private in the Second. I had no part of the events which came to either of them in the service.

No, what I have wished to write about has been a day in our national life, or in one side of it, which has gone on and which was drawing to a close when we came to Fort Wayne. However, I cannot speak of Washington without mentioning them. Not the least of which made Washington the dream city of urban life was the making of new friends and the renewing of old friendships which took place there. It was in the hospitable home of Mame Smith, daughter of General C. H. Smith, the old colonel of our regiment, who had become Mrs. Irving Hall Dunlap, that the man I was to marry spent the night preceding our wedding. This took place in St. Thomas's Church near Du Pont Circle.

Of the man who took my heart above all others in the love of my life, and who repaid with unvarying devotion, I have said but little, as the golden years of happiness he brought me are a chapter apart. Like his forebears he is an army-minded man, his father and grandfather serving with distinction in the armies of our country and of England. He himself has remained by occupation a civilian. Both in this relation and in his military service he has given the best that is in him to his country and the community, unselfishly and with a vision not always given or understood by the average man. Our son is like him in this respect. Neither has any use for the narrowness which would restrict opportunity and recognition for those of any creed, race, or color and their indignation has flamed to bold utterance when this has been shown.

My marriage to such a man and the crowning happiness of my life with him in all places has not altered my love for that beautiful city which is the shrine of our national life. It is to Washington that I hope someday to return. When the sun goes down for me finally it is my hope that I may be laid to rest in that same hallowed spot across the Potomac where my dear father and mother now lie.

Editor's Note: Mary Leefe Laurence died 19 July 1945, just after completing these memoirs. She is buried with her parents and brother in Arlington National Cemetery.

NOTES

Introduction

1. While not a completely exhaustive list, accounts by "army brats" include, in chronological order of experience, from the antebellum era, Henry Hunt Snelling, *Memoirs of a Boyhood at Fort Snelling*, ed. Lewis Beeson (Minneapolis: Private Printing, 1939). This thirty-six-page memoir describes his childhood, mostly Indian tales and adventure in early Minnesota, but does not include much on garrison social life. He was the son of post commander Josiah Snelling, colonel of the Fifth Infantry during the 1820s. Charlotte Ouisconsin Van Cleve, *"Three Score Years and Ten," Life-Long Memories of Fort Snelling, Minnesota and Other Parts of the West* (3d ed. Minneapolis: Harrison & Smith, 1895) offers one hundred pages on her childhood consisting mostly of biographical accounts of acquaintances and famous people she knew, with some local history. She is spare on details of childhood but was with Henry Hunt Snelling at Fort Snelling in the 1820s. Her father, Nathan Clark, was a lieutenant and later a major of the Fifth Infantry.

Accounts from the post–Civil War era include Guy V. Henry Jr.,

"A Brief Narrative of the Life of Guy V. Henry, Jr." (unpublished manuscript, Special Collections, United States Military Academy Library, West Point, New York). This is the carbon of the original manuscript in the U.S. Army Military History Institute, U.S. Army War College, Carlisle Barracks, Pennsylvania. This unpublished memoir provides seventeen pages of very vivid text and excellent details of childhood in the 1870s and 1880s on frontier cavalry posts in Nebraska, Kansas, Oklahoma, and Wyoming. Henry was the son and grandson of army officers — his father was a Civil War brevet brigadier general and regular captain in the Third Cavalry. Charles M. Hough, "Memoir" (typescript, University of Colorado Library), offers the view of an infantry officer's son at Fort Douglas, Utah, in the 1870s. Bertha Barnitz B. Peelle, "Autobiography" (typescript, Special Collections, United States Military Academy Library, West Point, New York), is forty-four pages of typescript, about thirty pages of which is on her childhood. She was the daughter of Captain Albert Barnitz, Seventh Cavalry. Her father was retired of wounds received in Custer's Washita Campaign of 1868–69, but the family spent most of her youth in close association with army families and she eventually married a Sixth Infantry officer. The son of an Eighth Infantry officer, Reynolds J. Burt wrote twenty good pages describing childhood army life in Nebraska, California, and Illinois in the 1870s and 1880s. His memoir, "Boyhood Data," is part of the Don Rickey Jr. Collection at the U.S. Army Military History Institute at Carlisle Barracks, Pennsylvania. Although lacking the detail of Mary Leefe Laurence, "Cricket" Cooper's experiences as the daughter of Lieutenant Charles Cooper at Fort Sill, Oklahoma, in 1877 and later Fort Concho, Texas, are recorded and edited in Barbara E. Fisher, ed., "Forrestine Cooper Hooker's Notes and Memoirs on Army Life in the West, 1871–1876" (master's thesis, University of Arizona, 1963). Fiorello H. La Guardia, *The Making of an Insurgent: An Autobiography, 1882–1919* (Philadelphia: J. B. Lippincott Company, 1948), has thirty pages of excellent narrative devoted to childhood at Fort Huachuca and Whipple Barracks, Arizona. He was the son of an Italian immigrant and the enlisted bandmaster of the Eleventh Infantry in the late 1880s. Douglas MacArthur (*Reminiscences*, New York: McGraw-Hill Book Company, 1964) was the son of a Thirteenth Infantry captain who was a nineteen-year-old

Civil War brevet colonel. The book has seven pages on his life with his father in the 1880s in New Mexico, Kansas, and Texas. Jack W. Heard, *The Pictorial Military Life History of Jack Whitehead Heard* (San Antonio TX: Schneider Printing Company, 1969), has twenty excellent pages describing his life as the son of a Third Cavalry officer on the Texas frontier and in upper Vermont posts in the late 1880s. It also contains an unusual and very interesting account of the Philippine Islands, where he lived with his father during a portion of the insurrection in 1900, as well as Fort Assiniboine, Montana, in 1904. For an account of the 1920s and 1930s, see William J. Smith, *Army Brat: A Memoir* (Brownsville OR: Story Line Press, 1980). Smith was the son of an enlisted man at Jefferson Barracks, Missouri.

2. It is probable that Mary Leefe Laurence completed the manuscript just a month before her death on 19 July 1945. In chapter 9 she mentions a remark on black soldiers made by General Dwight D. Eisenhower, a quote that first appeared in the *New York Times* on 16 June 1945. Guy Vernon Henry Jr. was born at Camp Robinson, Nebraska, in January 1875 and graduated from West Point in 1898. He served in the Philippine Insurrection, was the commandant of the United States Military Academy at West Point from 1916 to 1918, became a cavalry brigadier general in 1918, and was the chief of cavalry from 1930 to 1934. He retired as a major general in 1939 but returned to active duty for World War II. He died in 1967. His father, Guy Vernon Henry, was a class of 1861 graduate of West Point and rose to the rank of brigadier general of volunteers in the Civil War, earning a Medal of Honor at Cold Harbor, Virginia. In the postwar years Henry served extensively on the frontier in both the Third and Ninth Cavalry Regiments, losing an eye at the Battle of Rosebud Creek in 1876. The elder Henry died as a brigadier general in 1899. Brevet Major-General George W. Cullum, *Biographical Register of the Officers and Graduates of the U.S. Military Academy at West Point, N.Y. from Its Establishment, in 1802, to 1890 . . .* 3 vols. (New York: Houghton, Mifflin and Company, 1891), 2: 796–98; idem, *Biographical Register of the Officers and Graduates of the U.S. Military Academy at West Point, N.Y. since Its Establishment, in 1802, Supplement IV . . .* , ed. Edward S. Holden (Cambridge: Riverside Press, 1901), 4: 653–54; *Register of Graduates and Former Cadets, 1802–1964, of the United States Military Academy*

(West Point NY: West Point Alumni Foundation, 1964), 294; Francis B. Heitman, *Historical Register and Dictionary of the United States Army* . . . , 2 vols. (Washington DC: GPO, 1903), 1: 523.

3. Sherry L. Smith, "Stanley Vestal," in *Historians of the American Frontier* . . . ed. John R. Wunder (Westport CT: Greenwood Press, 1988), 697–712. Stanley Vestal, or "Walter S. Campbell," published more than 20 books and 150 articles on the West. Born on a homestead in 1887 in Severy, Kansas, Vestal was a Rhodes Scholar at Oxford and a distinguished professor in the English Department at the University of Oklahoma. He died in 1957 and was buried at the National Cemetery at the Custer Battlefield National Monument. Vestal was not an academic historian, but his informal histories were popular and widely read.

4. John F. Laurence, son of Mary Leefe Laurence, interview by editor, Glen Harbor, New York, 21 February 1994.

5. The military biography of Lieutenant Colonel John George Leefe was compiled from the following sources: Laurence interview; National Archives and Records Service (NARS), Records of the United States Army Adjutant General's Office, 1780–1917, Record Group (RG) 94, Appointment, Commission, and Personal Branch, Documents Files, Box 51, 1871, 3303–394, ACP 3393 Service File, John George Leefe (hereafter cited as Adjutant General's Records, ACP 3393); Special Orders, Headquarters of the Army, Special Orders 217, 20 September 1901, retiring Lieutenant Colonel Leefe; "Obituary, Lieut. Col. J. G. Leefe," *New York Times* (12 June 1903): 9, col. 6; Heitman, *Historical Register* . . . , 1: 626; Guy V. Henry, *Military Record of Civilian Appointments in the United States Army* . . . , 2 vols. (New York: Carleton, Publishers, 1869), 1: 370.

6. Leefe's efficiency reports are in Adjutant General's Records, ACP 3393; Captain J. G. Leefe, "Buttons," in *Captain Dreams* . . . , ed. Captain Charles King (Philadelphia: J. B. Lippincott Company, 1895), 173–210. For a historical treatment of the impact of Captain Charles King and the public perception of the frontier army, see Oliver Knight, *Life and Manners in the Frontier Army* (Norman: University of Oklahoma Press, 1978).

7. Laurence interview; courtesy of John F. Laurence, Mary Leefe Laurence collection of newspaper clippings from the period 1905 to

1910. Many of the newspapers are not identified but do include columns in the *Washington Times, Musical Courier, Evening Star,* and *Newark News.*

8. Henry, "A Brief Narrative," 1–17; MacArthur, *Reminiscences,* 19–23; Heard, *Pictorial Military Life History,* 2–21; Van Cleve, *"Three Score Years and Ten,"* 8–100; La Guardia, *The Making of an Insurgent,* 19–33.

9. MacArthur, *Reminiscences,* 20; Henry, "A Brief Narrative," 4; Van Cleve, *"Three Score Years and Ten,"* 45–46; Heard, *Pictorial Military Life History,* 7.

10. Laurence manuscript, 1–3.

11. Laurence manuscript, 22, 24; Henry, "A Brief Narrative," 3, 5, 116; MacArthur, *Reminiscences,* 21; Heard, *Pictorial Military Life History,* 4.

12. Laurence manuscript, 136; Henry, "A Brief Narrative," 7, 9; MacArthur, *Reminiscences,* 21; Heard, *Pictorial Military Life History,* 19.

13. Laurence manuscript, 21, 145; Heard, *Pictorial Military Life History,* 15; Henry, "A Brief Narrative," 3, 6.

14. Henry, "A Brief Narrative," 7–8; Laurence manuscript, 21, 31, 154.

15. Laurence manuscript, 146, 154.

16. La Guardia, *The Making of an Insurgent,* 20; Heard, *Pictorial Military Life History,* 15.

17. MacArthur, *Reminiscences,* 20; Laurence manuscript, vi.

18. Lillian Schissel, Byrd Gibbens, and Elizabeth Hampsten, *Far from Home: Families of the Westward Journey* (New York: Schocken Books, 1989), vii, xvii.

19. Elizabeth Hampsten, *Settlers' Children: Growing Up on the Great Plains* (Norman: University of Oklahoma Press, 1991), 29–34, 165. For a more positive view of women's experiences on the frontier, see Glenda Riley's excellent *The Female Frontier: A Comparative View of Women on the Prairie and the Plains* (Lawrence: University Press of Kansas, 1988) and *A Place to Grow: Women in the American West* (Arlington Heights IL: Harlan Davidson, 1992). Riley does integrate a few accounts of army women in her studies. In general she concludes that children were relied upon as domestic labor within the family, but

those chores and labor were important training for their future gender-based duties as wives or husbands. She also finds that the freedom of the plains was liberating for some young women, women who later refused to surrender that sense of independence for early marriage. In some respects this could apply to Mary Leefe, who married relatively late in life. Riley, *The Female Frontier*, 84–86, and *A Place to Grow*, 201–4. For a good collection of primary accounts, letters, and diary excerpts from adolescents on the Kansas plains, see C. Robert Haywood and Sandra Jarus, *"A Funnie Place, No Fences": Teenagers' Views of Kansas, 1867–1900* (Lawrence: Division of Continuing Education, University of Kansas, 1992).

20. Elliott West, *Growing Up with the Country: Childhood on the Far Western Frontier* (Albuquerque: University of New Mexico Press, 1989), 245, 262.

21. West, *Growing Up with the Country*, 35, 43; Laurence manuscript, 8, 9.

22. West, *Growing Up with the Country*, 35; Laurence manuscript, 28, 24–25. In her study of army perceptions of Plains Indians, Sherry L. Smith finds that army families and Indians shared a mutual distrust that the other would steal their children. Sherry L. Smith, *The View from Officers' Row: Army Perceptions of Western Indians* (Tucson: University of Arizona Press, 1990), 76.

23. West, *Growing Up with the Country*, 19, 152; Laurence manuscript, 155, 175.

24. West, *Growing Up with the Country*, 126, 149; Laurence manuscript, 22.

25. West, *Growing Up with the Country*, 55, 73, 233, 246; Hampsten, *Settlers' Children*, 54, 77, 197; Laurence manuscript, 51, 60–61, 132–33. Guy V. Henry Jr. relates that his young sister died of diphtheria at Fort Sanders, Wyoming, in 1880. Henry, "A Brief Narrative," 4. Until the 1930s and mass immunization, the highly contagious bacterial disease diphtheria was one of the most significant causes of childhood mortality. The bacterial toxin of the organism created paralysis of the throat and eventually heart failure.

26. Patricia Yeary Stallard, *Glittering Misery: Dependents of the Indian Fighting Army* (Fort Collins CO: Old Army Press, 1978; reprint,

with a foreword by Darlis A. Miller, Norman: University of Oklahoma Press, 1992); Edward M. Coffman, *The Old Army: A Portrait of the American Army in Peacetime, 1784–1898* (New York: Oxford University Press, 1986); Knight, *Life and Manners.* For an excellent case study of the domestic aspects of the army, see Robert Wooster, *Soldiers, Sutlers, and Settlers: Garrison Life on the Texas Frontier* (College Station: Texas A&M University Press, 1987). For a good article-length treatment of army kids on the Texas frontier, see Shirley Leckie, "Fort Concho: A Paradise for Children," *Fort Concho Report* 19, no. 1 (spring 1989): 1–15.

27. On the composition of the army in 1878, see "Report of the General of the Army, 7 Nov. 1878," in "Report of the Secretary of War, 19 Nov. 1878," *House Exec. Doc.*, 45th Cong., 3d sess., no. 1, pt. 2, serial 1843, 3, 12–21. On the first report on civilians with the army, see "Report of the Surgeon General, 22 Sept. 1891," in "Report of the Secretary of War, 3 Nov. 1891," *House Exec. Doc.*, 52d Cong., 1st sess., no. 1, vol. 1, pt. 2, serial 2921, 605–7; Stallard, *Glittering Misery*, 57.

28. E. A. Bode, *A Dose of Frontier Soldiering: The Memoirs of Corporal E. A. Bode, Frontier Regular Infantry, 1877–1882*, ed. Thomas T. Smith (Lincoln: University of Nebraska Press, 1994), 17–18; Knight, *Life and Manners*, 163.

29. Knight, *Life and Manners*, 4, 31, 43; Laurence manuscript, 165.

30. Stallard, *Glittering Misery*, 15, 23, 26, 36; Coffman, *The Old Army*, 126, 289; Knight, *Life and Manners*, 40, 76, 112; Laurence manuscript, 101.

31. Stallard, *Glittering Misery*, 75, 94–95, 99; Coffman, *The Old Army*, 322–26; Laurence manuscript, 49, 98, 103, 110, 132. Reynolds J. Burt, the son of an Eighth Infantry officer, found in 1880 to 1882 an "opportunity for two years systematic schooling" when his father was on recruiting duty in Chicago. Afterward at Angel Island in San Francisco Bay there was "no schooling . . . though mother held 'sketchy' classes for me." At Fort Bidwell, California, the post school, shared by a few town kids, was taught by an Irish soldier. Burt, "Boyhood Data," 1–2, 14.

32. Stallard, *Glittering Misery*, 43, 46, 47, 51, 83; Coffman, *The Old Army*, 294; Knight, *Life and Manners*, 120, 138, 149–53; Laurence manuscript, 98, 109, 113–14, 135, 140.

33. Coffman, *The Old Army*, 138; Laurence manuscript, 140–41, 143.

34. Laurence manuscript, 33; Coffman, *The Old Army*, 302.

35. Huntington built upon a similar "army in isolation" thesis, originally offered in 1924 by William A. Ganoe. Ganoe, in one of the earliest survey histories of the U.S. Army, has a chapter titled "The Army's Dark Ages." Samuel P. Huntington, *The Soldier and the State: The Theory and Politics of Civil-Military Relations* (Cambridge MA: Harvard University Press, 1957), 227–29; William Addleman Ganoe, *The History of the United States Army* (New York: D. Appleton and Company, 1924), 348–54. Other historians, such as Russell Weigley and Robert M. Utley, have followed the Ganoe thesis. See, for example, Russell F. Weigley, *History of the United States Army* (New York: Macmillan, 1967), 265–92; Robert M. Utley, *Frontier Regulars: The United States Army and the Indian, 1866–1891* (New York: Macmillan, 1973), 61. Oliver Knight writes that army officers were isolated, elite exiles, the aristocrats of the West. Knight, *Life and Manners*, 3. A challenge to the Ganoe thesis of isolation is found in John M. Gates, "The Alleged Isolation of U.S. Army Officers in the Late 19th Century," *Parameters* 10 (September 1980): 32–45. Gates points out that in 1881 almost a third of the officer corps was stationed in the East or in the urban West and that social contact with civilians was considered a part of military life. In spite of his inclusion of the isolation thesis, Oliver Knight acknowledges that army officers' contact with civilian frontiersmen was more immediate and frequent than their contact with relatives back East. Sherry Smith found that officers socialized freely with townspeople and moved in local social circles. See Knight, *Life and Manners*, 223, 227; Smith, *The View from Officers' Row*, 10.

36. Laurence manuscript, 78, 88, 102, 122, 191–94.

37. Quotes from Don Rickey Jr., *Forty Miles a Day on Beans and Hay: The Enlisted Soldier Fighting the Indian Wars* (Norman: University of Oklahoma Press, 1963), 5; Laurence manuscript, 163.

38. Smith, *The View from Officers' Row*, 61–62; Laurence manuscript, 18–19. Coffman finds that it was not uncommon for Indians

to try to buy officers' wives or children. Coffman, *The Old Army*, 299. More recent scholarship has begun to suggest that historians have long undervalued the power and roles of women in Plains Indian cultures. See, for example, Patricia Albers and Beatrice Medicine, *The Hidden Half: Studies of Plains Indian Women* (Washington DC: University Press of America, 1983).

39. Smith, *The View from Officers' Row*, 114; Laurence manuscript, 28. See also Coffman, *The Old Army*, 317.

40. Coffman, *The Old Army*, 295; Knight, *Life and Manners*, 93. One little-studied aspect of the old army is the challenge of single parenting. While uncommon, it did occur, as in the case of Captain Simon Snyder of the Fifth Infantry. His diaries are filled with poignant worry over his daughter Lillian while he was away campaigning in the Montana Territory in the 1880s. "Simon Snyder Papers," U.S. Army Military History Institute, Carlisle Barracks, Pennsylvania. The scandal in the Nineteenth Infantry occurred when Assistant Surgeon William S. Tremaine and Major Jacob H. Smith were both in Chicago's Clifton House on sick leave. Smith returned to his room one night and, apparently finding Tremaine with his wife, shot the surgeon twice. Tremaine lived but lost a finger. Although both officers refused to discuss the matter, the story made the Chicago newspapers and received major play in the Dodge City paper. "A Military Melee," *Ford County Globe* (Dodge City, Kansas; 23 December 1879): 2.

41. Stallard, *Glittering Misery*, 76, 101; Coffman, *The Old Army*, 290, 314.

1. Fort Dodge, Kansas, 1878–1880

1. The forty-nine-year-old commander of Fort Dodge, Lieutenant Colonel William H. Lewis, Nineteenth Infantry, died 28 September 1878 of wounds received in battle against the Cheyenne on 27 September at Punished Woman's Fork, Kansas. Born in Alabama and appointed to West Point from New York, Lewis graduated from the United States Military Academy in 1849. Prior to the Civil War Lewis served in the First, Fourth, and Fifth Infantry Regiments in Texas, Florida, New Mexico, and Utah and as a tactics instructor at West Point. In New Mexico during the war he earned a brevet to major in March 1862 at the Battle of Apache Canyon and one to lieutenant

colonel in April 1862 at Peralta, New Mexico. Lewis served in various infantry regiments during the remainder of the war before becoming the lieutenant colonel of the Nineteenth Infantry in 1873. The remains of Colonel Lewis were eventually interred at Fort Leavenworth. The Civil War veterans of Dodge City named their Grand Army of the Republic post in honor of Lewis. Cullum, *Biographical Register,* 2: 382–84; Heitman, *Historical Register,* 1: 631.

2. After the Battle of the Little Big Horn most of the Northern Cheyenne were sent to Indian Territory to be placed on the Cheyenne and Arapaho Reservation. Following a miserable winter of starvation in 1877 Dull Knife and Little Wolf determined to return to their northern hunting grounds, breaking out with three hundred members of their bands in September 1878. Ordered to intercept the flight of the Cheyennes, Colonel William H. Lewis at Fort Dodge sent several companies of the Fourth Cavalry, each of which was defeated in turn by the Indians. Taking to the field himself and anxious to end criticism of the army's failure, Lewis led a column of five companies of the Fourth Cavalry and detachments from the Nineteenth Infantry by rail and route march until he caught the Cheyennes at Punished Woman's Fork of the Smoky Hill River, thirty miles south of Fort Wallace, Kansas. The Cheyennes had an excellent defensive position and during the first assault mortally wounded Colonel Lewis and killed three enlisted men. Lewis bled to death from a bullet wound to the thigh that severed the femoral artery.

The Cheyenne band slipped away during the night, continuing their journey northward, and, contrary to the account offered by Mary Leefe Laurence, Major Mauck's column did not catch them. In October 1878 Dull Knife surrendered in Nebraska and the army sent his group to Fort Robinson. During a break-out attempt from there in January 1879 the army killed sixty-four and recaptured seventy-eight Cheyennes. With some support from sympathetic officers Dull Knife settled on the Pine Ridge Agency in the Dakota Territory. He was not forced to return to Indian Territory. Little Wolf's band of 126 eluded capture until March 1878, when they surrendered in Montana. They eventually settled there on the Tongue River Reservation. "Colonel W. H. Lewis," *Ford County Globe* (Dodge City, Kansas; 1 October 1878): 2; David Kay Strate, *Sentinel to the Cimarron: The Frontier*

Experience of Fort Dodge, Kansas (Dodge City KS: Cultural Heritage and Arts Center, 1970), 100–105; Stanley Vestal, "Notes on the Battle of Punished Woman's Fork," from the original appendix of the Mary Leefe Laurence manuscript; Paul Andrew Hutton, *Phil Sheridan and His Army* (Lincoln: University of Nebraska Press, 1985), 334–37; Utley, *Frontier Regulars,* 291–92.

3. Transferring from Fort Lyon, Colorado, the Leefe family arrived at Fort Dodge, Kansas, on 29 April 1876. Although he was the regular first lieutenant of Company B, Nineteenth Infantry Regiment, George Leefe had been assigned to be the post quartermaster with the temporary or brevet rank of captain. At their arrival in 1876 Fort Dodge had two companies of Nineteenth Infantry and a company of Fifth Cavalry, a total of 6 officers and 125 enlisted men. Located on the north bank of the Arkansas River and designed to protect the Santa Fe Trail, the post of Fort Dodge was established by the Eleventh Kansas Cavalry in April 1865. The post served as a base of operations for Major General Philip H. Sheridan's winter campaign of 1868–69 and was an important post in the Red River War of 1874–75. The arrival of the Santa Fe Railroad in 1872 made the town a railhead for cattle herds and defined the nature of Dodge City, the prototypical wild cowtown. The U.S. Army closed the post in 1882, but its numerous stone buildings are used by the state as part of a soldiers' home. Post Returns, Fort Dodge, Kansas, January 1866–October 1882, microfilm no. M617, roll 319, in Returns from United States Military Posts 1800–1916, Records of the United States Army Adjutant General's Office, 1780–1917, Record Group (RG) 94 (hereafter cited as Post Returns, Fort Dodge); Strate, *Sentinel to the Cimarron;* National Park Service, *Soldier and Brave: Historic Places Associated with Indian Affairs and the Indian Wars in the Trans-Mississippi West,* National Survey of Historic Sites and Buildings, vol. 12, ed. Robert G. Ferris (Washington DC: U.S. Department of the Interior, National Park Service, 1971), 139–40; Robert W. Frazer, *Forts of the West* (Norman: University of Oklahoma Press, 1965), 52–53.

4. The Leefes were stationed at Fort Lyon, Colorado, from 1874 to 1876.

5. The report of the secretary of war for 1869 states that on 6 October 1868 near Sand Creek, Colorado, a Mrs. Blinn and child were

abducted by unknown Indians and afterward murdered during Custer's attack on Black Kettle's camp in November 1868. "Report of the Secretary of War, 20 Nov. 1869," *House Exec. Doc.*, 41st Cong., 2d sess., no. 1, pt. 2, serial 1412, 53–55.

6. Mary Leefe Laurence is referring to the infamous Sand Creek Massacre. Volunteer Colonel John M. Chivington and seven hundred of the First and Third Regiments Colorado Volunteer Cavalry surprised the unsuspecting band of Cheyenne chief Black Kettle at their camp on 29 November 1864. During the attack over two hundred Cheyennes were killed, three-quarters of them women and children. Robert M. Utley, *Frontiersmen in Blue: The United States Army and the Indian, 1848–1865* (New York: Macmillan, 1967; reprint, Lincoln: University of Nebraska Press, 1981), 290–97.

7. Custer was not stationed at Fort Lyon at the time, as Mary Leefe Laurence states. The garrison was Troop L of the Seventh Cavalry and three companies of the Third and Fifth Infantry Regiments, all commanded by Captain W. H. Penrose. Penrose pursued but could not find the Indians involved, continuing east as part of three large columns converging on the lower Indian Territory. Custer, meanwhile, was in Kansas preparing for the preplanned winter expedition down into the Washita and Canadian River Valleys of Indian Territory. Custer launched his winter expedition out of Camp Supply on 23 November and crossed a trail that led him to Black Kettle's camp, which he attacked on the morning of 27 November 1868 in what came to be known as the Battle of the Washita. Custer's memoirs record that in the middle of the fight an Indian woman was seen running hand in hand with a captive white boy. Refusing to surrender, she stabbed and killed the boy before she herself was shot. "Report of the Secretary of War, 20 Nov. 1868" and "Report of Major General Philip H. Sheridan, Headquarters, Department of the Missouri, 15 Oct. 1868," *House Exec. Doc.*, 40th Cong., 3d sess., no. 1, pt. 1, serial 1367, 17–20, 732; General G. A. Custer, USA, *My Life on the Plains, or Personal Experiences with Indians* (New York: Sheldon and Company, 1874), 165; Utley, *Frontier Regulars*, 154–58.

8. During the Battle of the Washita at Black Kettle's camp Major Joel Elliott and a group of seventeen troopers pursued Indians trying to escape east of the village. Elliott and his soldiers were apparently

cut off by other Indians coming to the aid of Black Kettle. Lieutenant Edward Godfrey told Custer he heard heavy firing in the direction Elliott had taken, but Custer ignored the information. After a short search failed to turn up Elliott's group Custer became concerned his own command would be overwhelmed by the growing numbers of Indians. Custer returned to Camp Supply and reported to Major General Phil Sheridan that Elliott had been surprised and killed. The next month, in December 1868, Sheridan was with the party that discovered the bodies of Elliott and his force. It was apparent from the spent cartridges and defensive arrangement of the position that the soldiers held out for a considerable period before being killed, perhaps long enough to be rescued by Custer had he chosen to do so. A good portion of the Seventh Cavalry lost faith in Custer after he abandoned Elliott. The discovery of the bodies increased the stormy relations of the Seventh into pro- and anti-Custer factions. Philip H. Sheridan, *Personal Memoirs of P. H. Sheridan, General United States Army*, 2 vols. (New York: Charles L. Webster and Company, 1888), 2: 320; Hutton, *Phil Sheridan and His Army*, 71–80; Stan Hoig, *The Battle of the Washita: The Sheridan-Custer Indian Campaign of 1867–69* (New York: Doubleday & Company, 1976), 156–61.

9. Probably a version of the famous story of Captain Nicholas Nolan's Troop A, Tenth Cavalry, on the Staked Plains of Texas in the summer of 1877. The men were desperately thirsty enough to drink the blood of their horses. Colonel Martin L. Crimmins, "Captain Nolan's Lost Troop on the Staked Plains," in *The Black Military Experience in the American West*, ed. John M. Carroll (New York: Liveright, 1971), 287–92.

10. Mary Leefe Laurence reflects the perspective of many army ladies; their view of the stereotypical gender relations of the Plains Indians is described in Sherry L. Smith's study of officer attitudes toward Indians. Smith, *The View from Officers' Row*, 61–62.

11. The quartermaster's department was usually short of officers to fill this important duty, so it routinely had to have commanders detail officers from the line to fill the post. Leefe was a regular first lieutenant of infantry but by becoming the post quartermaster earned the privileges and status, but not the pay, of a captain. He remained, off and on, as a regimental quartermaster officer for ten years. His

organization at Fort Dodge consisted of forty-five individuals, a structure larger than an infantry company. He had working for him a clerk, twenty teamsters, nine purchasing agents, the post guide or scout, seven herders, as well as a group of technical craftsmen such as the wheelwright, blacksmith, saddler, and farrier. Leefe's responsibilities included all wagon transportation, purchasing and distributing supplies and forage, and transporting the food and rations purchased by the commissary department. For the army wives at a fort the post quartermaster was an individual central to the quality of their domestic life. Many wives took great pains to cultivate influence and a friendly relationship with the quartermaster, for it was he who controlled the supply of paint, lumber, and workmen to repair or remodel living quarters. Of course it was also he on whom they heaped blame for the dilapidated condition of most army quarters, living spaces which Congress had directed be built with soldier labor, preferably at no expense to the government. Post Returns, Fort Dodge, Kansas, May 1876; Adjutant General's Records, ACP 3393; Knight, *Life and Manners*, 124–25.

12. This record of Leefe's company having no desertion for six years is incorrect. For details, see chapter 10.

13. The Utes of the Upper Colorado Basin and White River Agency exploded in the autumn of 1879 over their treatment at the inept hands of agent Nathan C. Meeker, whom they killed, along with nine others at the agency. After several bloody skirmishes with the army the band surrendered. As a result of a negotiated settlement the White River Utes were moved to Utah to the Uintah Reservation in September 1881. The army movement of the Utes did not pass through Fort Dodge, so when Mary Leefe Laurence saw the camp she may have been visiting Fort Garland, Colorado, a post her father often visited on temporary duty. Rather than Frank Lawton, Mary Leefe Laurence is referring to Henry W. Lawton of the Fourth Cavalry, who gained fame as Colonel Ranald Mackenzie's industrious quartermaster during the Red River War of 1874–75 and was the tenacious pursuer of Geronimo for two thousand miles in Mexico in 1886. Beginning his career as a Civil War volunteer sergeant in the Ninth Indiana Infantry in 1861, Lawton finished the war as a volunteer major general. He was killed in action in the Philippines in December 1899. Robert

Emmitt, *The Last War Trail: The Utes and the Settlement of Colorado* (Norman: University of Oklahoma Press, 1954), 94; Utley, *Frontier Regulars*, 341–51; Heitman, *Historical Register*, 1: 620.

14. Both Indian and white parents shared a mutual distrust and fear that the other would steal their children. Smith, *The View from Officers' Row*, 76.

2. Diversions at Fort Dodge

1. A search of enlisted records, Indian War pension applications, and Nineteenth Infantry Regiment company muster rolls in the National Archives did not yield a match with a single enlisted man's name in this memoir. In spite of her professed admiration and affection for them Mary Leefe Laurence apparently had a poor memory for their proper names. Strikers, or "dog-robbers" as they were sometimes called, were enlisted men who served as an officer's personal man. Paid an extra five dollars a month by the officer, these strikers were often older, reliable soldiers with families and a greater financial incentive. With age it became more difficult to perform field service, from which they were usually excused to look after the officer's family, and likewise their own, while the unit went on campaigns and scouts. They were also excused from the routine of guard duty, drill, and roll calls. Most of the army ignored the 1870 congressional prohibition against the practice until the regulations of 1881 finally outlawed strikers. Coffman, *The Old Army*, 305, 347; Stallard, *Glittering Misery*, 29; Knight, *Life and Manners*, 128.

2. Contrary to this view, the enlisted memoirs complain of monotonous rations, however nutritious. Officers were paid about twenty-five cents in lieu of the daily issue, but the ration of the 1870s issued to the enlisted man consisted of a twenty-ounce portion of fresh or salt beef, twelve ounces of bacon or pork with a similar small portion of flour, bread, or cornmeal, peas or beans, rice or hominy, sugar, and coffee beans or tea. Companies maintained gardens to supplement the ration with fresh vegetables. In garrison the main meals were breakfast and lunch, with a supper of bread and coffee. Bode, *A Dose of Frontier Soldiering*, 17–18; "Report of the Commissary-General of Subsistence, 10 Oct. 1881," *House Exec. Doc.*, 47th Cong., 1st sess., no. 1,

pt. 2, serial 2010, 484–85; Coffman, *The Old Army,* 340; Rickey, *Forty Miles a Day,* 39.

3. A viol is a seventeenth-century stringed instrument, played with a bow. It is similar to a viola.

4. The only Protestant Episcopal Bishop "LaTourette" was Kenneth S. La Tourette, who was not born until 1886, well after the period referenced by Mary Leefe Laurence. Thomas H. Vail was the Episcopal bishop of Kansas from 1864 to 1889. *Notable Names in American History: A Tabulated Register,* 3d ed. (Clifton NJ: James T. White and Company, 1973), 520, 534.

5. While true in the 1940s, currently once again household goods are shipped at government expense within the rank weight allowance. The older method of government-provided furniture still holds true for assignments to Germany, where most soldiers have a very restricted weight allowance of a few thousand pounds.

6. The Leefes departed Fort Dodge on 5 March 1880. First Lieutenant Leefe was reassigned to his rifle command, Company B, Nineteenth Infantry. Special Orders No. 57, Headquarters, Department of Missouri, 18 February 1880, Post Returns, Fort Dodge, Kansas, March 1880.

3. Fort Leavenworth, Kansas, 1880–1881

1. After a two-day journey from Fort Dodge the Leefes arrived at Fort Leavenworth on 7 March 1880. Post Returns, Fort Leavenworth, Kansas, January 1870–December 1890, microfilm no. M617, roll 612, in Returns from United States Military Posts 1800–1916, Records of the United States Army Adjutant General's Office, 1780–1917, Record Group (RG) 94 (hereafter cited as Post Returns, Fort Leavenworth).

2. Mary Leefe Laurence is referring to the old army practice known as "ranking out," in which an incoming, more senior officer could lay claim to the quarters of a more junior officer. That junior officer would then "rank out" someone else until, at times like falling dominos, half a dozen families might have to move, demoralizing all of the wives. There were incidents of officers having to move several times in a single month to successively smaller quarters. The most infamous example occurred at Fort Clark, Texas, where a lieutenant

with a new bride was ranked down to living in a hallway between a set of quarters. When a senior ranked him out of the hallway he resigned the service in disgust. Stallard, *Glittering Misery*, 23–24; Knight, *Life and Manners*, 123.

3. The Leefes were assigned to 43 West End Parade Field, a row of six spacious two-story duplexes on what is now Kearney Avenue. The quarters were torn down during the 1902–3 construction of the artillery barracks. Edwin Green, *Green's Directory of Ft. Leavenworth, 1880–81* (Leavenworth KS: Private Printing, 1881), 220; personal communication, Stephen J. Allie, Director, Frontier Army Museum, Fort Leavenworth, Kansas.

4. At the time of the arrival of the Leefes the commander of the Nineteenth Infantry, Colonel Charles H. Smith, commanded the post. The garrison consisted of 11 officers and 126 enlisted men belonging to headquarters, the band, and Companies B and H of the regiment. In October 1880 Companies D, E, and F, Nineteenth Infantry returned from detached service in Colorado, bringing the garrison strength to 14 officers and 286 enlisted men, a large population for a western fort of the era. Leefe was the first lieutenant of Company B, which was commanded by Captain William J. Lyster. Edward B. Ives served as the second lieutenant. The company had forty-three enlisted men, a full company for that period. In addition to the Nineteenth Infantry garrison the post also served as the headquarters for the Department of the Missouri under Brigadier General John Pope. Post Returns, Fort Leavenworth, March and October 1880.

5. Established by Colonel Henry Leavenworth in May 1827 to protect the Santa Fe Trail, Fort Leavenworth, Kansas, is the oldest active post west of the Mississippi River. The post was one of the key frontier locations, on the left bank of the Missouri River and contiguous to the major western immigration routes. It became a major supply point and a base of operations for numerous frontier exploration and punitive expeditions in the nineteenth century. In the 1870s the post served as headquarters for the Department of the Missouri. Although an infantry post when the Leefes arrived in 1880, the post soon filled with all arms, as Mary Leefe Laurence recalls. The post was designated as the School of Application for Infantry and Cavalry in late 1881, and in January 1882 the garrison doubled to 582 to include

companies from the Third, Fourth, Seventh, and Eighth Cavalry Regiments, Second Artillery Regiment, and First, Eleventh, and Twentieth Infantry Regiments. Since the 1880s Fort Leavenworth has been essential to the army professional schools system. The School of Application was reorganized as the General Service and Staff School in 1901 as part of the army officer education program in the renewed drive for officer professional development. Currently Fort Leavenworth houses the U.S. Army Command and General Staff College and is the site of a military prison, the U.S. Disciplinary Barracks, which was built in 1874. "Report of the General of the Army, 14 Nov. 1882," and "Report of Brevet Major General John Pope, 2 Oct. 1882," *House Exec. Doc.*, 47th Cong., 2d sess., no. 1, pt. 2, serial 2091, 32–33, 102; National Park Service, *Soldier and Brave*, 146–48; Frazer, *Forts of the West*, 56; Elvid Hunt and Walter E. Lorence, *History of Fort Leavenworth, 1827–1937* (Fort Leavenworth KS: Command and General Staff School Press, 1937), 122–29.

6. Mary Leefe's school was the Cathedral Female School run by the Sisters of Charity. Her brothers went to a similar boys' school at the same location, on the corner of Kickapoo and Fifth in Leavenworth. The buildings have subsequently been torn down and replaced by another school. Edwin Green, *Edwin Green's Municipal Record and City Register, 1880–81* (Leavenworth KS: Private Printing, 1881), 24.

7. After their outbreak over the loss of tribal lands in 1877, eight hundred Nez Percé under Looking Glass and Joseph outpaced the army on a 1,700-mile chase across the West that earned the sympathy and respect of both the public and many officers. When four hundred finally surrendered in October 1877 they were temporarily held at the old racetrack grounds on Fort Leavenworth. In July 1878 the majority were sent to Indian Territory, and eventually some transferred back to Washington. Chief Joseph, the political leader who so captured the public imagination, lived until 1904. Mary Leefe's memory is faulty in that the Nez Percé had left Fort Leavenworth two years before her family transferred there. She may be remembering Joseph from a family visit to the post while still stationed at Fort Dodge. There is no U.S. Army documentary evidence proving that Lieutenant Leefe accompanied Joseph to Indian Territory; however, he is not present at Fort Dodge, his normal duty station, during July 1878, when the Nez

Percé moved, and the post returns offer no explanation for his absence. Because Leefe was a seasoned quartermaster officer it is possible he was informally attached to the relocation mission of the Nez Percé. It is also possible that he accompanied Joseph on the return leg of the chief's two trips to Washington DC in 1879. Post Returns, Fort Dodge, June–July 1878; Merrill D. Beal, "I *Will Fight No More Forever*": *Chief Joseph and the Nez Percé War* (Seattle: University of Washington Press, 1963), 274–84; Bruce Hampton, *Children of Grace: The Nez Percé War of 1877* (New York: Henry Holt and Company, 1994), 311–37; Utley, *Frontier Regulars*, 305–30.

8. The Carlisle Indian Industrial School was established by Lieutenant Richard A. Pratt in 1879 at the post of Carlisle Barracks, Pennsylvania. The vocational school for Native Americans produced such graduates as Olympic stars Jim Thorpe and Louis Tewanima. It closed in 1918. Richard H. Pratt, *Battlefield and Classroom: Four Decades with the American Indian, 1867–1904,* ed. Robert M. Utley (New Haven CT: Yale University Press, 1964).

9. The fourth-century BC Greek Athenian soldier-scholar Xenophon lead an army of mercenaries in a one-thousand-mile withdrawal from Persia to Greece after a failed military adventure, described in his classic *Anabasis.*

10. Captain Leefe was on detached service to Fort Garland, Colorado, from April to December 1880. Post Returns, Fort Leavenworth, Kansas, December 1880.

11. The Leefes came to know Gorgas on the Texas frontier in the 1880s. Assistant Surgeon William Crawford Gorgas was at this time, 1880–81, serving on the Rio Grande frontier at Texas Forts Brown, McIntosh, and Duncan. It was during the Fort Brown yellow fever epidemic of the early 1880s that Gorgas first became interested in techniques to eradicate the disease. Following up on army surgeon Walter Reed's discovery that yellow fever was carried by a mosquito, Gorgas was instrumental in the eradication of the disease in Havana during the Spanish-American War and in Panama, which allowed for the construction of the canal. Gorgas went on to become the president of the American Medical Association in 1908 and surgeon general of the army in 1914. He retired in 1918 as a major general. Born in Alabama in 1854, Gorgas died in 1920. Although Mary Leefe Laur-

ence offers praise for army doctors, they did not enjoy the universal esteem offered to such medical talent as Gorgas, Leonard Wood, Walter Reed, and George M. Sternberg. The army medical department, always shorthanded, improved considerably after the Civil War and underwent an increasingly rigorous qualification process, but army doctors were generally regarded by soldiers as lacking the competence of their civilian peers. In fairness the army doctors struggled against a difficult environment and commanders who had little notion of modern hygiene. Samuel Smith, an army doctor at Fort Concho, Texas, in 1879 became so frustrated at a company commander's reluctance to introduce simple measures to prevent scurvy that the good doctor declared, "The head of the average Army officer is as thick as a board." On Gorgas, see Roger J. Spiller and Joseph G. Dawson III, eds., *Dictionary of American Military Biography*, 3 vols. (Westport CT: Greenwood Press, 1984), 1: 392–94; John M. Gibson, *Physician to the World: The Life of General William C. Gorgas* (Durham NC: Duke University Press, 1950). For views on the army medical department, see Stallard, *Glittering Misery*, 76–77; Coffman, *The Old Army*, 381–90; Utley, *Frontier Regulars*, 89–90; Rickey, *Forty Miles a Day*, 131–33. The Smith quote is from John Neilson, ed., " 'I Long to Return to Fort Concho': Acting Assistant Surgeon Samuel Smith's Letters from the Texas Military Frontier, 1878–1879," *Military History of the West* 24 (fall 1994): 164.

12. The Leefes attended St. Paul's Episcopal Church, founded in 1856. The stone church, built in 1864 on Seventh Street in Leavenworth, still holds services and appears very much as Mary Leefe described it. Green, *Green's Municipal Record*, 25; The Right Reverend Goodrich Robert Fenner and the Right Reverend Edward Clark Turner, *The First 100 Years: The Diocese of Kansas* (Lawrence KS: Private Printing, 1959).

13. The Leefes departed Fort Leavenworth for Fort Gibson, Oklahoma, on 19 September 1881. Post Returns, Fort Leavenworth, September 1881.

4. Fort Gibson, Indian Territory, 1881

1. Brevet Major General of Volunteers Russell A. Alger served in the Second, Fifth, and Sixth Michigan Cavalry Regiments, had a term

as governor of Michigan (1885 to 1886), and became the secretary of war in the McKinley administration in March 1897. Criticized for the inadequate preparation of the War Department during the Spanish-American War, Alger resigned in August 1899. He died in 1907 while a U.S. senator. William Gardner Bell, *Secretaries of War and Secretaries of the Army: Portraits and Biographical Sketches* (Washington DC: Center of Military History, 1992), 98.

2. The elder brother was Fred, whom everyone called Dick. The youngest brother, Sydney, called Tom, was wounded in the Spanish-American War and did not recover, spending the remainder of his life in Washington DC at St. Elizabeth Hospital. Laurence interview.

3. Kate Leefe, the older sister of Mary, was born 18 September 1871 and died in Elizabeth, New Jersey, on 14 July 1948. While the family was stationed at Fort Brady, Michigan, she met and married Albert von Mangelsdorf, a former German officer who had immigrated and settled in Detroit and was working as an engineer doing surveys of the Great Lakes near the post. He died on 23 January 1925. Their only child, Mary Emile Mangelsdorf, was born 20 July 1902 and lives in Elizabeth, New Jersey. Interview with Mary Emile Mangelsdorf, 23 August 1994.

4. In 1824 the army established Fort Gibson, Oklahoma, in the Indian Territory during the conflict between the Cherokee and Osage Indians. It was constructed three miles up on the Grand River near the confluence of the Grand, Verdigris, and Arkansas Rivers. It became an important depot and upper terminal of navigation on the Arkansas River, supplying expeditions and surveys of the Great Plains during the antebellum period. Abandoned by the U.S. Army in 1857, the stockaded fort served Confederate forces before being reoccupied by the Union during the Civil War. It remained an active post until 1890. Brad Agnew, *Fort Gibson: Terminal on the Trail of Tears* (Norman: University of Oklahoma Press, 1980), 25–62; National Park Service, *Soldier and Brave,* 264–66.

5. The Leefes arrived at Fort Gibson, Indian Territory, on 21 September 1881 after a two-day train journey from Fort Leavenworth. Leefe assumed command of the post and of Company I, Nineteenth Infantry. The post garrison at that time consisted of Companies I and K, Nineteenth Infantry, a total of three officers and eighty enlisted

men. Post Returns, Fort Gibson, Oklahoma, July 1872–October 1897, microfilm no. M617, roll 406, in Returns from United States Military Posts 1800–1916, Records of the United States Army Adjutant General's Office, 1780–1917, Record Group (RG) 94 (hereafter cited as Post Returns, Fort Gibson).

6. Captain Alexander M. Wetherill from Pennsylvania was appointed as a second lieutenant in the Sixth Infantry in 1867 and became the regimental quartermaster in 1887. As a captain he was killed at the Battle of San Juan at Santiago, Cuba, on 1 July 1898. Heitman, *Historical Register,* 1: 1021.

7. In 1842 Charles Dickens made his first trip to America, where he was entertained by a number of distinguished Americans, including President Tyler. The literary results of the trip, a cranky commentary titled *American Notes,* was not well received by his former hosts. Edgar Johnson, *Charles Dickens: His Tragedy and Triumph,* 2 vols. (New York: Simon and Schuster, 1952), 1: 304–95, 441–42.

8. In October 1881 Lieutenant Leefe was detailed by the regimental commander to go to general recruiting service on Davids Island, New York. Post Returns, Fort Gibson, October 1881.

5. David's Island, New York, 1881–1882

1. The Leefes arrived at Davids Island on 10 November 1881. Lieutenant Leefe commanded Company B, a training company of the general recruiting service. The commander of the post was Lieutenant Colonel Henry M. Black of the Eighteenth Infantry. At the post were nine officers, the lieutenant colonel, a major, three captains, and four lieutenants from seven different regiments. The training battalion had an organization of four companies and taught the recruits the basics of marching and marksmanship before sending them on to their units on the frontier. Leefe's Company B had 106 recruits plus 4 sergeants, 4 corporals, and 4 musicians. In addition, the command had recruiting sergeants in most of the major cities on the East Coast. The total post garrison was 541 enlisted and 9 officers. Post Returns, Davids Island, New York, July 1878–June 1896, microfilm no. M617, roll 294, in Returns from United States Military Posts 1800–1916, Records of the United States Army Adjutant General's Office, 1780–1917, Record Group (RG) 94 (hereafter cited as Post Returns, Davids Island).

2. Adna Romanza Chaffee Sr., born in Ohio in 1842, enlisted in the Sixth Cavalry during the Civil War, rising to the rank of first sergeant before being commissioned in 1863. He served in the postwar Sixth, Ninth, and Third Cavalry Regiments, gaining distinction for his service during the Indian Wars on the frontier. Chaffee became a volunteer major general during the Cuban Campaign in the Spanish-American War and led the relief of the legations at Peking during the Boxer Rebellion in 1900. Chaffee, as regular army major general, was military governor of the Philippines and, in 1904, became a lieutenant general and chief of staff of the army. He retired in 1906 and died on 1 November 1914. Chaffee had three daughters and one son, Adna R. Jr., who became a major general and key figure in the development of the armored force in the U.S. Army before he died of cancer in 1941. Heitman, *Historical Register,* 1: 292; Spiller and Dawson, *Dictionary of American Military Biography,* 1: 164–67; Trevor N. Dupuy, Curt Johnson, and David L. Bongard, *The Harper Encyclopedia of Military Biography* (New York: HarperCollins, Publishers, 1992), 141–42.

3. Davids Island, New York, later known as Fort Slocum, is an eighty-acre island in Long Island Sound that was fortified in 1861 to protect New York City during the Civil War. Located near New Rochelle, the post's name was later changed to honor the former colonel of the Twenty-Seventh New York, Major General Henry W. Slocum, a distinguished division and corps commander of the Army of the Potomac and the commander of the Army of Georgia in Sherman's march to the sea. The post remained active until 1965, serving as a POW camp, Air Force Headquarters, U.S. Army Chaplain School, and Nike-Atlas missile base. Contrary to Mary Leefe Laurence and old army records, modern maps often refer to it as Davids Island without the apostrophe. Robert B. Roberts, *Encyclopedia of Historic Forts: The Military, Pioneer, and Trading Posts of the United States* (New York: Macmillan Publishing Company, 1988), 580.

4. Born in London in 1820, the author, songwriter, and entertainer Stephen Massett often went by the stage name of "Jeems Pipes of Pipesville." As a young man he came to New York and gained local fame as the composer of a number of popular songs in the 1840s such as "When the Moon on the Lake Is Beaming," "My Darling's Face," and "Shadows in the Lane." Massett never married and was a colorful

character and eccentric. When he died in August 1898 he had his body cremated and spread on Fresh Pond in New York City. His will expressly forbade his relatives and "so-called" friends from attending the funeral. "Obituary, Stephen Massett," *New York Times* (22 August 1898): 5, col. 5; "Will of Stephen Massett," *New York Times* (9 October 1898): 10, col. 2.

5. Pelham Priory had been the home of Robert Bolton, the Episcopal minister at Bolton Church in Pelham, New York. In the early 1880s Bolton's daughters, both older women, lived there and ran a school in the priory. The priory, built in 1838, is a New York State historic landmark one mile north of the Bartlow-Pell Mansion in Pelham Bay Park. Telephone interview with Nancy Wixon, Curator, Bartow-Pell Mansion, Pelham Bay Park, Bronx, New York, 8 September 1994.

6. Lieutenant Leefe was released from recruiting duty and departed Davids Island on 23 December 1882. Post Returns, Davids Island, December 1882.

6. Fort Ringgold, Texas, 1883–1886

1. Named for Captain Sam Ringgold, who died at Palo Alto, Ringgold Barracks, or Fort Ringgold, was one of the oldest of the frontier posts in Texas. Established on the Rio Grande in October 1848, at the close of the Mexican War, near the site of Davis Landing and Rio Grande City, the post was abandoned by the army during the Civil War. Rebuilt in 1869, it remained active until 1906, was reoccupied during the border troubles of 1913, and was finally completely deactivated in 1944. Many of the buildings of the post remain in use by the local school district. Although considered the hottest post in Texas, Fort Ringgold, in the post–Civil War era, had very good quarters and could boast of some of the finest barracks in the army. Four large two-story barracks each held ample dormitory space for one company, sergeants' rooms, washrooms, and even reading rooms for the soldiers. Wooster, *Soldiers, Sutlers, and Settlers,* 30, 35; Frazer, *Forts of the West,* 158–59.

2. Fort McIntosh was at Laredo. Son of the late Major General Edwin V. "Bull" Sumner, Major Samuel S. Sumner of the Eighth Cavalry commanded at Fort McIntosh with one company each of the

Eighth Cavalry and Sixteenth and Nineteenth Infantry Regiments. "Report of the Secretary of War, 14 Nov. 1882," 34.

3. Mrs. E. H. Liscum, like most of the regimental wives, was very sensitive to the spread of illness among the families. The previous summer, in August 1882, yellow fever made a sudden and dramatic appearance in the lower Rio Grande Valley, particularly affecting the Nineteenth Infantry companies at Fort Brown. Ten percent of the garrison caught the disease, but only six people died, thanks in part to a rigorous quarantine established by the post commander, Colonel C. H. Smith. Smith had been ordered to attend a court-martial in Kentucky but sent an urgent request to the War Department seeking permission to remain at Fort Brown and share the peril of the fever with his regiment. His actions earned him lasting respect throughout the army. Smith moved the bulk of his command and families into a clean camp fourteen miles downriver, where they remained until fall. William C. Gorgas, the assistant surgeon at Fort Brown, caught the fever but recovered. Gorgas went on to do his famous pioneering work in eradicating the disease in Cuba and Panama. The threat of yellow fever during the summer months led the War Department to wait until the late fall before issuing orders for soldiers to transfer into the region from other areas. The Leefes arrived at the ideal time, in January, after the onset of the short winter season. "Report of Brigadier General C. C. Augur, 2 Oct. 1882," *House Exec. Doc.*, 47th Cong., 2d sess., no. 1, pt. 2, serial 2091, 105; Theo. F. Rodenbough and William L. Haskin, *The Army of the United States* (*New York: Maynard, Merrill, & Co.*, 1896), 664; Edgar W. Howe, *The History of the Class of 'Seventy-Eight at the U.S. Military Academy* (New York: Homer Lee Bank Note Co., 1881), 84, 87.

4. This warning from the signal officer about the approaching norther is an interesting confirmation of the efficiency of the fledgling weather early-warning system established by the Signal Corps of the U.S. Army. After the American Civil War the army began an extensive project to install a military telegraph system linking the frontier posts. In concert with this system Congress authorized in 1870 for certain telegraph stations to have army operators trained in weather observation and equipment in order to furnish data to centralized collection points. The meteorological observation system provided public warn-

ing of approaching storms and dangerous weather changes to farmers and sailors, resulting in an enormous benefit to the public good and nearly universal praise from citizens. By 1879 the system was very sophisticated, with 133 stations making observations and reports. This system is generally the progenitor of the National Weather Service of today. "Report of the Chief Signal Officer, 15 Nov. 1879," *House Exec. Doc.*, 46th Cong., 2d sess., no. 1, pt. 2, vol. 4, serial 1908, 10.

5. The Leefes arrived at Fort Ringgold on 24 January 1883. Lieutenant Leefe joined his new command, Company I, Nineteenth Infantry. Captain E. H. Liscum commanded the company and the second lieutenant was E. D. Smith. Major R. H. Offley commanded the post, which consisted of Company B, Eighth Cavalry, 2 officers and 47 men, and Companies A, H, and I of the Nineteenth Infantry, 8 officers and 100 men. The total garrison was 13 officers and 150 enlisted men, a sizable post for the Texas frontier. The Nineteenth Infantry had transferred to Texas in 1881 from the Department of the Missouri. By the period 1882 to 1883 the Indian Wars were over in Texas, and there were few reports of hostile raids by the tribes. However, the dangerous border area was fraught with peril from the bands of Mexican and Texan outlaw bands that infested the region on both sides of the Rio Grande. Post Returns, Fort Ringgold, Texas, January 1875–December 1884, microfilm no. M617, roll 1021, and January 1883–June 1886, microfilm no. M617, roll 1022, in Returns from United States Military Posts 1800–1916, Records of the United States Army Adjutant General's Office, 1780–1917, Record Group (RG) 94 (hereafter cited as Post Returns, Fort Ringgold); "Report of Brigadier General C. C. Augur, 2 Oct. 1882," 106.

6. In this letter by Mary Leefe Laurence's grandmother Pinckney the "Jack" she refers to is the family name for Lieutenant John G. Leefe. Mary is his wife, the mother of Mary Leefe Laurence.

7. During this period both Leefe and Smith were in Company I. Leefe was promoted to captain in October 1886 and took command of Company K and later Company B. Edmund D. Smith, from Connecticut, graduated from West Point in 1879 and served in the Nineteenth Infantry until, as a captain, he died of wounds near Fort Amia, Philippines, on 5 February 1900. Smith was an assistant professor at the United States Military Academy from 1891 to 1895. Regimental

Returns, Nineteenth Infantry, January 1880–December 1888, microfilm no. M665, roll 205, July 1886, in Returns from Regular Army Infantry Regiments, June 1821–December 1916, Adjutant General's Records, NARS (hereafter cited as Regimental Returns, Nineteenth Infantry); Heitman, *Historical Register,* 1: 896; *Register of Graduates,* 269.

8. Rio Grande City, 120 miles from the mouth of the river, was the upper terminal of river navigation. Shallow-draft steamers had been going up the river since the Mexican War. Most of the supplies moved by water to the lower river forts in the post–Civil War era were contracted to the firm of C. A. Witney & Company of New Orleans or to Kenedy and King. Mifflin Kenedy and Richard King built huge Texas ranching empires from their government freight business. "Report of the Quartermaster General, 10 Oct. 1879," *House Exec. Doc.,* 46th Cong., 2d sess., no. 1, pt. 2, vol. 2, serial 1903, 343.

9. Immigrating to Rio Grande City from Monterrey, Mexico, after the American Civil War, local merchant George Decker and his family were prominent in the town during the period 1865 to 1900. Telephone interview with Mr. George Edgerton, Starr County Historical Society, Rio Grande City, Texas, 18 September 1994.

10. Leefe left the post in September 1885 and returned in February 1886. The regimental commander put him on temporary duty as a recruiter at Davids Island, New York, to give him time to deal with the illness of Mrs. Pinckney. When he returned to Fort Ringgold in February 1886 he was put on special duty as the post quartermaster until he left the post in June 1886. Post Returns, Fort Ringgold, November 1885, February, May, June 1886.

11. Lieutenant Harris L. "Polly" Roberts, from Washington DC, graduated from West Point in the class of 1880 and served in the Nineteenth Infantry for most of his long career, including the Puerto Rico Expedition and the Philippine Insurrection. He was a colonel when he died in Chicago on 27 December 1918. Heitman, *Historical Register,* 1: 835; *Register of Graduates,* 271.

12. There is no documentary evidence that either Major General O. O. Howard or any of his sons were at Fort Ringgold. At this time Howard was the commander of the Division of the Pacific and would have had no authority or reason to be inspecting in Texas. His son, Guy, was a Twelfth Infantry officer during this period, but not his

aide and not in Texas. Another son, John, was an officer in the Nineteenth Infantry, but not until 1891. The story related by Mary Leefe Laurence could have its origins in two later inspection trips by O. O. Howard, both of which involved her father or other officers of the Nineteenth Infantry. While the Leefes were at Mount Vernon Barracks, Alabama, in 1889 General Howard made an inspection there as part of his efforts to help the Apache Indian prisoners. In this case he had no sons with him. However, in 1898 it is probable that his sons John and Guy were with him at Mobile, Alabama, when he inspected the camp of the regiments preparing to depart for the Spanish-American War. It is possible that the episode described by Mary Leefe Laurence occurred at this 1898 inspection. Oliver Otis Howard, *Autobiography of Oliver Otis Howard, Major General United States Army*, 2 vols. (New York: Baker & Taylor Company, 1907), 2: 510, 545, 550, 566.

13. Company laundresses of the nineteenth-century army were often the wives of noncommissioned officers; thus the name "Laundress Row" for married enlisted quarters. The hiring of four laundresses per company for purposes of sanitation began in the 1780s and was formalized in the regulations of 1802. The women were paid a set fee per soldier for cleaning clothes and were issued a ration per day as well as a set of quarters. The official hiring of laundresses ceased with congressional legislation of 1876, but the law allowed those in place to continue to work. In 1883 army regulations halted the practice of issuing rations to the laundresses. Miller J. Stewart, "Army Laundresses: Ladies of 'Soap Suds Row,' " *Nebraska History* 61 (winter 1980): 421–36; Stallard, *Glittering Misery*, 53–75; Coffman, *The Old Army*, 24–25, 112–15, 308.

14. Captain James M. Ropes of the Eighth Cavalry Regiment at Fort Ringgold was from New York. Joining the Second Cavalry as a lieutenant at the start of the Civil War, he finished the conflict a brevet major. Reappointed as a second lieutenant in 1867, Ropes served several decades in the Eighth Cavalry, retiring as a captain in 1891. He died 4 June 1897. Heitman, *Historical Register*, 1: 845.

15. Riding a horse sidesaddle or astride was a gender issue. The "proper" or traditional method for females was the sidesaddle. Some women on the frontier resisted this societal limitation and in defiance

of the restrictions of propriety rode horses astride as men did. It is interesting to note that although Mary Leefe Laurence could be considered proper in every respect she is pointed in her disregard of convention in this case, apparently with the blessing of her mother. Riley, *The Female Frontier*, 2, 4.

16. Among the papers of a sergeant from Company D, Nineteenth Infantry, stationed at Fort Ringgold with the Leefes during this period is a flyer outlining the program of one of these post entertainment events. At 9:30 PM on the night of 20 October 1886 the Frontier Glee Club, composed of soldiers of the regiment, presented a series of minstrel selections with songs such as "Old Folks Are Gone." This was followed by a magic lantern exhibition showing slides of places of interest in cities of the world. Following this three skits were presented by members of the garrison. The post band furnished the music for the program. Admission was fifty cents for reserve seats or twenty-five cents for general admission. "Ambrose H. Davidson File," Don Rickey Jr. Collection, U.S. Army Military History Institute, Carlisle Barracks, Pennsylvania.

17. As the lieutenant colonel of the Second Cavalry Robert E. Lee had a lengthy stay at Ringgold Barracks in 1856 while assigned there to conduct several courts-martial. Phil Sheridan had been on the Rio Grande at Fort Duncan in 1854 as a second lieutenant in the First Infantry. As she will later relate, Mary Leefe Laurence met him at Fort Clark while Sheridan was on an inspection trip as commanding general of the army. Douglas Southall Freeman, *R. E. Lee: A Biography*, 4 vols. (New York: Charles Scribner's Sons, 1936), 1: 368–69; Sheridan, *Personal Memoirs*, 1: 15–34.

18. In 1882, 9 of the 11 Texas posts had schools. In attendance were 125 soldiers, 29 officers' children, 129 enlisted men's children, and 58 children of civilians. In the army as a whole there were 105 posts with schools and 32 without. The total attendance for all post schools was 1,586 soldiers, 370 officers' children, 987 enlisted men's children, and 417 children of civilians. The chaplain in charge of army education noted that the major problem of all of the schools was the lack of competent teachers, in that a "full one-half are not at all fitted by education and experience for the work." A second major difficulty was that post funds were usually insufficient to provide the required

numbers of books and lamp lights. "Report of the General of the Army, 14 Nov. 1882" and "Report of Chaplain George C. Mullins, Chaplain, Twenty-Fifth Infantry, in Charge of Education in the Army, 20 Oct. 1882," *House Exec. Doc.*, 47th Cong., 2d sess., no. 1, pt. 2, serial 2091, 26, 190–92.

19. Mary Leefe Laurence is referring to fifteenth-century Florentine artists that idealized the Madonna and child; Raphael (1483–1520), Fra Angelico (1387–1455), and Fra Filippo Lippi (1406–1469).

20. The Leefes departed Fort Ringgold on 1 June 1886 en route to Fort Duncan, Texas. Post Returns, Fort Ringgold, June 1886.

7. Fort Duncan, Texas, 1886

1. In 1848, during the Mexican War, the Texas Mounted Volunteer Regiment established Camp Eagle Pass near an important crossing point where the Rio Escondido empties into the Rio Grande. Paso del Aguila, or Pass of the Eagle, was a ford across the nearby Rio Escondido in Mexico on the Guerrero–Monclova Viejo military road. Shortly afterward James Campbell established a trading station in the vicinity known as Campbell's Store that became the origin of civilian settlement at the site. At the war's end the U.S. Army established a frontier fort three miles north of the old outpost. Founded by Captain Sidney Burbank in 1849 along a main route of international trade, Fort Duncan served to guard the Rio Grande line until the outbreak of the Civil War. Reoccupied in 1868, the post became one of the ten forts in Texas the government attempted to purchase. When the contract could not be arranged the post was abandoned in 1883. The fort was used off and on as a patrolling camp for the next decade. The federal government finally succeeded in buying the site in 1894. Garrisoned during the border troubles and the Mexican Revolution, the site was used intermittently until 1920. The city of Eagle Pass purchased the fort from the government in 1938. Fort Duncan suffered from a shortage of water, and the post buildings left much to be desired as the army did little in the way of permanent construction. Post Returns, Fort Duncan, Texas, March 1868–August 1883, microfilm no. M617, roll 336, in Returns from United States Military Posts 1800–1916, Records of the United States Army Adjutant General's Office, 1780–1917, Record Group (RG) 94; William T. Field, "Fort Duncan

and Old Eagle Pass," *Texas Military History* 6 (summer 1967): 160–71; Frazer, *Forts of the West,* 148–49.

2. The regimental commander transferred Lieutenant Leefe to Fort Duncan, Texas, to be the senior lieutenant of Company K and the quartermaster at the site. Fort Duncan was not active at that time as a Texas federal fort but instead was treated as a temporary camp, called Camp at Eagle Pass. In 1886 the departmental commander, Brigadier General David S. Stanley, ordered a Nineteenth Infantry company and a Third Cavalry troop to occupy the site because of robberies occurring in the vicinity of Eagle Pass. Leefe's Company K, Nineteenth Infantry, commanded by Captain George Towle, had two officers and forty-four men. The Leefes arrived at Fort Duncan 12 June 1886. Regimental Returns, Nineteenth Infantry, June, July 1886; "Report of Brigadier General D. S. Stanley, Headquarters, Department of Texas, 4 Sept. 1886," *House Exec. Doc.,* 49th Cong., 2d sess., no. 1, pt. 2, serial 2461, 125.

3. The Leefes and Company K transferred to Fort Clark, Texas, 14 July 1886 via Special Orders No. 69, Headquarters, Department of Texas. Regimental Returns, Nineteenth Infantry, July 1886.

8. Fort Clark, Texas, 1886–1889

1. The train tracks of the Galveston, Harrisburg & San Antonio Railroad division of the Southern Pacific ended at Spofford Junction. A daily stage ran from there ten miles north to Fort Clark. The Leefes arrived at Fort Clark on 16 July 1886. "Report of the Lieutenant General of the Army, 10 Oct. 1886," *House Exec. Doc.,* 49th Cong., 2d sess., no. 1, pt. 2, serial 2461, 98; Post Returns, Fort Clark, Texas, July 1886–December 1892, microfilm no. M617, roll 215, in Returns from United States Military Posts 1800–1916, Records of the United States Army Adjutant General's Office, 1780–1917, Record Group (RG) 94 (hereafter cited as Post Returns, Fort Clark).

2. Throughout its long life Fort Clark had a fairly large garrison and, of all the remote posts in Texas, enjoyed a universal reputation for a pleasant setting and a gay social life. At the time of the Leefes' arrival in July 1886 Colonel Charles H. Smith, Nineteenth Infantry, commanded Fort Clark. The garrison contained 22 officers and 490 enlisted men, a total of 6 infantry companies, 6 cavalry troops, and a

detachment of 19 Seminole Indian scouts. From the Nineteenth Infantry were Headquarters and Companies A, B, C, E, H, and K from the Third Cavalry, Troops G and E, and from the Eighth Cavalry, Troops F, G, H, and L. For much of the antebellum and post–Civil War years Fort Clark was one of the key posts on the Texas frontier. Established on Las Moras Creek in 1852 by the First Infantry Regiment, the post served as a guard to the border and the San Antonio–El Paso military road. Briefly used by Confederate Texas troops in the Civil War, Fort Clark was reoccupied by the Fourth Cavalry in 1866. It was the base of Colonel Ranald S. Mackenzie and his Fourth Cavalry in many operations against the Lipan, Comanche, and Kickapoo in the Indian Wars of the 1870s. The post remained a cavalry and infantry training center until it closed in 1946. Leefe took command of Company K, Nineteenth Infantry, in August 1886, just after his arrival at Fort Clark. His infantry company was very typical of the period. Leefe had one additional officer, Second Lieutenant Woodbridge Geary. His total authorized strength was three officers and forty-eight enlisted men, yet Leefe had but one and thirty, while the companies in the Nineteenth averaged two officers and forty-two men. His complement of enlisted men was a first sergeant, three sergeants, three corporals, one musician, and twenty-two privates. Of the twenty-two privates twelve were on extra duty at the quartermaster's yard, three were sick, two were on detached service, and one was on leave, giving him a total effective rifle strength of twelve men, consisting of four privates and eight noncommissioned officers. Leefe therefore had but 25 percent of his authorized strength for daily operations. In the previous two months the company had received only two recruits, had one man discharged for disability, lost one to transfer, and, remarkably, had no desertions. The great strength of his company was in the long service and experience of his soldiers. His first sergeant had fifteen years of service, the corporals had at least five years, eleven of his privates had over five years in uniform, and one private, Patrick Dillon, had fifteen years in the army. Frederick V. Abbot, *History of the Class of 'Seventy-Nine at the U.S. Military Academy* (New York: G. P. Putnam's Sons, Knickerbocker Press, 1884), 128; Mrs. Orsemus Bronson Boyd, *Cavalry Life in Tent and Field* (New York: J. S. Tait, 1894; reprint, with an introduction by Darlis A. Miller, Lincoln: University of Nebraska

Press, 1982), 277, 279; Lydia Spencer Lane, *I Married a Soldier; Or, Old Days in the Old Army* (Philadelphia: Lippincott, 1893; reprint, Albuquerque: University of New Mexico Press, 1988), 37; Post Returns, Fort Clark, July 1886; Regimental Returns, Nineteenth Infantry, July 1886; National Park Service, *Soldier and Brave*, 319–20; Frazer, *Forts of the West*, 146; Caleb Pirtle III and Michael F. Cusack, *Fort Clark: The Lonely Sentinel* (Austin: Eakin Press, 1985); Army Muster Rolls, Nineteenth Infantry Regiment, Box 572, Company K, 31 December 1866 to 31 August 1902, National Archives and Records Service, Washington DC; Regimental Returns, Nineteenth Infantry, August 1886.

3. At Fort Clark on one of his many inspection tours Lieutenant General Philip H. Sheridan was at that time the commanding general of the army, a post he had held since the retirement of William T. Sherman in 1884. The famous Civil War incident of "Sheridan's Ride" occurred at the Battle of Cedar Creek at the end of Sheridan's Shenandoah Valley campaign during October 1864. With Sheridan away at a conference, Confederate Lieutenant General Jubal Early surprised Sheridan's army and put part of it to flight. Sheridan arrived on the scene at a gallop; riding through his retreating and panicked columns, he inspired his men to return to battle and win the day. The exaggeration of the legend caused some bitterness in the army from members of G. W. Getty's Second Division of VI Corps who did not panic but instead fought it out with Early until Sheridan could organize the remainder of his army. Some historians also credit VIII Corps commander George Crook and Third Cavalry Division commander George A. Custer with key roles in saving Sheridan's command that day. During the battle John G. Leefe was a captain and adjutant of the First Division of William H. Emory's XIX Corps. Hutton, *Phil Sheridan and His Army*, 14, 386; George Crook, *General George Crook: His Autobiography*, ed. Martin F. Schmitt (Norman: University of Oklahoma Press, 1960), 98, 127, 141; Gregory J. W. Urwin, *Custer Victorious: The Civil War Battles of George Armstrong Custer* (Lincoln: University of Nebraska Press, 1983), 206–19; Jeffery D. Wert, *From Winchester to Cedar Creek: The Shenandoah Campaign of 1864* (Carlisle PA: South Mountain Press, 1987).

4. The satellite village to Fort Clark, the rough-and-tumble town

of Brackettville had, in 1887, fifteen saloons and fifty professional gamblers. It had been known in army circles as a wild town since the antebellum era. Florence Fenley, *Oldtimers: Frontier Days in Uvalde Section of South West Texas* (Uvalde TX: Hornby Press, 1939; reprint, Austin TX: State House Press, 1991), 185; Boyd, *Cavalry Life in Tent and Field*, 256.

5. Post schools had improved little in the decade of the 1880s. In the final report on education in the army for the decade the adjutant general reported that there were in Texas 10 post schools with an attendance of 128 enlisted men, 5 children of officers, 54 children of enlisted men, and 4 children of civilians. Six of the schools lacked books, all schools needed furniture, and there was a general shortage of competent teachers. "Report of the Adjutant General, 7 Oct. 1890," *House Exec. Doc.,* 51st Cong., 2d sess., no. 1, pt. 2, serial 2831, 62.

6. A small band of Seminole Negro-Indian scouts served in the U.S. Army on the Rio Grande frontier in the decade of the 1870s. Patrolling out of Fort Duncan or out of Fort Clark under the command of Lieutenant John L. Bullis, they proved to be effective fighters and a crucial instrument of command intelligence on the frontier. Their general ancestry was a mixture of southern Seminole or Creek Indian and Negro runaway slaves. The Seminoles were removed from Florida and Alabama to Indian Territory during the 1830s and 1840s. Dissatisfied with conditions in Indian Territory, several hundred moved to Mexico in 1849 and 1850. Eventually some of the Seminoles became army scouts in 1870 and about two hundred belonging to various bands settled in the vicinity of Fort Duncan at Eagle Pass and Fort Clark at Brackettville. By 1876 the scouts had been consolidated at Fort Clark, and there they served for many years. The final order disbanding the scouts came in 1914, but some of their descendants currently remain in the region. Kenneth Wiggins Porter, "The Seminole Negro-Indian Scouts, 1870–1881," *Southwestern Historical Quarterly* 55 (January 1952): 358–77.

7. Orders No. 11, 12 January 1889, Fort Clark, Texas, by order of Colonel A. G. Brackett, Third Cavalry. Laurence manuscript, 141.

8. Colonel Charles H. Smith began his career as a volunteer captain in the First Maine Cavalry at the beginning of the Civil War, fought in most of the major cavalry actions of the Eastern Theater,

earned the Medal of Honor at St. Mary's Church, and finished the war as a brevet major general. In the reorganization after the war Smith was the colonel of the Twenty-Eighth Infantry Regiment before transferring to the Nineteenth Infantry in 1869. He retired in 1891 and died in 1902. Heitman, *Historical Register,* 1: 895.

9. The Third Cavalry served in Arizona generally from 1882 to 1885, when it moved to Texas. The only Third Cavalry company grade officer named "George" present at Fort Clark in 1889, at the time of this incident, was Captain George F. Chase, commanding Troop M. The only available decoration of the period was the Indian War Medal of Honor. Army records do not document a white recipient with the last initial *T* for actions against the Apache in Arizona, nor do any of the award narratives match the action described. It is possible that T—— was promoted or mentioned in dispatches, a more common form of reward than a decoration during this period. The general history of the Third Cavalry does not include a battle that matches the combat actions described in the passage, particularly with such severe losses of soldiers. Post Returns, Fort Clark, April 1889; U.S. Army Public Information Division, *The Medal of Honor of the United States Army* (Washington DC: Government Printing Office, 1948), 206–38; Ralph C. Deibert, *A History of the Third United States Cavalry* (Harrisburg PA: Telegraph Press, 1933), 30–32.

10. Captain Leefe gained command of Company B in April 1889. The company and the Leefes departed Fort Clark for Mount Vernon Barracks, Alabama, on 12 May 1889. Post Returns, Fort Clark, April, May 1889.

9. Mount Vernon Barracks, Alabama, 1889–1890

1. In 1890 most of the Nineteenth Infantry went from Texas to the Division of the Atlantic and the Great Lakes region. The Leefes, with Companies B and C, Nineteenth Infantry, arrived by train at Mount Vernon Barracks, Alabama, on 15 May 1889, replacing four batteries of the Second Artillery Regiment as post garrison. Captain Charles Witherell, the commander of Company C, commanded the post until the October arrival of Major William L. Kellogg, Nineteenth Infantry. The post garrison consisted of 6 officers and 93 enlisted men who were to guard the 380 Chiricahua and Warm Springs Apache

prisoners of war. Founded as an arsenal in 1829 and abandoned in 1894, Mount Vernon Barracks was not a healthy post and was consistently on the surgeon-general's "worst twenty" list for disease and alcoholism. In the period 1889 to 1891 fewer than half the soldiers at the post were healthy enough to perform daily duties, a "constantly noneffective" rate of 64.17 percent, the second highest in the army and compared to 28.47 percent for the army average. However, during the first year that the Nineteenth Infantry replaced the Second Artillery Regiment at the post the alcoholism admission rate dropped from 137 per 1,000 in 1889 to 45 in 1890 to 0 in 1891. Upon arrival at Mount Vernon Barracks, Leefe's Company B had for duty three officers, eight noncommissioned officers, two musicians, two artificers, and nineteen privates, for a total strength of thirty-four, or about 66 percent of the authorized strength. Not present for duty were fourteen men; of these one was sick, one was on detached service, and twelve were on extra duty. In the previous two months Leefe had received two recruits, had one reenlistment, and had no desertions. The low desertion rate is a good indicator of strong unit discipline and effective leadership. All of the soldiers in the company were under five-year enlistments. Post Returns, Mount Vernon Barracks, Alabama, January 1879–December 1894, microfilm no. M617, roll 612, in Returns from United States Military Posts 1800–1916, Records of the United States Army Adjutant General's Office, 1780–1917, Record Group (RG) 94 (hereafter cited as Post Returns, Mount Vernon Barracks); Rodenbough and Haskin, *The Army of the United States*, 664; "Report of the Surgeon-General of the Army, 22 Sept. 1891," *House Exec. Doc.*, 52d Cong., 1st sess., no. 1, pt. 2, vol. 1, serial 2921, 633, 646–67; Army Muster Rolls, Nineteenth Infantry Regiment, Box 557, Company B, 31 October 1861 to 31 October 1897, National Archives and Records Service, Washington DC.

2. In 1886 five hundred Apache prisoners from the southwestern Apache wars were sent into captivity from Arizona to Fort Marion, Florida. The high death rate among the Chiricahua and Warm Springs Apache families spurred various humanitarian organizations and Generals George Crook and O. O. Howard to lobby to move the Indians to the 2,100-acre reserve at Mount Vernon Barracks, Alabama. A detail of 1 officer and 8 soldiers of the Second Artillery Regiment escorted

355 Apache prisoners to Mount Vernon Barracks, arriving by train on 28 April 1887. The group consisted of 69 men, 167 women, and 119 children. In 1888 28 Apache leaders, including Naiche, or "Nachez," and Geronimo, were brought to Mount Vernon Barracks from their prison at Fort Pickens, Florida. In May 1889, when the Leefes arrived, there remained but 380 of the prisoners; 76 men, 168 women, 7 boys over twelve years old, 66 boys under twelve, 4 girls over twelve, 59 girls under twelve years old. The death toll among the Apache children and women was alarming. In June, the month after the Leefes arrived, five died, in July two died, one in August, five in September, and four in October. During this same period four Indian children were born. The "coughing sickness," tuberculosis, was a major threat and took the life of Geronimo's son Chapo as well as Lozen, the sister of Chief Victorio. The death rate of the Apache prisoners in the southern camps was about 24 percent. For several years the Indians were living in crude huts without chimnies that originally were intended to be temporary quarters, but Congress failed to appropriate funds for further construction. Eventually sturdy log cabins were constructed, but the damp, swampy terrain of the reserve remained a breeding ground for disease. Indians who worked for the post were paid thirty-five cents a day, and some, in 1891, enlisted in an Apache infantry company formed by the army as Company I, Twelfth Infantry. Eventually, in 1894, Congress passed legislation moving the Apache to Fort Sill, Indian Territory, and in 1914 some returned to New Mexico, released after twenty-eight years as prisoners of war. "Report of Major General Howard, Headquarters, Division of the Atlantic, 30 Sept. 1890," *House Exec. Doc.*, 51st Cong., 2d sess., no. 1, pt. 2, serial 2831, 152; Post Returns, Mount Vernon Barracks, April 1887, May–October 1889; National Park Service, *Soldier and Brave*, 120; Eve Ball, Nora Henn, and Lynda A. Sanchez, *Indeh: An Apache Odyssey* (Norman: University of Oklahoma Press, 1988), 154–55, 158–59; C. L. Sonnichsen, *The Mescalero Apaches* (Norman: University of Oklahoma Press, 1973), 220–29; Frank C. Lockwood, *The Apache Indians* (New York: Macmillan Company, 1938), 307–30; Crook, *General George Crook*, 289–300; Donald E. Worcester, *The Apaches: Eagles of the Southwest* (Norman: University of Oklahoma Press, 1979), 308–24.

3. The Indians made bows, arrows, and various articles of Apache

craftsmanship and were allowed to sell them at the train station or in town to tourists. Many of the craftsmen gave their wares to Geronimo; he would sell them to tourists, who believed they were made by his own hands. Ball, *Indeh*, 153.

4. In 1824 Congress authorized the construction of Mount Vernon Arsenal, twenty-eight miles north of Mobile on the west side of the Mobile River. Construction of the post was completed in 1828 and the arsenal was established the following year, primarily for the assembly of rifles whose parts were manufactured elsewhere. Taken over by the Confederates, the arsenal served the southern states during the Civil War. The post was reoccupied by the federal government after the war. The army changed the name and made the site a troop post in 1873. Mount Vernon Barracks, as it came to be called, was abandoned in December 1894 and given to the state of Alabama. Roberts, *Encyclopedia of Historic Forts*, 12.

5. Here Mary Leefe Laurence reflects the white view that Apache political organization was monolithic like that of the whites. The Apache had little overall tribal organization but were a loose confederation of small bands, with the leader of the band, or "chief," chosen or elected by the followers. When in a group situation such as Mount Vernon Barracks the various band chiefs had influence but not control, particularly over other bands within the group. The military officers at Mount Vernon had given Geronimo real power by making him the tribal judge. One of the young Apache there at the time recalled that Geronimo was harder on the Apaches than were army officers. In the mountains of Mexico the legendary Juh was the primary leader but did not survive to surrender to captivity. Geronimo began as a relatively minor leader but because he was one of the final holdouts gained great stature. More influential than Geronimo was Naiche, sometimes referred to as "Nachez," the second son of Cochise and the leader of the Warm Springs band of the reservation Chiricahua. Nana, Victorio's successor, was the elder statesman of the Chiricahua. The intelligent and able Chihuahua of the Warm Springs Chihenne led a band of raiders but did not join the final breakout of Geronimo in 1886. Geronimo died in 1909, Naiche lived until 1921. Ball, *Indeh*, 43–45, 154; Utley, *Frontier Regulars*, 367, 379, 385, 395; Sonnichsen, *The Mescalero Apaches*, 229; Lockwood, *The Apache Indians*, 324; Dan L.

Thrapp, *The Conquest of Apacheria* (Norman: University of Oklahoma Press, 1967), 177, 234–36, 290.

6. Loco, a Chiricahua, was part of the original breakout of the San Carlos Reservation with the Mimbres Apaches under Chief Victorio in 1877. Loco had lost an eye to a grizzly bear as a young man and was one of the most respected of all the war leaders. Although he counseled that there was no future in a war with the white men, Loco participated in many skirmishes and was wounded before he surrendered to Crook in 1883. Thrapp, *The Conquest of Apacheria*, 177, 234–35, 290; Utley, *Frontier Regulars*, 385–86.

7. One of the Apache children, Eugene Chihuahua, the son of Chief Chihuahua, recalled that Geronimo acted as a very strict disciplinarian for all the Indian children at Mount Vernon Barracks. Ball, *Indeh*, 154.

8. Miss Sophie Shepard, rather than "Shepherd," ran the missionary school for the Indian children on funds from a ladies charitable group from Boston. A dozen of the Apache children, suffering from tuberculosis, had been sent to Mount Vernon Barracks from the Indian School at Carlisle, Pennsylvania. "Report of Major General Howard, Headquarters, Division of the Atlantic, 30 Sept. 1890," *House Exec. Doc.*, 51st Cong., 2d sess., no. 1, pt. 2, serial 2831, 152; Worcester, *The Apaches*, 316.

9. Captain Leefe was ordered to inspect the troops and camp of the First Regiment, Alabama State Troops, in June 1889. At this time the Alabama State Troops consisted of three white regiments and two companies of black troops. As part of the military reform movement of the 1880s regular army officers such as Leefe were periodically assigned to help train and inspect various state volunteer militia organizations. Not until the midnineties would these state militia units become known universally as the National Guard, and even then some southern states, such as Texas and Georgia, retained the old name "Volunteers." In his inspection Captain Leefe cast the critical eye of a seasoned regular upon the 301 militiamen of the First Alabama Regiment, reporting them lacking marksmanship, drill, and camp hygiene and in want of a dependable supply system. However, he tempered his remarks by noting their "creditable" appearance, their notable "absence of intoxication," and the fact that their shortcomings were due

to lack of opportunity to practice their skills as soldiers. Leefe found a social, rather than military, atmosphere about the camp, in general "a good-natured frolic," which included a visit from the state governor and "throngs of visitors until late at night." National Archives and Records Service, Records of the United States Army Adjutant General's Office, 1780–1917, Record Group (RG) 94, Appointment, Commission, and Personal Branch, Documents Files, Box 51, 1871, 3303–394, ACP 3393 Service File, John George Leefe; Special Orders No. 22, Headquarters of the Army, 27 May 1889; "Report of the Inspector-General of the Army, 1 Oct. 1890," *House Exec. Doc.*, 51st Cong., 2d sess., no. 1, pt. 2, serial 2831, 293; Graham A. Cosmas, *An Army for Empire: The United States Army in the Spanish-American War* (Columbia: University of Missouri Press, 1971; 2d ed., Shippensburg PA: White Mane Publishing Company, 1994), 6–7, 44–46. For Leefe's inspection report, see "Report of the Adjutant General of the Army, 10 Oct. 1889," *House Exec. Doc.*, 51st Cong., 1st sess., no. 1, pt. 2, serial 2715, 258–61.

10. Jefferson Davis was an 1828 graduate of the United States Military Academy at West Point, a Mexican War regimental commander, a U.S. senator, the U.S. secretary of war from 1853 to 1857, and the president of the Confederate States of America. He died in New Orleans on 6 December 1889 and was buried in New Orleans. Later the body was moved to Richmond, Virginia. Bell, *Secretaries of War,* 64.

11. For excellent studies of the creation and experience of the black infantry and cavalry regiments, see William H. Leckie, *The Buffalo Soldiers: A Narrative of the Negro Cavalry in the West* (Norman: University of Oklahoma Press, 1967) and Arlen Fowler, *Black Infantry in the West, 1869–1891* (Westport CT: Greenwood Publishing, 1971).

12. When he graduated from West Point in 1915 Dwight D. Eisenhower served as a lieutenant at Fort Sam Houston, Texas, in the Nineteenth Infantry Regiment from 1915 to 1916. The original quote from Eisenhower as paraphrased by Mary Leefe Laurence came at a press conference in Paris and was recorded in the *New York Times* on 16 June 1945. When asked about the performance of black soldiers in the European Theater of Operations, Ike replied, "I do not differentiate among soldiers. I do not say white soldiers or negro soldiers, and

I do not say American or British soldiers. To my mind I have had a task in this war that makes me look upon soldiers as soldiers." Notes from Eisenhower's service record and quote from telephone interview, Mr. Dwight Strandberg, Staff Archivist, Dwight D. Eisenhower Library, Abilene, Kansas, 17 October 1994; Stephen E. Ambrose, *Eisenhower: Soldier, General of the Army, President Elect, 1890–1952* (New York: Simon and Schuster, 1983), 55–57.

13. Two companies of the Fifteenth Infantry arrived 30 April 1890 from Fort Randall, Dakota Territory, to replace the Nineteenth Infantry companies at Mount Vernon Barracks. The Leefes and the infantry companies departed by train on 5 May 1890. Post Returns, Mount Vernon Barracks, May 1890.

10. Fort Brady, Michigan, 1890–1896

1. The Leefes and Company B, Nineteenth Infantry, arrived at Fort Brady, Michigan, on 8 May 1890 to replace two companies of the Twenty-third Infantry who were sent to Texas. Company E, Nineteenth Infantry, arrived from Texas on 13 May 1890, giving the post a total strength of five officers and seventy-nine enlisted men. The commander of Company E, Captain Richard Vance, served as garrison commander. In the period June to December 1892 Leefe was the garrison commander until the arrival of Lieutenant Colonel Charles A. Wikoff. The addition of another rifle company at that time gave the garrison a strength of 7 officers and 157 enlisted men. In October 1894 Fort Brady became a four-company post with the addition of Company C, Nineteenth Infantry. The total garrison strength was 8 officers and 226 enlisted men. Post Returns, Fort Brady, Michigan, May 1890–September 1896, microfilm no. M617, roll 135, in Returns from United States Military Posts 1800–1916, Records of the United States Army Adjutant General's Office, 1780–1917, Record Group (RG) 94 (hereafter cited as Post Returns, Fort Brady).

2. On the site of a 1751 French outpost called Fort Repentigny, Fort Brady was established in 1822 by Colonel Hugh Brady and five companies of the Second Infantry. An important post on the upper frontier line, Fort Brady was located on the south bank of the Sault Sainte Marie River, fifteen miles from Lake Superior. The bulk of the garrison was withdrawn and sent to Fort Snelling, Minnesota, in 1857,

but the post was reoccupied in 1866 by the Fourth Infantry Regiment. In 1892, as Mary Leefe Laurence recalled, a new post, also called Fort Brady, was located closer to the town of Sault Sainte Marie. This post was finally abandoned by the government in October 1945. Roberts, *Encyclopedia of Historic Forts*, 415–16.

3. Episcopalian bishop Peter Trimble Rowe, born in Canada in 1856, was an 1880 graduate of Trinity College, Toronto. Rowe did missionary work in Canada and was the first missionary bishop of the Alaskan Territory from 1895 to 1943. *Notable Names in American History*, 508, 519; Albert Nelson Marquis, ed., *Who's Who in America, 1936–1937*, vol. 19 (Chicago: A. N. Marquis Company, 1936), 2111.

4. Lieutenant Frank McIntyre, born in Alabama, graduated from the United States Military Academy in the class of 1886, joining the Nineteenth Infantry until his return to West Point to teach math in 1890. Rejoining his regiment in 1894, McIntyre served in the Philippine Insurrection until transferred to the War Department's Bureau of Insular Affairs, where he remained until 1929, retiring as a major general. On 16 February 1944 in Florida, McIntyre died at the age of seventy-nine. Heitman, *Historical Register*, 1: 669; *Register of Graduates*, 277.

5. Lieutenant Arthur Foster, United States Military Academy, class of 1887 was born in Illinois and served in the Nineteenth Infantry with the Leefes at Mount Vernon Barracks, Alabama, and at Fort Brady, and with Captain Leefe in Puerto Rico and the Philippine Insurrection. He died as a major in the Philippine Scouts in Manila, 18 December 1909, at the age of forty-six. Heitman, *Historical Register*, 1: 431; *Register of Graduates*, 280; Cullum, *Biographical Register*, 4: 453.

6. The "Fighting McCooks of Ohio," as they were known, had seventeen men of the family serving the Union in the Civil War, six of which were volunteer general officers. Brothers Robert L., Daniel, and Alexander M. were volunteer generals, the first two being killed. Their cousins Edward M. and Anson G. were also generals, while twelve others, including their father, served as army or navy officers or in the ranks. Born in 1849, Alexander McCook "Robbie" Guard was a forty-five-year-old first lieutenant when Mary Leefe Laurence knew him at Fort Brady. This advanced age was not uncommon in the

old army. Guard graduated in the class of 1871 at West Point and served on the frontier and in the Philippine Insurrection before he retired as a disabled major in 1899. He died in Michigan on 19 July 1905. Mark Mayo Boatner III, *The Civil War Dictionary* (New York: David McKay Company, 1959), 526; Ezra J. Warner, *Generals in Blue: The Lives of the Union Commanders* (Baton Rouge: Louisiana State University Press, 1964), 294–97; *Register of Graduates*, 261.

7. According to the regimental returns, Leefe's company had no desertions for two years, rather than the six years as stated by Mary Leefe Laurence. From 17 May 1894 to 6 April 1896 Company B, Nineteenth Infantry had not a single desertion, thus ending what was certainly an unusually good record for the regiment and for the old army. Desertion rates from the army had steadily declined from a high of 33 percent in 1873 to about 4 percent by the end of the 1890s. Army leaders attributed this to the reforms and improvements in soldiers' lifestyle, health, and recreation as well as a closer screening of recruits. Regimental Returns, Nineteenth Infantry, January 1889–December 1897, M665, roll 206; Coffman, *The Old Army*, 372–74; Weigley, *History of the United States Army*, 270.

8. Captain Richard Vance, from Kentucky, earned a Civil War commission to first lieutenant, was given a regular commission in the Nineteenth Infantry in 1866, and retired as a captain in November 1892. Vance died 17 February 1902. Heitman, *Historical Register*, 1: 981.

9. Lieutenant Theodore H. Eckerson, from Oregon, graduated from West Point in 1874 and served most of his career in the Nineteenth Infantry. At Fort Brady he was the post quartermaster and signal officer, ran the canteen, and commanded Company F. He retired of disabilities as a captain in January 1895 and died in January 1941. Lieutenant John Howard, son of Major General O. O. Howard, was appointed to the Nineteenth Infantry as a second lieutenant in 1891, served as a major of volunteers in the Spanish-American War, and returned to the Nineteenth as a captain in 1901. Heitman, *Historical Register*, 1: 396, 546; *Register of Graduates*, 264; Cullum, *Biographical Register*, 4: 251.

10. On 5 July 1894 Companies B and E, Nineteenth Infantry, were ordered by telegraph to be "armed and equipped for field service"

and to depart immediately for Chicago for strike duty. Leefe and his command departed that afternoon by rail and established a camp in Lake Front Park in Chicago. In 1894 regiments of the army were ordered to maintain order along railroad routes and to suppress labor strikes in the coal fields of Indian Territory and Idaho, railroad strikes in Montana and the Dakotas, and the Pullman Strike in Chicago. The Pullman Strike affected the railroads west of the major hub of Chicago. These railroads were considered a military asset, some were in receivership and protected by federal courts, and all carried the U.S. mail and interstate commerce. President Cleveland saw the strike as a challenge to federal authority, particularly in the case of Eugene Debs and the American Railway Union. In the majority of the eleven times between 1877 and 1900 that the U.S. Army intervened in a labor-capital conflict the request for troops came from beleaguered state officials. The Pullman Strike was unique in that the federal government initiated the decision to send troops. Regular officers in general found labor conflict duty disagreeable but believed that the chaos and disorder of the industrial strikes were harmful to society. They were not sympathetic to the militant methods of organized labor. When the Pullman Palace Car Company slashed unskilled labor wages by 25 percent in the winter of 1893–94 the workers appealed for support from the Railway Union, whose switchmen subsequently boycotted by refusing to handle Pullman cars. When management fired the switchmen and touched off a railroad strike that involved workers in 27 states, over 1,900 soldiers were sent to strike duty in the Chicago area along with 4,000 state militia. Eventually government lawyers got a court injunction for union officials to halt the strike and the interference with mails and interstate commerce. Ignoring the injunction, Debs and others were arrested and sentenced to six months in prison, effectively breaking the strike. Telegraphic Order No. 50, Headquarters, Department of the Missouri, 5 July 1894, in Post Returns, Fort Brady, July 1894; Colston E. Warne, *The Pullman Boycott of 1894: The Problem of Federal Intervention* (Boston: D. C. Heath and Company, 1955), 8, 19–50; Jerry M. Cooper, "The Army and Industrial Workers: Strikebreaking in the Late 19th Century," in *Soldiers and Civilians: The U.S. Army and the American People*, ed. Timothy K. Nenninger and Garry D. Ryan (Washington DC: National Archives and Records Administration, 1987;

reprint in *American Military Developments: From the Colonial Wars to the Root Reforms,* ed. Joseph G. Dawson III [New York: American Heritage Custom Publishing Group, 1993]), 129–44; Cosmas, *An Army for Empire,* 56.

11. Leefe and Company B, Nineteenth Infantry, returned to Fort Brady from duty at the Chicago Pullman strike in September 1894. Special Orders 93, Headquarters, Department of the Missouri, 4 September 1894, in Post Returns, Fort Brady, September 1892.

12. In September 1896 the Leefes and their battalion, Companies B, C, D, and F of the Nineteenth Infantry, departed for Fort Wayne, Michigan. They were replaced at Fort Brady by another Nineteenth Infantry battalion consisting of Companies A, E, G, and H. Paragraph 2, Special Orders 132, Headquarters, Department of the Missouri, 5 August 1896, in Post Returns, Fort Brady, August 1896.

11. Fort Wayne, Michigan, 1896–1898

1. The Leefes arrived at Fort Wayne, Michigan, on 10 September 1896. The garrison, commanded by Colonel Simon Snyder, consisted of the headquarters and the band of the Nineteenth Infantry and Companies B, E, D, F, I, and K, a total strength of 16 officers and 252 enlisted men. In the wake of tensions between the United States and England over the occupation of the Oregon Territory, Fort Wayne was begun in 1843 and completed in 1851. The post was built on the right bank of the Detroit River, two and a half miles from the town center. It is a massive formal bastioned fortress with barracks constructed of stone and walls seventeen feet thick. The post was not garrisoned until 1861 and functioned as a major support base through the later part of the nineteenth century. It was a training facility in both world wars and was turned over to the city of Detroit in 1949. Post Returns, Fort Wayne, Michigan, September 1896–April 1898, microfilm no. M617, roll 1403, and January 1898–December 1907, roll 1404, in Returns from United States Military Posts 1800–1916, Records of the United States Army Adjutant General's Office, 1780–1917, Record Group (RG) 94 (hereafter cited as Post Returns, Fort Wayne); Wade Millis, "Fort Wayne, Detroit" (Detroit: Private Printing, 1934, pamphlet, Special Collections, United States Military Academy Library); Roberts, *Encyclopedia of Historic Forts,* 424.

2. The Nineteenth Infantry departed Fort Wayne by rail for their Spanish-American War assembly camp at Mobile, Alabama, on 19 April 1898, leaving behind one officer and five enlisted men as a rear detachment. In October 1898 the post was occupied by the Seventh Infantry Regiment. Post Returns, Fort Wayne, April, October 1898.

BIBLIOGRAPHY

Archives

National Archives and Records Service, Washington DC (NARS) Records of the United States Army Adjutant General's Office, 1780–1917, Record Group (RG) 94

> Appointment, Commission, and Personal Branch, Documents Files, Box 51, 1871, 3303–394, ACP 3393 Service File, John George Leefe
>
> Army Muster Rolls, Nineteenth Infantry Regiment
>> Box 557, Company B, 31 October 1861 to 31 October 1897
>> Box 572, Company K, 31 December 1866 to 31 August 1902
>
> Letters Received, Adjutant General's Office
>> Annual Reports, 1886, Headquarters, Department of Texas, General Order 24, 30 August 1886, results of annual rifle competition, microfilm no. M689, roll 502
>
> Returns from United States Military Posts 1800–1916
>> Post Returns, Fort Brady, Michigan, January 1883–December 1896, microfilm no. M617, roll 135

Post Returns, Fort Clark, Texas, January 1882–December 1892, microfilm no. M617, roll 215

Post Returns, Davids Island, New York, July 1878–June 1896, microfilm no. M617, roll 294

Post Returns, Fort Dodge, Kansas, January 1866–October 1882, microfilm no. M617, roll 319

Post Returns, Fort Duncan, Texas, March 1868–August 1883, microfilm no. M617, roll 336

Post Returns, Fort Gibson, Oklahoma, July 1872–October 1897, microfilm no. M617, roll 406

Post Returns, Fort Leavenworth, Kansas, January 1870–December 1890, microfilm no. M617, roll 612

Post Returns, Fort Ringgold, Texas, January 1875–December 1884, microfilm no. M617, roll 1021, and January 1883–June 1886, microfilm no. M617, roll 1022

Post Returns, Mount Vernon Barracks, Alabama, January 1879–December 1894, microfilm no. M617, roll 820

Post Returns, Fort Wayne, Michigan, January 1886–December 1897, microfilm no. M617, roll 1403, and January 1898–December 1907, microfilm no. M617, roll 1404

Returns from Regular Army Infantry Regiments, June 1821–December 1916

Regimental Returns, Nineteenth Infantry, January 1880–December 1897, microfilm no. M665, rolls 205, 206

Special Orders, Headquarters of the Army

Special Orders 122, 27 May 1889, detailing Captain Leefe for inspection duties

Special Orders 217, 20 September 1901, retiring Lieutenant Colonel Leefe

Special Collections, United States Military Academy Library, West Point, New York

Henry, Guy V., Jr. "A Brief Narrative of the Life of Guy V. Henry, Jr." Manuscript carbon of the original manuscript in the U.S. Army Military History Institute, Carlisle Barracks, Pennsylvania.

Laurence, Mary Leefe. "A Rainbow Passes." Unpublished manuscript.

Millis, Wade. "Fort Wayne, Detroit." Detroit: Private Printing, 1934. Pamphlet.

Peelle, Bertha Barnitz B. "Autobiography." Typescript.
U.S. Army Military History Institute, Carlisle Barracks, Pennsylvania
Burt, Reynolds J. "Boyhood Data." Don Rickey Jr. Collection
Davidson, Ambrose H. "Ambrose H. Davidson File." Don Rickey
Jr. Collection
Snyder, Simon. "Simon Snyder Papers."

Government Documents

United States Congressional Records
40th Congress, 3d Session

House Executive Documents, no. 1, pt. 1, serial 1367 ("Report of the Secretary of War, 20 Nov. 1868"; Report of Major General Philip H. Sheridan, Headquarters, Department of the Missouri, 15 Oct. 1868").

41st Congress, 2d Session

House Executive Documents, no. 1, pt. 2, serial 1412 ("Report of the Secretary of War, 20 Nov. 1869").

45th Congress, 2d Session

House Executive Documents, no. 1, pt. 2, serial 1843 ("Report of the Secretary of War, 19 Nov. 1878"; "Report of the General of the Army, 7 Nov. 1878").

46th Congress, 2d Session

House Executive Documents, no. 1, pt. 2, vol. 2, serial 1903 ("Report of the Quartermaster General, 10 Oct. 1879").

House Executive Documents, no. 1, pt. 2, vol. 4, serial 1908 ("Report of the Chief Signal Officer, 15 Nov. 1879").

47th Congress, 1st Session

House Executive Documents, no. 1, pt. 2, serial 2010 ("Report of the Commissary-General of Subsistence, 10 Oct. 1881").

47th Congress, 2d Session

House Executive Documents, no. 1, pt. 2, serial 2091 ("Report of the Secretary of War, 14 Nov. 1882"; "Report of the General of the Army, 14 Nov. 1882"; "Report of Brevet Major General John Pope, 2 Oct. 1882"; "Report of Chaplain George C. Mullins, Chaplain, Twenty-Fifth Infantry, in Charge of Education in the Army, 20 Oct. 1882"; "Report of the Adjutant-General, 1882"; "Report of Brigadier General C. C. Augur, 2 Oct. 1882").

49th Congress, 2d Session
>House Executive Documents, no. 1, pt. 2, serial 2461 ("Report of Brigadier General D. S. Stanley, Headquarters, Department of Texas, 4 Sept. 1886"; "Report of the Lieutenant General of the Army, 10 Oct. 1886").

51st Congress, 1st Session
>House Executive Documents, no. 1, pt. 2, serial 2715 ("Report of the Adjutant General of the Army, 10 Oct. 1889").

51st Congress, 2d Session
>House Executive Documents, no. 1, pt. 2, serial 2831 ("Report of Major General Howard, Headquarters, Division of the Atlantic, 30 Sept. 1890"; "Report of the Inspector-General of the Army, 1 Oct. 1890"; "Report of the Adjutant-General, 7 Oct. 1890").

52d Congress, 1st Session
>House Executive Documents, no. 1, pt. 2, serial 2921 ("Report of the Surgeon-General of the Army, 22 Sept. 1891").

52d Congress, 2d Session
>House Executive Documents, no. 1, pt. 2, vol. 4, serial 3084 ("Report of the Inspector-General, 15 Sept. 1892").

Books

Abbot, Frederick V. *History of the Class of 'Seventy-Nine at the U.S. Military Academy.* New York: G. P. Putnam's Sons, Knickerbocker Press, 1884.

Agnew, Brad. *Fort Gibson: Terminal on the Trail of Tears.* Norman: University of Oklahoma Press, 1980.

Albers, Patricia, and Beatrice Medicine. *The Hidden Half: Studies of Plains Indian Women.* Washington DC: University Press of America, 1983.

Alexander, Eveline Martin. *Cavalry Wife: The Diary of Eveline M. Alexander, 1866–1867.* Ed. Sandra L. Myres. College Station: Texas A&M Press, 1977.

Ambrose, Stephen E. *Eisenhower: Soldier, General of the Army, President Elect, 1890–1952.* New York: Simon and Schuster, 1983.

Athern, Robert G. *William Tecumseh Sherman and the Settlement of the West.* Norman: University of Oklahoma Press, 1956.

Ball, Eve, Nora Henn, and Lynda A. Sanchez. *Indeh: An Apache Odyssey.* Norman: University of Oklahoma Press, 1988.

Beal, Merrill D. *"I Will Fight No More Forever": Chief Joseph and the Nez Percé War.* Seattle: University of Washington Press, 1963.

Bell, William Gardner. *Secretaries of War and Secretaries of the Army: Portraits and Biographical Sketches.* Washington DC: Center of Military History, 1992.

Boatner, Mark Mayo, III. *The Civil War Dictionary.* New York: David McKay Company, 1959.

Bode, E. A. *A Dose of Frontier Soldiering: The Memoirs of Corporal E. A. Bode, Frontier Regular Infantry, 1877–1882.* Ed. Thomas T. Smith. Lincoln: University of Nebraska Press, 1994.

Boyd, Mrs. Orsemus Bronson. *Cavalry Life in Tent and Field.* New York: J. S. Tait, 1894. Reprint, with an introduction by Darlis A. Miller, Lincoln: University of Nebraska Press, 1982.

Chief of Military History. *The Army Lineage Book.* Vol. 2, *Infantry.* Washington DC: GPO, 1953.

Coffman, Edward M. *The Old Army: A Portrait of the American Army in Peacetime, 1784–1898.* New York: Oxford University Press, 1986.

Cosmas, Graham A. *An Army for Empire: The United States Army in the Spanish-American War.* Columbia: University of Missouri Press, 1971. 2d ed., Shippensburg PA: White Mane Publishing Company, 1994.

Crook, George. *General George Crook: His Autobiography.* Ed. Martin F. Schmitt. Norman: University of Oklahoma Press, 1960.

Cullum, Brevet Major-General George W. *Biographical Register of the Officers and Graduates of the U.S. Military Academy at West Point NY from Its Establishment, in 1802, to 1890.* 3 vols. New York. Houghton, Mifflin and Company, 1891.

———. *Biographical Register of the Officers and Graduates of the U.S. Military Academy at West Point NY since Its Establishment, in 1802, Supplement IV.* Ed. Edward S. Holden. Cambridge: Riverside Press, 1901.

Custer, General G. A., USA. *My Life on the Plains, or Personal Experiences with Indians.* New York: Sheldon and Company, 1874.

Deibert, Ralph C. *A History of the Third United States Cavalry.* Harrisburg PA: Telegraph Press, 1933.

Dupuy, Trevor N., Curt Johnson, and David L. Bongard. *The Harper Encyclopedia of Military Biography.* New York: HarperCollins, Publishers, 1992.

Emmitt, Robert. *The Last War Trail: The Utes and the Settlement of Colorado.* Norman: University of Oklahoma Press, 1954.

Fenley, Florence. *Oldtimers: Frontier Days in Uvalde Section of South West Texas.* Uvalde TX: Hornby Press, 1939. Reprint, Austin TX: State House Press, 1991.

Fenner, The Right Reverend Goodrich Robert, and The Right Reverend Edward Clark Turner. *The First 100 Years: The Diocese of Kansas.* Lawrence KS: Private Printing, 1959.

Fowler, Arlen. *Black Infantry in the West, 1869–1891.* Westport CT: Greenwood Publishing, 1971.

Frazer, Robert W. *Forts of the West.* Norman: University of Oklahoma Press, 1965.

Freeman, Douglas Southall. *R. E. Lee: A Biography.* 4 vols. New York: Charles Scribner's Sons, 1936.

Ganoe, William Addleman. *The History of the United States Army.* New York: D. Appleton and Company, 1924.

Gibson, John M. *Physician to the World: The Life of General William C. Gorgas.* Durham NC: Duke University Press, 1950.

Green, Edwin. *Edwin Green's Municipal Record and City Register, 1880–81.* Leavenworth KS: Private Printing, 1881.

———. *Green's Directory of Ft. Leavenworth, 1880–81.* Leavenworth KS: Private Printing, 1881.

Grierson, Alice Kirk. *The Colonel's Lady on the Western Frontier: The Correspondence of Alice Kirk Grierson.* Ed. Shirley Anne Leckie. Lincoln: University of Nebraska Press, 1989.

Hampsten, Elizabeth. *Settlers' Children: Growing Up on the Great Plains.* Norman: University of Oklahoma Press, 1991.

Hampton, Bruce. *Children of Grace: The Nez Percé War of 1877.* New York: Henry Holt and Company, 1994.

Hart, Herbert M. *Tour Guide to Old Western Forts.* Fort Collins CO: Old Army Press, 1980.

Haywood, C. Robert, and Sandra Jarus. *"A Funnie Place, No Fences":*

Teenagers' Views of Kansas, 1867–1900. Lawrence: Division of Continuing Education, University of Kansas, 1992.

Heard, Jack W. *The Pictorial Military Life History of Jack Whitehead Heard.* San Antonio TX: Schneider Printing Company, 1969.

Heitman, Francis B. *Historical Register and Dictionary of the United States Army.* 2 vols. Washington DC: GPO, 1903.

Henry, Guy V. *Military Record of Civilian Appointments in the United States Army.* 2 vols. New York: Carleton Publishers, 1869.

Hoig, Stan. *The Battle of the Washita: The Sheridan-Custer Indian Campaign of 1867–69.* New York: Doubleday & Company, 1976.

Howard, Oliver Otis. *Autobiography of Oliver Otis Howard, Major General United States Army.* 2 vols. New York: Baker & Taylor Company, 1907.

Howe, Edgar W. *The History of the Class of 'Seventy-Eight at the U.S. Military Academy.* New York: Homer Lee Bank Note Company, 1881.

Hunt, Elvid, and Walter E. Lorence. *History of Fort Leavenworth, 1827–1937.* Fort Leavenworth KS: Command and General Staff School Press, 1937.

Huntington, Samuel P. *The Soldier and the State: The Theory and Politics of Civil-Military Relations.* Cambridge MA: Harvard University Press, 1957.

Hutton, Paul Andrew. *Phil Sheridan and His Army.* Lincoln: University of Nebraska Press, 1985.

Johnson, Edgar. *Charles Dickens: His Tragedy and Triumph.* 2 vols. New York: Simon and Schuster, 1952.

Knight, Oliver. *Life and Manners in the Frontier Army.* Norman: University of Oklahoma Press, 1978.

La Guardia, Fiorello H. *The Making of an Insurgent: An Autobiography, 1882–1919.* Philadelphia: J. B. Lippincott Company, 1948.

Lane, Lydia Spencer. *I Married a Soldier; Or, Old Days in the Old Army.* Philadelphia: Lippincott, 1893. Reprint, Albuquerque: University of New Mexico Press, 1988.

Leckie, William H. *The Buffalo Soldiers: A Narrative of the Negro Cavalry in the West.* Norman: University of Oklahoma Press, 1967.

Lenny, John J. *Rankers: The Odyssey of the Enlisted Regular Soldier of America and Britain.* New York: Greenburg, 1950.

Lockwood, Frank C. *The Apache Indians.* New York: Macmillan Company, 1938.

MacArthur, Douglas. *Reminiscences.* New York: McGraw-Hill Book Company, 1964.

Marquis, Albert Nelson, ed. *Who's Who in America, 1936–1937.* Vol. 19. Chicago: A. N. Marquis Company, 1936.

National Park Service. *Soldier and Brave: Historic Places Associated with Indian Affairs and the Indian Wars in the Trans-Mississippi West.* National Survey of Historic Sites and Buildings. Vol. 12. Ed. Robert G. Ferris. Washington DC: U.S. Department of the Interior, National Park Service, 1971.

Notable Names in American History: A Tabulated Register. 3d ed. Clifton NJ: James T. White and Company, 1973.

Pirtle, Caleb, III, and Michael F. Cusack. *Fort Clark: The Lonely Sentinel.* Austin TX: Eakin Press, 1985.

Pratt, Richard H. *Battlefield and Classroom: Four Decades with the American Indian, 1867–1904.* Ed. by Robert M. Utley. New Haven CT: Yale University Press, 1964.

Register of Graduates and Former Cadets, 1802–1964, of the United States Military Academy. West Point NY: West Point Alumni Foundation, 1964.

Rickey, Don, Jr. *Forty Miles a Day on Beans and Hay: The Enlisted Soldier Fighting the Indian Wars.* Norman: University of Oklahoma Press, 1963.

Riley, Glenda. *The Female Frontier: A Comparative View of Women on the Prairie and the Plains.* Lawrence: University Press of Kansas, 1988.

———. *A Place To Grow: Women in the American West.* Arlington Heights IL: Harlan Davidson, 1992.

Roberts, Robert B. *Encyclopedia of Historic Forts: The Military, Pioneer, and Trading Posts of the United States.* New York: Macmillan, 1988.

Rodenbough, Theo. F., and William L. Haskin. *The Army of the United States.* New York: Maynard, Merrill, & Company, 1896.

Schissel, Lillian, Byrd Gibbens, and Elizabeth Hampsten. *Far from*

Home: Families of the Westward Journey. New York: Schocken Books, 1989.

Schmitt, Martin F., and Dee Brown. *Fighting Indians of the West.* New York: Bonanza Books, 1968.

Sheridan, Philip H. *Personal Memoirs of P. H. Sheridan, General, United States Army.* 2 vols. New York: Charles L. Webster & Company, 1888.

Smith, Sherry L. *The View from Officers' Row: Army Perceptions of Western Indians.* Tucson: University of Arizona Press, 1990.

Smith, William J. *Army Brat: A Memoir.* Brownsville OR: Story Line Press, 1980.

Snelling, Henry Hunt. *Memoirs of a Boyhood at Fort Snelling.* Ed. Lewis Beeson. Minneapolis: Private Printing, 1939.

Sonnichsen, C. L. *The Mescalero Apaches.* Norman: University of Oklahoma Press, 1973.

Spiller, Roger J., and Joseph G. Dawson, III, eds. *American Military Leaders.* New York: Praeger, 1989.

————. *Dictionary of American Military Biography.* 3 vols. Westport CT: Greenwood Press, 1984.

Stallard, Patricia Yeary. *Glittering Misery: Dependents of the Indian Fighting Army.* Fort Collins CO: Old Army Press, 1978. Reprint, with a foreword by Darlis A. Miller, Norman: University of Oklahoma Press, 1992.

Stout, Joseph A., Jr. *Apache Lightning: The Last Great Battles of the Ojo Calientes.* New York: Oxford University Press, 1974.

Strate, David Kay. *Sentinel to the Cimarron: The Frontier Experience of Fort Dodge, Kansas.* Dodge City KS: Cultural Heritage and Arts Center, 1970.

Summerhayes, Martha. *Vanished Arizona: Recollections of My Army Life.* Philadelphia: Lippincott, 1908. Reprint, Lincoln: University of Nebraska Press, 1979.

Thrapp, Dan L. *The Conquest of Apacheria.* Norman: University of Oklahoma Press, 1967.

Urwin, Gregory J. W. *Custer Victorious: The Civil War Battles of George Armstrong Custer.* Lincoln: University of Nebraska Press, 1983.

U.S. Army Public Information Division. *The Medal of Honor of the United States Army.* Washington DC: GPO, 1948.

Utley, Robert M. *Frontier Regulars: The United States Army and the Indian, 1866–1891.* New York: Macmillan, 1973.

———. *Frontiersmen in Blue: The United States Army and the Indian, 1848–1865.* New York: Macmillan, 1967. Reprint, Lincoln: University of Nebraska Press, 1981.

Van Cleve, Charlotte Ouisconsin. *"Three Score Years and Ten," Life-Long Memories of Fort Snelling, Minnesota and Other Parts of the West.* 3d ed. Minneapolis: Harrison & Smith, 1895.

Warne, Colston E. *The Pullman Boycott of 1894: The Problem of Federal Intervention.* Boston: D. C. Heath and Company, 1955.

Warner, Ezra J. *Generals in Blue: The Lives of the Union Commanders.* Baton Rouge: Louisiana State University Press, 1964.

Weigley, Russell F. *The American Way of War: A History of United States Military Strategy and Policy.* New York: Macmillan, 1973. Reprint, Bloomington: Indiana University Press, 1977.

———. *History of the United States Army.* New York: Macmillan, 1967.

Wert, Jeffery D. *From Winchester to Cedar Creek: The Shenandoah Campaign of 1864.* Carlisle PA: South Mountain Press, 1987.

West, Elliott. *Growing Up with the Country: Childhood on the Far Western Frontier.* Albuquerque: University of New Mexico Press, 1989.

Woodward, Grace Steele. *The Cherokees.* Norman: University of Oklahoma Press, 1963.

Wooster, Robert. *The Military and United States Indian Policy, 1865–1903.* New Haven CT: Yale University Press, 1988.

———. *Soldiers, Sutlers, and Settlers: Garrison Life on the Texas Frontier.* College Station: Texas A&M University Press, 1987.

Worcester, Donald E. *The Apaches: Eagles of the Southwest.* Norman: University of Oklahoma Press, 1979.

Articles and Theses

"A Military Melee." *Ford County Globe* (Dodge City, Kansas; 23 December 1879): 2.

Brackett, Albert G. "Our Cavalry on the Frontier." *Army and Navy Journal* (10 November 1883): 283–84.

"Colonel W. H. Lewis." *Ford County Globe* (Dodge City, Kansas; 1 October 1878): 2.

Cooper, Jerry M. "The Army and Industrial Workers: Strikebreaking in the Late 19th Century." In *Soldiers and Civilians: The U.S. Army and the American People*. Ed. Timothy K. Nenninger and Garry D. Ryan. Washington DC: National Archives and Records Administration, 1987. Reprint in *American Military Developments: From the Colonial Wars to the Root Reforms*. Ed. Joseph G. Dawson III. New York: American Heritage Custom Publishing Group, 1993.

―――. "The Army's Search for a Mission, 1865–1890." In *Against All Enemies: Interpretations of American Military History from Colonial Times to the Present*. Ed. Kenneth J. Hagan and William R. Roberts. Westport CT: Greenwood Press, 1986.

Crimmins, Colonel Martin L. "Captain Nolan's Lost Troop on the Staked Plains." In *The Black Military Experience in the American West*. Ed. John M. Carroll. New York: Liveright, 1971.

Ellis, Richard N. "The Humanitarian Generals." *Western Historical Quarterly* 3 (April 1972): 169–78.

Field, William T. "Fort Duncan and Old Eagle Pass." *Texas Military History* 6 (summer 1967): 160–71.

Fisher, Barbara E., ed. "Forrestine Cooper Hooker's Notes and Memoirs on Army Life in the West, 1871–1876." Master's thesis, University of Arizona, 1963.

Gates, John M. "The Alleged Isolation of U.S. Army Officers in the Late 19th Century." *Parameters* 10 (September 1980): 32–45.

Leckie, Shirley. "Fort Concho: A Paradise for Children." *Fort Concho Report* 19, no. 1 (spring 1989): 1–15.

Leefe, Captain J. G. "Buttons." In *Captain Dreams*. Ed. Captain Charles King. Philadelphia: J. B. Lippincott Company, 1895.

Neilson, John, ed. " 'I Long to Return to Fort Concho': Acting Assistant Surgeon Samuel Smith's Letters from the Texas Military Frontier, 1878–1879." *Military History of the West* 24 (fall 1994): 123–86.

"Obituary, Lieut. Col. J. G. Leefe." *New York Times* (12 June 1903): 9, col. 6.

"Obituary, Stephen Massett." *New York Times* (22 August 1898): 5, col. 5.

Porter, Kenneth Wiggins. "The Seminole Negro-Indian Scouts,

1870–1881." *Southwestern Historical Quarterly* 55 (January 1952): 358–77.

Rickey, Don, Jr. "Enlisted Men of the Indian Wars." *Military Affairs* 23 (1959–60): 91–96.

Smith, Sherry L. "Stanley Vestal." In *Historians of the American Frontier*. Ed. John R. Wunder. Westport CT: Greenwood Press, 1988.

Stewart, Miller J. "Army Laundresses: Ladies of 'Soap Suds Row.' " *Nebraska History* 61 (winter 1980): 421–36.

———. "A Touch of Civilization: Culture and Education in the Frontier Army." *Nebraska History* 65 (summer 1984): 257–82.

Utley, Robert M. "The Frontier and the American Military Tradition." In *Soldiers West: Biographies from the Military Frontier*. Ed. Paul Andrew Hutton. Lincoln: University of Nebraska Press, 1987.

Walker, Henry P. "The Enlisted Soldier on the Frontier." In *The American Military on the Frontier: The Proceedings of the 7th Military History Symposium, U.S. Air Force Academy, 30 Sept.–1 Oct. 1976*. Ed. James P. Tate. Washington DC: GPO, 1978.

"Will of Stephen Massett." *New York Times* (9 October 1898): 10, col. 2.

Interviews

Edgerton, George, Starr County Historical Society, Rio Grande City, Texas. Interview by editor. Telephone. 18 September 1994.

Laurence, John F., son of Mary Leefe Laurence, Glen Harbor, New York. 21 February 1994.

Mangelsdorf, Mary Emile, niece of Mary Leefe Laurence. Interview by editor. Telephone. 23 August 1994.

Strandberg, Dwight, staff archivist, Dwight D. Eisenhower Library, Abilene, Kansas. Interview by editor. Telephone. 17 October 1994.

Wixon, Nancy, curator, Bartow-Pell Mansion, Pelham Bay Park, Bronx, New York. Interview by editor. Telephone. 8 September 1994.

INDEX

27, 91, 172 n.1
—duty, concept of, xxi, 6, 105, 132
—education, xxiv, xxvi, 37, 43, 49, 68, 71, 75–76, 91, 121, 143 n.31, 154 n.6, 165 n.18, 170 n.5
—electric light, 113, 127
—enlisting, 126
—food. *See* Army life: —rations
—funerals, xviii, 8
—gambling, 29
—gardens, 25, 151 n.2
—guard duty, xxv, xxvii, 27, 97
—guardhouse, 27, 38, 63, 73, 105
—health and hygiene, xxiv, 42, 67, 142 n.25, 161 n.3, 171 n.1. *See also* Army life: —medical corps, doctors
—holidays: Christmas, 27, 77; Fourth of July, 61
—Indians: soldiers' attitudes toward, xxix, 13, 16, 21, 40, 41, 149 n.10; soldiers' relations with, 18, 21
—inspections, xxv, 73
—labor, soldier, 27, 129–30
—latrines, 88, 121, 130
—Laundress Row, laundresses, 73, 164 n.13
—marching, drill, 32, 36, 73, 129
—medical corps, doctors, 42, 155 n.11
—militia and volunteers, relations with, xxix, 14, 112, 113, 129, 175 n.9
—music, xxvii, 23, 24, 29, 38, 43,

60, 62, 72, 74, 75, 93, 124. *See also* Army life: —bands, military
—moves, xxiii, xxviii, 31, 34, 35, 42–43, 44, 55, 58, 64, 66, 79, 80, 83, 89, 103, 106, 108, 119, 128, 129, 130, 152 n.5
—officers: chaplains, xxvi; character of, 46, 62, 75, 105, 132; officer of the day, 12; quartermaster, 16, 87, 149 n.11; wives of, xxv, 62, 64, 113
—orderlies. *See* Army life: —servants, strikers, and orderlies
—outhouses, 88, 121, 130
—parades, 97
—pay, xxvii
—photographer, traveling, 30–31
—promotion, 87
—punishment, 27, 63, 105
—quartermaster, 16, 87, 149 n.11
—quarters, of families, xxiv, xxvi, 11, 28, 35, 51, 58, 67–68, 70, 85–86, 97, 121, 150 n.11
—ranking out, 35, 152 n.2
—rations, 11, 25, 29, 38, 43, 56, 67, 68, 70–71, 92, 93, 121, 151 n.2
—recreation, xxvii, 18, 24, 27, 38, 43, 71, 74, 75, 77–78, 88, 93, 98, 99, 112–13, 122, 124, 131, 165 n.16. *See also* Army life: —dancing; music; sports
—relocation. *See* Army life: —moves

Caesar, Don, 77
Camargo, Mex., 68, 77
Campbell, Walter S. (Stanley Vestal), xii, 140 n.2
Camp Robinson NE, 139 n.2
Canada, 120, 127
Canadian River, 14
Carlisle Indian Industrial School PA, 40, 155 n.8, 175 n.8
Carton, Sydney, 72
Catholic Church, 37
Catholic school, xxvi, 37, 43, 154 n.6
Celeste (nursemaid), 16, 24, 31
Central Park, NYC, 58
Chaffe, Gen. Adna, 59, 159 n.2
Chase, Capt. George F., 171 n.9
Chestnut, Corporal, 123
Chicago IL, 145 n.40; strike of 1894, 129, 180 n.10
Chihuahua (Apache), 109, 114, 175 n.5 n.7
Chippewa House (hotel), 121, 127
Chivington, Col. John M., 13, 148 n.6
Church of England, 124
Clark, Maj. Nathan, 137 n.1
Clarke (cook), 92, 93
Cleveland, Pres. Grover, 129, 180 n.10
Cody, Col. William "Buffalo Bill," xxviii
Coffman, Edward M., xxiv
Coleman, Laura, 91
Colorado, xxi

Colorado Volunteer Cavalry, 13, 148 n.6
Congressional Medal of Honor, 15
Constitution Hall, Washington DC, xvi, 134
Cooper, Lt. Charles, 138 n.1
Cowboys, 24, 32
Custer, Elizabeth B., 5
Custer, Lt. Col. George A., 13, 14, 15, 75, 125, 126, 169 n.3
Cypress Hill Cemetery, NYC, xv

Daughters of the American Revolution, xvi, 134
Davids, Thaddeus, 59
David's Island NY: described, 59, 159 n.3; mentioned, xxvi, xxviii, 55, 57, 63, 64, 66, 67, 68, 69, 76, 90, 119
Davis, Jefferson, 115, 176 n.10
Debs, Eugene V., 180 n.10
Decker, George, 71, 163 n.9
De La Salle Institute, NYC, xv
Detroit MI, 131, 133, 181 n.1
Detroit River, 131, 181 n.1
Dickens, Charles, 53, 158 n.7
Dodge City KS: described, 11; mentioned, 18, 23, 24, 25, 29, 32
Donizetti, Gaetano, xxx
Dudu, Frank (striker), 24, 25, 26, 53, 100
Dunlap, Mrs. Irving Hall, 134
Duvenck, Frank, xvi
Dull Knife (Cheyenne), 9, 10, 146 n.2

Eagle Pass TX, 79, 82–83, 90

Eckerson, Lt. Theodore H., 128, 179 n.9

Egmond (striker), 131–32

Egypt, 77, 78

Eighth Infantry Regiment, 138 n.1

Eisenhower, Gen. Dwight D., 118, 139 n.1, 176 n.11

Eleventh Infantry Regiment, xviii, 138 n.1

Eli (cook), 82, 85, 92

Eliot, George, 70

Elliott, Maj. Joel H., 15, 125, 148 n.8

England, 135

Englewood NJ, 91

Episcopalian Church: of Dodge City KS, 31; of Fort Gibson OK, 54; of Fort Smith AR, 43; of Leavenworth KS, 43, 156 n.12; mentioned, xxvi, 37, 123

Falkenberg (striker), 96

Fifth Infantry Regiment, xviii, 137 n.1

First Michigan Infantry Regiment, xiv, 47

First World War, 62, 128, 134

Ford, John, xvi

Fort Assiniboine MT, 139 n.1

Fort Bidwell CA, 143 n.31

Fort Brady MI: described, 120–21, 177 n.2; mentioned, 100, 119, 123, 125, 126, 129

Fort Brown TX, 155 n.11, 161 n.3

Fort Clark TX: described, 90–91;

167 n.2; mentioned, xiii, xix, xxvi, xxvii, 75, 87, 92, 97, 103, 107, 113, 121, 152 n.2

Fort De Russey LA, xv

Fort Dodge KS: described, 11, 147 n.3; mentioned, xviii, xxx, 7, 9, 10, 12, 14, 18, 22, 26, 30, 31, 34, 35, 36, 44, 53, 75, 87, 100, 125, 150 n. 11, 154 n.7

Fort Douglas UT, 138 n.1

Fort Duncan TX: described, 87, 166 n.1; mentioned, xxviii, 75, 79, 82, 83, 84, 88, 92, 167 n.2

Fort Garland CO, 150 n.13

Fort Gibson OK, xxviii, 41, 45, 50, 51, 52, 53, 55, 125, 157 n.4

Fort Huachuca AZ, 138 n.1

Fort Lauderdale FL, 106

Fort Leavenworth KS: described, 35, 153 n.5; mentioned, xxvi, 31, 34, 41, 43, 44, 45, 50, 76, 90, 91, 146 n.1, 154 n.7

Fort Lyon CO, 9, 13, 22, 147 n.3 n.4

Fort Mackinac MI, 70

Fort McIntosh TX, 67, 160 n.2

Fort Repentigny MI, 177 n.2

Fort Ringgold TX, xviii, xxvi, xxvii, xxviii, 64, 66, 68, 69, 70, 71, 72, 73, 75, 80, 100, 119, 121, 160 n.1

Fort Robinson NE, xviii

Fort Sanders WY, 142 n.25

Fort Selden NM, xviii

Fort Sill OK, 138 n.1

Fort Slocum NY. *See* David's Island NY

Fort Smith AR, xiv, 43, 47
Fort Snelling MN, xviii, 137 n.1
Fort Supply OK, 14, 15
Fort Wallace KS, 9, 146 n.2
Fort Wayne MI, xxviii, 100, 129, 131, 134, 181 n.1
Fort Wingate NM, xviii
Foster, Lt. Arthur, 124, 178 n.5
Frank Leslie's Magazine, 125
Frascatti AL, 112
Frog Bayou AR, xiv, 47

Geary, Lt. Woodbridge, 168 n.2
Germany, 105, 126, 128
Geronimo (Apache), 6, 108, 109, 110, 111, 150 n. 13, 173 n.2, 174 n. 3 n.5, 175 n.7
Gibbens, Byrd, xxi,
Glen Head NY, xiv
Godfrey, Lt. Edward, 149 n.8
Gorgas, Dr. William C., 42, 155 n.11, 161 n.3
Governor's Island NY, 133
Great Lakes Survey, 50, 128
Guard, Lt. Alexander McCook "Robbie," 124, 127, 179 n.6

Hampsten, Elizabeth, xxi, xxii
Heard, Jack W., xvii, xviii, xix, xx, 139 n.1
Henry (striker), 54
Henry, Maj. Gen. Guy V., 139 n.1
Henry, Maj. Gen. Guy V., Jr., xi, xiii, xvii, xviii, xix, xx, 4, 137 n.1, 139 n.1, 142 n.25

Hooker, Forrestine Cooper, 138 n.1
Hough, Charles M., 138 n.1
Howard, Lt. John, 129, 164 n.12, 179 n.9
Howard, Maj. Gen. Oliver O., 40, 72, 129, 163 n.12, 172 n.2, 179 n.9
Huntington, Samuel P., xxviii

Idaho, 40
Indian School, Carlisle PA, 40, 155 n.8, 175 n.9
Indian Territory, 14, 39, 40, 45, 50, 57, 67
Indian tribes:
—Apache, Chiricahua and Warm Springs: Chihuahua, 109, 114, 175 n.5 n.7; Cochise, 174 n.6; dress, 107, 110; education, 175 n.3; Geronimo, 6, 108, 109, 110, 111, 150 n. 13, 173 n.2, 174 n. 3 n.5, 175 n.7; Juh, 174 n.5; Loco, 110, 175 n.6; Naiche, 108, 173 n.2, 174 n.5; Nana, 174 n.5; prisoners of war, 106, 172 n.1; tribal organization, 174 n.4; Victorio, 173 n.2, 174 n.6; mentioned, 52, 87, 119
—Apache, Lipan, 87
—Cheyenne: Battle of Punished Woman's Fork KS, 8, 145 n.1, 146 n.2; Black Kettle, 13, 15, 148 n.6 n.7; Dull Knife, 9, 10, 146 n.2; Little Wolf, 9, 146 n.2; mentioned, xviii, 13, 18

Mount Vernon Barracks AL: described, 107, 110, 172 n.1, 173 n.2, 174 n.4; mentioned, xxvi, 103, 106, 112, 113, 119, 164 n.12

Muskogee OK, xxviii, 50, 53, 55

Naiche (Apache), 108
Nancy (maid), 92
Nebraska, xvii
Neilson, Christine, 23, 24
New Hampshire, xiv
New Jersey, xxvii
New Mexico, xvii, xxi, 119
New Orleans LA, 111, 176 n.10
Newport RI, 67
New Rochelle NY, 55, 58, 63, 68
New York, 93, 133
New York City NY, xv, xvi, 53, 55, 57, 64, 71, 133
Nineteenth Infantry Regiment, xv, xix, 9, 46, 69, 72, 87, 90, 129, 132, 157 n.5, 162 n.5, 171 n.1, 179 n.10, 182 n.2
Ninth Cavalry Regiment, 118, 139 n.1
Nolan, Capt. Nicholas, 149 n.9
North Dakota, xxi

Offley, Maj. R. H., 162 n.5
Oklahoma, xvii, 45
162nd New York Infantry Regiment, xv
Ontario, Can., 124
Oregon Territory, xxi

Panama Canal, 42

Peele, Bertha Barnitz, 138 n.1
Pelham Priory NY, 63, 160 n.5
Penrose, Capt. W. H., 148 n.7
Peralta NM, 146 n.5
Philippine Islands, xv, xviii, xxi, 69, 89, 132, 139 n.1, 150 n.13
Philippine Occupation and Insurrection, xv, 46, 139 n.1
Piedras Negras, Mex., 83
Pinckney, Charles Clarence (grandfather of Mary Leefe Laurence), xiv, 47
Pinckney, Emily Keene ("Grandmother Pinckney"), xiv, 19, 22, 27, 30, 37, 38, 41, 42, 46, 47, 49, 66, 71, 72, 88
Pinckney, Henry, 49
Pinckney, Mary Comfort. See Leefe, Mary Comfort Pinckney
Pittsburgh PA, 49
Plymouth Colony MA, 47
Plymouth Rock MA, 22
Pope, Brig. Gen. John, 153 n.4
Port Hudson LA, xv
Port Washington NY, xi, 55, 59, 123, 134
Puerto Rico, xv, 132

Raphael, 78
Rickey, Don, Jr., xxix
Riley, Glenda, 141 n.19
Rio Grande, 66, 68, 79, 83, 87
Rio Grande City TX, 67, 68, 71, 74, 160 n.1, 163 n.8
Roberts, Lt. Harris L. "Polly," 72, 163 n.11

Roosevelt, Pres. Theodore, 134
Ropes, Capt. James M., 73, 164
  n.14
Rowe, Rev. Peter Trimble, 123,
  178 n.3

Sabine TX, xv
Saint Marys River MI, 120, 122
San Antonio TX, 67, 70, 90
Sand Creek CO, 147 n.5
Sand Creek Massacre, 148 n.6
Sands Point NY, 55
Sault Sainte Marie MI, 120
Saxony, king of, 50, 125
Schissel, Lillian, xxi
Second World War, 62, 128, 134
"Seechy" (striker), 100
Seventh Cavalry Regiment, 14,
  138 n.1
Seventh Infantry Regiment, 129,
  182 n.2
Seventh New York Infantry
  Regiment Armory, NYC, 133
Shenandoah Valley Campaign,
  1864, xv
Shepard, Sophie, 110, 111, 175 n.8
Sheridan, Lt. Gen. Philip H.,
  xv, 40, 75, 91, 149 n.8, 165 n.17,
  169 n.3
Severy KS, 140 n.3
Sixth Infantry Regiment, 138 n.1
Smith (teamster), 16, 100
Smith, Col. Charles H., 98, 134,
  153 n.4, 161 n.3, 167 n.2, 170
  n.8
Smith, Lt. Edmund D., 69, 70,
  162 n.5 n.7

Smith, Maj. Jacob H., 145 n.40
Smith, Mame, 134
Smith, Sherry L., xii, xxix
Smith, William J., 139 n.1
Snelling, Henry Hunt, 137 n.1
Snelling, Col. Josiah, 137 n.1
Snyder, Lillian, 145 n.40
Snyder, Capt. Simon, 145 n.40,
  181 n.1
South Carolina, 47
Spanish-American War, xv, 46,
  132, 157 n.1, 182 n.2
Stallard, Patricia E., xxiv
State Volunteer Forces, 14
St. James Church, Sault Sainte
  Marie MI, 123
St. John's Cathedral, NYC, 123
St. Luke's Hospital, NYC, 71
St. Thomas's Church, Washing-
  ton DC, 134
Sturgis, Col. Samuel A., 40
Sudlon, Cebu Island, Philip-
  pines, xv
Suez Canal, 122
Sullivan, Archbishop, 124
Sumner, Maj. Gen. Edwin V.,
  160 n.2
Sumner, Maj. Samuel S., 67, 160
  n.2

Taft, Pres. William H., 134
Tennessee, xiv, 43, 47
Tenth Cavalry Regiment, 149
  n.9
Tenth Infantry Regiment, 118,
  129
Texas, xv, xvii, xviii, 76, 121

Third Cavalry Regiment, xvii, xix, 90, 138 n.1, 171 n.9
Thirteenth Infantry Regiment, xvii, 129, 138 n.1
Thirtieth Infantry Regiment, xv, 132
Thompson, Willie, 115
Tremaine, Asst. Surgeon William S., 145 n.40
Twelfth Infantry Regiment, 129
25th Infantry Regiment, 118
24th Infantry Regiment, 87, 118

United States Military Academy, West Point NY, xvi, 118, 124, 138 n.1
University of Michigan, 49
U.S. Army Signal Corps, 67, 161 n.4
U.S. Marine Corps Band, xvi, 28, 134

Van Buren AR, 47
Vance, Capt. Richard, 124, 126–27, 177 n.1, 179 n.8
Van Cleve, Charlotte Ouisconsin, xviii, 137
Vermont, xviii
Vernon NY, xiv
Vestal, Stanley (Walter S.

Campbell), xi, 140 n.2
Vigan, Philippines, xxi
Virginia, 104

Wang, General, 134
War: First World War, 62, 128, 134; prisoners of, 106, 172 n.1; Second World War, 62, 128, 134. *See also* Spanish-American War
Washington DC, xvi, 6, 31, 40, 97, 124, 133, 134, 135
Washita River OK, 14
West, Elliott, xxii, xxiii
West Point, xvi, 118, 124, 134 n.1
Wetherill, Capt. Alexander M., 51, 158 n.6, 171 n.1
Whipple Barracks AZ, xx, 138 n.1
White, John and Mary, 47
White, Peregrine, 47
White House, 28, 134
Wilhelmus Capricornus (pet goat), xxvii, 97–98
Wilkinson, Captain, 113
Willard Hotel, Washington DC, xvi, 133
Windsor, Can., 131
Wyoming, xvii

Xenophon, 40, 155 n.9

THOMAS TYREE SMITH is a native Texan and Regular Army Major of Infantry. He served in Vietnam with the U.S. Navy and earned a B.S. in education from Southwest Texas State University and an M.A. in history from Texas A&M University. He commanded an infantry company in Germany, served as an assistant professor of military history at the United States Military Academy at West Point, and is currently on assignment to the United States Army Command and General Staff College at Fort Leavenworth, Kansas. His previous books are *Fort Inge: Sharps, Spurs, and Sabers on the Texas Frontier, 1849–1869* (1993) and *A Dose of Frontier Soldiering: The Memoirs of Corporal E. A. Bode, Frontier Regular Infantry, 1877–1882* (1994).